Ja B——,

Buen Camino,

Bill Wal—

The Best Way

To See the Old Continent

by Bill Walker

Skywalker Publishing

Printer: Createspace.com

ISBN-13 978-1467960229

ISBN-10 1467960225

Dedication

To the tireless *hospitaleiros* at the countless albergues along El Camino de Santiago. Your selfless performance of critical tasks helps make the Camino the very best way.

Disclaimer

This book describes the author's experiences while walking the Camino de Santiago and reflects his opinions relating to those experiences. Others may recall these same events differently. A couple names and identifying details mentioned in the book have been changed to protect their privacy.

Also by Bill Walker

Skywalker—Close Encounters on the Appalachian Trail (2008)

Skywalker—Highs and Lows on the Pacific Crest Trail, (2010)

Map of the Camino Frances

THE MAJOR PILGRIM ROUTES THROUGH FRANCE & SPAIN TO THE SHRINE OF ST JAMES IN THE MIDDLE AGES

The Way

To See The Old Continent

Part One

THE CAMINO FRANCES

"A pilgrimage is the practice of every major religion. It is profoundly human."

Scott Peck, *In Search of Stones*

Chapter 1

Catholics, Protestants, and Jews

"Man, this road must lead to the whole world. Ain't nowhere else it can go, right?"

Jack Kerouac, *On the Road*

This particular group of pilgrims would have made almost anyone envious.

A delightful, thirtyish French woman named Carol lolled along in dilettantish fashion. At turns, she sampled flowers, puffed on cigarettes that she visibly savored, and conversed pleasantly in a variety of languages. Traipsing along at her side was an elfin-built, blonde-headed Frenchman, as well as a Hungarian girl afflicted with a severe case of *Francophilia*. The way they had all been chatting when we had come upon them, made me assume they were all close friends. In fact, they had all just met.

"Catholicism in France isn't so much a religion, as a birthright," wrote Dan Brown in *The DaVinci Code*. Given that this pilgrimage to Santiago de Compostela has Catholic roots going back to early medieval times, hordes of French would surely be a fact of life for the next 800 kilometers (500 miles).

My traveling companion was my eighteen year-old nephew, Gavin. He was arguably the single coolest and most irresponsible member of the entire 2010 high school graduating class in the United States of America. Add cheeky to that description, as well. After all, Americans study Spanish as our second language. Not Gavin, though. He had chosen the storied French language as his foreign elective. This was a statement unto itself, especially given that he came from a family and country chock-full of French haters. Gavin had cleverly played it to his advantage, as well. This summer of his graduation was going to be when his mother put him to work. But when he had heard about my plans to do the Camino, he had deftly maneuvered his way onto the traveling team. That most rare species—an American Francophile (which some might call a *Frankenstein*)—was in the making.

Gavin and I joined up with the three French-speaking pilgrims. They seemed genuinely glad of our company. We felt the same. The war in Iraq and 'patriot fries' were historical arguments for bitter, old men. What we were doing was arguably even more important anyway. We were on a 'spiritual pilgrimage,' which is a less controversial term than the more combustible 'religious pilgrimage' – especially here in Europe.

Our group, which was now a fivesome, turned a bend in the trail. We came upon another threesome lying pleasantly alongside a stream. It was a scene that surely has played out countless times on this thousand year-old pilgrimage route. Two middle-aged men were doing their utmost to evoke laughs from a younger woman.

"*Buenos dias,*" I pleasantly said to them. I didn't really think they were from Spain. But we Americans have the unfortunate reputation of being the lepers and dolts of the world of multilingualism. I was obsessed with not fitting this stereotype. Each member of the threesome saluted back in foreign-accented English. "Where are you from?" is the default question on such an international trek. I was not any more imaginative.

"My father is Italian," the young lady answered, "and my mother is Swedish."

"Which are you?" I asked.

"I'm European," she said plainly. "My name is Martina." Martina had a strikingly athletic physique. Throw in her alluring personality and she was destined to be amongst male pilgrims all along the way.

Martina's two hiking companions soon revealed a surprise. "We're from Israel," the short, stocky one said. "I'm Avi. This is David." The conversation with these two Israelis would flow so freely over the next few days that I would never even think to clear up my initial confusion—*what in the world are two Israelis doing here on El Camino de Santiago?*

"Why are you doing the Camino?" Martina asked me.

"I'm here to meet European divorcees," I unhesitatingly replied. *That* drew the intended laughs.

"Good luck," Martina giggled a touch self-consciously.

My thoughts went back four years to the first time I had ever heard of El Camino de Santiago. A recently divorced American woman had recently given me a copy of Shirley MacLaine's book, *The Camino*. For two years, the book had sat on top of my john; every time I had assumed a seated position over that time period, I would grab Shirley's book and pick out a different section. *It has to get better,* I kept thinking. Alas, it didn't. Every section I delved into had more of her spiritual flights of fancy, topped off with unconvincing accounts of killer dogs harassing pilgrims along the Camino. Finally, I ran into the lady who had lent me the book.

"Sorry," I said, "but I just couldn't get into that book."

"Well," she had blushed, "you're either a Shirley MacLaine fan, or you're not."

"You can say that again," I had laughed. I also had written off the idea of ever doing The Camino.

A couple years later, however, in the summer of 2009, I was hiking on the Pacific Crest Trail in the American West. My hiking partner was a Danish journeyman who had trekked all over the world, including The Camino.

"You hiked The Camino?" I had asked in amazement.

"Yes, I greatly enjoyed it," he had said.

"But it's a religious trail," I had responded flummoxed. "You've said religion is a silly American thing."

"Ah, but El Camino is really the European Divorcee Trail," he had laughed knowingly.

European Divorcee Trail. Goose bumps had quickly broken out all over my body, several thousand miles away from The Camino. I had quickly forgotten about Shirley MacLaine's unfortunate book. One year later, here I was.

***

The eight of us—two French, one Hungarian Francophile, a European divorcee, two Israelis, a near 7-foot tall American Protestant (me), along with my 18 year-old French-speaking nephew—spontaneously joined together here in the Basque region of northeastern Spain. I was happy. This was the type of atmosphere and interesting group I had been hoping for.

We entered the first of countless anonymous villages we would pass through along the Camino. Like most Spanish pueblos, it was arrestingly ugly at first glance. Worse yet, two large dogs charged in our direction. "Oh boy," I muttered, "Shirley MacLaine's revenge." But nobody was laughing. These dogs were frothing at the mouth. All eight of us began backing away towards a low-roofed stone building.

"Hey, be careful," Gavin piped in. "These are Catholic dogs. They're trained to eat Protestants."

"I can assure you," Avi said in his distinctive Israeli accent, "they're trained to eat Jews, also."

Chapter 2

Sons of Thunder

One afternoon while mending their fishing nets along the Sea of Galilee, the two brothers, James and John, heard a call in their direction. It was *Jesus of Nazareth*. The two brothers must have been impressed with what they saw. For they immediately left their nets behind to become disciples of the mysterious Galilean. It was a decision to have far-reaching consequences. However, for the longest time it seemed like everybody would have been better off if the two brothers had just stuck to fishing.

"The disciples annoy the hell out of me, if you want to know the truth," writes Holden Caulfied in *Catcher in the Rye*. "They were alright after Jesus was dead. But while He was alive, they were about as much use to him as a hole in the head." Caulfield's assertion is not completely unfounded. When Jesus was rebuffed by the people of a Samaritan village, James and John angrily threatened to torch the village. Fortunately, Jesus took the time to patiently explain his concept of 'love thine enemies'. For their bombastic ways, he labeled the brothers *Sons of Thunder.*

At the *Last Supper*, James and John's mother, Salome, requested that her two sons be placed on Jesus' right and left hand, both at the dinner table and in heaven. In fact, Salome may even have paid the tavern bill for the Last Supper. But as to her request for preferential seating, Jesus sternly replied, "Ye' know not what ye' ask for."

The two brothers also may have had a bit too much wine at that Last Supper. For shortly afterwards in the Garden of Gethsemane, Jesus asked them to stay on the lookout for Roman centurions, while he headed off to pray. They fell asleep. Jesus returned awhile later to arouse them. But when he left to go pray a second time, it was again lights-out for the brothers. This allowed Jesus' captors to close in and arrest him. Of course, the next day he was crucified in the most grotesque fashion, with James and John looking helplessly on.

***

Fortunately, that wasn't the last chapter for the two brothers. Folk legend holds that the apostles then headed off all over the known world—India, Ethiopia, Armenia, Persia—to spread the word of Jesus. James was sent to Spain (ecclesiastical documents confirm this). In the total of twelve years he spent on the Iberian Peninsula, James is said to have converted a grand total of seven people to Christianity, a pace that even a Mormon missionary might find frustrating.

James became restless as well. In the year 42 CE (A.D.), he decided to return to Jerusalem. Suddenly he found the golden touch that had eluded him for so long. He began converting scores of awestruck observers, including the dreadful Hermogenes, exerciser of satanic powers. Unfortunately, the crafty old nemesis of the early Christians, Herod Agrippa, got wind of this. He had James arrested, brought before him with a rope gripped around his neck, and ordered executed. The man leading him to his execution, Josias, was also converted along the way, for which he, too, was executed. But James, the ever-loyal screw-up, had gained redemption, by going on a hot streak so late in life.

His body was thrown over the city walls, where wild animals awaited to devour it. But the small, but loyal, band of Christian brethren rushed to recover the body. Legend holds that the apostles then sent his body back to Spain in a rudderless stone boat. There in the Galician coast in northwestern Spain, the boat arrived, surrounded by scallop shells. All seven of James' converted Spanish disciples were waiting ashore to dutifully carry the body inland for a proper burial. Nothing much more was heard about James for the next 800 years.

***

Pelayo was a typical hermit. He contentedly passed his days praying and eating wild grass and honey. There were few surprises in his life.

However, one day in the year 814, Pelayo was walking in the Galician countryside in Northwest Spain when he was jolted out of his well-established rhythm. First, he noticed an especially gleaming star directly overhead in the atmosphere. Then he began to hear celestial-sounding music. Uncharacteristically, he rushed to the local bishop, who hurriedly notified the king. Soon a posse of locals, armed with picks and shovels, arrived at a deserted place in the hills. There in a dark cave, the party discovered a tomb. In it lay a body and a letter that read: "Here lies James, son of Zebede and Salome, brother of St. John, beheaded in Jerusalem. He came by sea, borne by his disciples."

The location became known as *Santiago de Compostela* (St. James Field of the Star). As Christians are wont to do, they quickly constructed a church on the site. Soon it was attracting *pilgrims.*

The timing of the discovery of his tomb was historically fortuitous—some would even say suspicious. All but the northernmost mountainous areas of Spain were now in the hands of their Muslim conquerors, the Moors. The remaining Spanish royalty were desperate for any means to combat these forces of anti-Catholicism. Having the ashes of an apostle with the prestige of St. James was to serve as a critical rallying point.

Better yet, the French bishops and kings were also ecstatic at the discovery. Their main rival was the Vatican in Rome. But now they could encourage French pilgrims to walk to Santiago in Spain, instead of to Rome. King and queens throughout France and northern Spain began showering Santiago with gifts.

It is difficult for anyone in modern times to understand just how powerful of a hold the idea of a pilgrimage had on medieval humans. "Belief in the Resurrection and Virgin Birth, a drawing away from hell, and immortality of the flesh," were just a few of the things promised pilgrims.

There was but one church, appropriately known as 'The Church'. It was considered an extraordinary blessing to be sent on such a far-flung peregrination on its behalf. Better yet, the pilgrimage to Santiago de Compostela effectively began to repopulate the northern part of Spain, after it had become hollowed out from the Islamic juggernaut. Soon pilgrim routes were formed in Italy and Germany, all converging at a mountain pass in the Pyrenees.

The greatest peaceful movement of people in European history had begun, one which would have a major effect on the development of Europe as we know it today.

Chapter 3

Spanish Love Affair Begins

"I have long believed that anybody interested in either the mystic or romantic aspects of life must define his attitude concerning Spain."

James Michener, *Iberia*

Gavin and I sat in a smoke-filled café in Madrid, after an all-night flight over the Atlantic. We were watching Spain's first round World Cup match against Switzerland. All eyes were fixated on the television set. The World Cup holds quasi-Holy Grail status in this emotional land. Amazingly, Spain had never won it.

The looks on the faces of this crowd of predominantly middle-aged men went from anticipatory, to worried, to downright grave when Switzerland scored to go ahead. Cigarettes and cappuccinos were being consumed in accelerating, almost helpless, fashion.

"*ETA, ETA, ETA* is celebrating right now," Gavin whispered to me. He was referring to the Basque terrorist group, *ETA*, which has demonstrated an especial fondness for blowing up high Spanish government officials over the years. Yeah, they probably were happy Spain was losing.

"Hey, we'd better hope this isn't like when England loses," I said a bit concerned, "and all hell breaks loose."

"Well, what do you want to do?" Gavin asked.

"We should probably get back to our hotel before the match ends," I said quietly.

Nonetheless, we stuck around to the end. Spain lost. Everyone in the café looked like they had just completed a bedside vigil of a dying family member. Slowly, dutifully they began shuffling out of the café. A glance out to the sidewalk revealed a funereal atmosphere. Collectively, everyone had the look of a people steeped in misfortune and adversity. God knows, Spanish history is just that.

A man who appeared to be pushing eighty was sitting by himself next to our table. He appeared especially traumatized.

"*Senor,* you had bad luck," I said sympathetically in the best Spanish I could muster. "We are from the United States and accustomed to losing in soccer."

This man's formative years probably were during the horrific Spanish Civil War, followed by 40 years under the odious Franco dictatorship. This could be his last chance to see Spain win the coveted Cup. It had just suffered a body blow. The man gave me a hard, stony-faced stare. He had that unmistakable *provincial look.* For all I knew, he had never even talked with an American. Lacking confidence in my Spanish, I decided to repeat myself slower and louder. "Spain still has much hope," I added.

He kept looking at me, not changing his expression. I stole a quick glance at his table to see if he might be drunk. But there was no sign of alcohol. It was simply littered with enough cigarettes and cappuccinos to eat up half his weekly pension. Finally, he looked me in the eye and quietly said, "*Espero* (I wait)".

His answer mixed Spanish stoicism, with a kind of childlike wonder. Its authenticity was overwhelming.

"You know," I turned to Gavin, "if we don't win the World Cup, I hope Spain does."

"Start pulling for Spain then," Gavin replied.

My low-grade love affair with Spain had begun.

"She says shut up," my Spanish interlocutor laughingly reported to me.

Gavin and I were standing there chatting with this woman in a 130 bed pilgrim's *albergue* (hostel) in Pamplona in northeastern Spain. We had spent most of the day on a bus coming up from Madrid. Our spirits were high as we neared the starting point of the Camino.

The Camino was reputed to be far and away the most popular footpath in Europe. But because it is just being discovered by Americans, I had remained dubious that it was as popular as cracked up to be. But here we were in a modern albergue, packed wall-to-wall with pilgrims. Everybody here had the same goal—to reach Santiago de Compostela for the July 25th Holy Day. Because the 25th of July fell on a Sunday this year, the Camino was expected to be especially teeming. Fully 200,000 pilgrims were expected.

In the midst of a sea of bunks, we had struck up a lively conversation with this attractive and personable Spanish girl. "How many kilometers do you walk every day? Is the trail well-marked? Where are most of the pilgrims from?" came my questions in rapid-fire fashion. I was talking in Spanish, and she was responding in English. Better yet, she was matching my level of enthusiasm. But then a harsh voice from a nearby bunk interrupted us. *Oh boy, if that's Spanish that person is speaking, then Gavin and I are in big trouble.* I didn't understand a word. Fortunately (or unfortunately), it wasn't Spanish. It was French.

"The lady says you are talking too loud," the Spanish girl reported to me, almost embarrassed. "She says to shut up."

I looked down into the bottom bunk, where I was greeted by the hard stare of a middle-aged French woman. It was that unmistakable look of studied disdain that certain Europeans reserve for Americans and other insects.

"Bill," my Francophile nephew warned, "looks like you're going to have to adapt with all these French around."

"We'll see about that," I muttered. But a pattern had just been established that would repeat itself intermittently throughout El Camino—French men and women telling me to shut up. Never in

English. And never in Spanish. Always in French. Yes, I was going to have to adapt.

Fortunately, it quickly became apparent that not all pilgrims were quiet-obsessed zealots. I went looking for somewhere to do some stretching exercises, after the long bus ride. Right next to the bunkroom was a small, open area that appeared immediately inviting. I assumed as much of a pretzel form as my 49 year-old, 6'11" physique could muster. Suddenly, unexpectedly, and, honest-to- God, helplessly, some clogged-up internal tube circuit malfunctioned, and did a re-enactment of Mount Vesuvius. This truly once-in-a-lifetime act of volcanic flatulence echoed throughout the sleeping quarters. *Are they really all that asleep? Miraculous.*

But then someone quietly cracked up on the far side of the cavernous bunkroom. Like a rave, the giggles rose steadily across the full length of the sleeping quarters, finally crescendoing into open delirium. It was like a hundred silly campers laughing in their bunks after lights out. Excuse me, 99 silly campers and one steamed French woman. Yes, this El Camino was going to require some adaptation on everybody's part.

Chapter 4

European Sophistication, American Amiability

I had been the biggest wimp on the entire Appalachian Trail. Well okay, maybe I had just been the tallest. In any event, it hadn't been pretty. But I had made it. On the even longer 2,663 mile Pacific Crest Trail, I had required considerably less wet nursing. But I was still anything but one of the more intrepid hikers. Now on El Camino de Santiago, I was resolved to be different. I was going to be confident. Maybe if there was a chance, I would even venture into the realm of the bold.

"Hey, what do you think about this idea?" I asked Gavin. "Instead of taking a taxi or bus over the French border to St. Jean Pied de Port (the beginning of the Camino Frances), let's try to walk through the mountains to get there."

"Why?"

"Well, the toughest day on El Camino is supposedly the very first day over the Pyrenees. This way, we'll get to do that part in both directions."

"Whatever," Gavin said. "Anything to get out of here."

This wasn't just a teenager's kneejerk apathy. We were in the northeastern Spanish border town of Roncesvalles, which was one of the grimmest places (notice I didn't say shithole) I've ever seen. We had shared a taxi with a group of pilgrims to get here. The closer we had gotten to Roncesvalles, the higher the elevation and worse the weather. It was June 18th. But it might as well have been the dead of winter.

"Okay, we'll stay at the albergue here in Roncesvalles tonight," I said to Gavin. Tomorrow morning, when everybody heads east, we'll go west to France."

"Sure, Bill."

His northern Virginia cool often flummoxed by middle Georgia, deep southern volubility.

***

Swedish women have the reputation for being—well, for being gorgeous. While I certainly wouldn't dissent, it should be noted that most Scandinavians – both make and female – appear inordinately healthy.

In the albergue in Roncesvalles, an especially athletic-looking Swedish girl, who spoke great English, helped bring Gavin and me into the running pilgrim conversation in the albergue in Roncesvalles. She introduced us to a Norwegian girl who had extensive trekking experience above the Arctic Circle. The two of them discussed their trek across the Pyrenees earlier in the day.

"The conditions were quite poor," the Norwegian quietly said. "Ten meters of visibility and heavy downpour."

"Tomorrow, we're thinking about hiking over the Pyrenees to get to St. Jean's," I said. "Do you think that is a good idea?"

"Do you mean go backwards?" she clarified.

"Nice idea, Bill, "Gavin interjected. "Leading us the wrong way."

"Honestly," I bore down, ignoring Gavin, "do you think it is a good idea from what you saw today?"

"Umm, I don't know," the Swede said. "I'm neutral."

"Neutral," the Norwegian girl laughed. "I seem to remember that."

Of course, the Norwegians had fought like hell in World War II, while the Swedes had posed for years with a dampened finger in the air. These two girls were also following standard European etiquette of joking about long-ago wars, as long as no Germans are standing around. I watched in admiration as the two of them conversed. The Swedish girl spoke Swedish, and the Norwegian spoke Norwegian.

"Do you understand each other?" I asked.

"We have to," the Norwegian said plainly. "It's northern European tradition." Actually, they sounded more alike than somebody from Mississippi attempting to converse with a New Yorker.

A college-age girl from Kentucky heard all this lively conversation, and quickly injected herself, American-style, into the discussion. "God, I thought I was gonna' die out there today," she gushed. "I swear I couldn't see my own hands by the time I got to the top."

"And you're never gonna' believe what I saw out there," she continued.

"Probably not," Gavin commented dryly.

"This huge wild boar came charging across the trail right in front of me."

"Did it have tusks?" I asked, perplexed.

"Well, yeah."

I would be even more perplexed a few days later when a Spaniard told me, "They killed all the heavy game around here 400 years ago." The Norwegian girl was also confused.

"How close did the boar get to you?" she inquired.

"About 20 yards," the American girl answered.

"But you said you couldn't see your hands," the Norwegian girl bore in. *Touche.*

But hey, if worldly sophistication isn't the leitmotif for us Americans, an easy familiarity with strangers is. Long live American friendliness.

Chapter 5

The Pyrenees

"Man, this weather is worse than I expected," I muttered to Gavin when we stepped out into the cold rain the next morning.

"So what are you saying?"

"Just that we've got to get out of here, somehow."

The impressive thing was that everybody had already gotten out of here. I had read in guidebooks that pilgrims were required to leave albergues every morning by 8 o' clock. *Yeah sure,* I had cynically thought. Dead wrong. Around 6 o'clock this morning, all types of racket had commenced. Gavin and I were practically the last people shoved out of the place by the hospitaleiros.

"The big problem," I said to Gavin, "is that nobody's gonna' be going the same direction as us. We could easily get lost." At dinner last night a local woman had strongly advised us not to attempt it. "It would be dangerous," she had warned. "It's an especially steep climb going towards France. And the *flechas* (yellow arrows) are all on the other side of the trees. Nobody ever walks that way."

"So what do you want to do then?" Gavin asked.

"A guy last night told me there was an alternate bad weather route around the mountain."

"Where does it go?"

"He told me," I said. "Let's try to find it."

***

I had been in virtually catatonic states before beginning the Appalachian and Pacific Crest Trails. But I hadn't worried about El Camino at all. Supposedly, it was less difficult. Yet as we headed into the woods and up the mountain in the rain and cold, the old familiar fears began stirring deep within.

We came to a turn in the trail. "The guy said take a left at the turn to avoid the big climb." We took the left fork, and started climbing through the forest. And climbing. After a half-hour of ascent directly up the face of the mountain, Gavin asked, "Do you think this is the alternate route?"

"Who knows," I said morosely.

Of course, both of us pretty much did know. We had taken the wrong turn and were headed into the high mountains along the so-called *Napoleon Way*. A minority of medieval pilgrims had actually taken this same route simply because it was less frequented by bandits.

Another hour of quad-roiling climbing later and we emerged onto an open, lunar-like landscape. The dense forest had shielded us from the worst vicissitudes of the weather. But now we were immediately exposed to a bullying wind and cold, slanting rain. Psychologically, we hadn't bargained for any of this in Spain in June. But this was the Pyrenees; anything could happen.

"Obviously, we blundered," I belatedly admitted. "This must be the main route."

"Do you think many people are out hiking in this today?" Gavin asked.

"I seriously doubt it," I said. "That's what worries me; we may not see a soul."

We came to a sign marking the French border. Soon after crossing over, we finally began seeing pilgrims. Waves of them followed, in plastic wrappings

Gavin and me at a recent Appalachian Trail event.

and various disguises. Many looked exhausted. The frozen faces of a few even hinted they were flirting with hypothermia. Yet they were headed to even higher elevations.

"Would you like these gloves," I asked Gavin. "They're pretty flimsy."

"No thanks." I looked over and noticed he had astutely found a home for his hands in his pants. I followed his lead.

We were going to be okay, because we had cleared the summit. A 4,300 foot downhill glide to the French border town of St. Jean Pied de Port lay ahead of us. It would get warmer for us every step of the way down. But what about our fellow pilgrims who were still ascending? In fact, this section of El Camino has seen far more deaths than any other over the centuries. And not just in medieval times. That night we would hear a wicked tale of someone perishing in this exact section a couple years before.

"Man, I'm honestly worried about some of these people," I said. "A lot of 'em don't look like they're in great shape."

"Hey look," Gavin said. "There's that big Brazilian man that was in the taxi with us yesterday. Do you think he's gonna' make it?"

"No," I quickly answered. "He should turn around and go back down the mountain with us." Thus commenced a pattern that would repeat itself throughout the Camino: our underestimating the determination of middle-aged and post middle-aged pilgrims. For many the Camino represented the journey of their lifetime, and they were acting like it.

***

"*Skywalker,* hey Skywalker." It was an unfamiliar voice, but it was calling out a familiar name. 'Skywalker' had been my trail name on the Appalachian and Pacific Crest Trails.

Soon a dozen-and-a-half college age pilgrims appeared out of the mist, along with a short, fit-looking middle-aged male. "Oh yeah, Kip," I finally said in realization.

Just a month before this man, Kip Reddick, a professor at Christopher Newport University, had approached me at the annual Trail Days Festival in Damascus, Virginia. He had informed me that he was going to lead a group of theology students on the Camino this summer.

We stood there chatting, when Kip gingerly broached the obvious subject. "Is there some problem up ahead?" He wasn't being nosy—just a good leader. I would have been jittery too, leading a bunch of impetuous college students to high elevations in conditions bordering on diabolical.

"We decided to walk to walk to St. Jean's, and then retrace it tomorrow."

"Great idea," he chortled, showing pilgrims look at things completely different from townspeople. "The Pyrenees are gorgeous."

"How do you know?" Gavin joked, looking around at the dense fog.

"You'll see," Kip assured us.

"You will too," I nodded, looking back up the mountain.

Kip laughed exultantly and headed off with his large class into the heavy fog and worsening weather.

Finally, Gavin and I got down low enough, where the fog density had somewhat abated. The French Pyrenees came into view. Rolling hills of wine-bottle green sloped down into lush, green valleys. Soon a stony, medieval-looking village nestled down deep in the valley came into view.

Gavin's *raison d' etre* for being on this trip was his supposed mastery of French. "Okay Gavin," I said, "here comes your fifteen minutes of fame."

"Do you want to hear all fifteen words right now?" he shot back.

"Can you get me to the bathroom?"

"Yes, but it might be the women's room."

"So am I required to adapt my style here?" I asked.

"Why do you ask?"

"Didn't DeGaulle say, *'Le style c'est l'homme'*" (The style is the man).

"Bill, I hope you don't have an inferiority complex already."

We crossed a stone bridge and began following the cobblestoned main thoroughfare of St. Jean's Pied de Port. Many a fragrant pilgrim over the centuries has surely been delighted to grace this picturesque little *village* surrounded by imposing peaks.

***

The French specialize in—well, in being French. We took our time ambling French-style through town, alternately peering through shop windows. The locals had us beat, however. They popped playfully in and out of the *vino shoppe, delicatessen, chocolaterias,* and *carnicerias,* all with their poodles in tow. Exquisite little houses fringed the town, within easy walking distance of their day's delights.

"Everything is more expensive here," I moaned.

"Bill, it's an honor to pay more if you're in France."

"Please find me the nearest WalMart."

Soon though, even your crusty-hearted narrator softened a bit at the delicate flavor of it all.

"How about finding out where pilgrims are supposed to stay here," I requested of my leader.

"They draw an arrow the same way in France, Bill."

We followed the yellow flechas almost until the main street became circumcised, where we came upon the other symbol of El Camino—the carnet shell. Medieval pilgrims are said to have used these shells when passing by stray homes to ladle out coffee and soup offered up by generous souls. Fortunately, a modern pilgrim is not required to be anywhere near so industrious.

A French woman who was perfectly happy to speak English directed us across the street to a pilgrim bunkroom. The price was five Euros per person. And let me just say this—I don't care what the Far Right xenophobic nationalists say, it's nice with the common European currency unit to not get raped at some currency exchange each time you enter a new European country.

We then deployed Gavin's admittedly impressive French to order up a sumptuous dinner. Afterwards, we ran into a school choir singing in a rustic cathedral. It was all very agreeable. Long live French *joie de vivre.*

Chapter 6

The Big Climb

"Old things are past away, all's become new and strange."

John Bunyan, *Pilgrim's Progress*, 1678

The clutter of boots, rattle of equipment, and click of walking staffs on the cobblestoned streets provided a steady din. The image of Caesar's hordes, or perhaps the French Foreign Legion heading off to battle, was inescapable. Gavin and I joined the masses the next morning on the ascent into the Pyrenees that would take us back into Spain.

Pilgrimage and war have long served eerily similar purposes. They have been the traditional means of those trapped in a provincial lifestyle to satiate their wanderlust. For the most part, human history has had a martial flavor. But we had no such aggressive purposes. Yes, pilgrimage is a step forward for humanity.

I've never been a father; this journey was going to be the closest I'd gotten to the role. My sister (Gavin's mother) had entrusted me with getting Gavin back home in one piece. Worse yet, because of my previous hiking experiences, I was perceived as having leadership skills and expertise.

To be sure, I was working with some pretty good protoplasm in Gavin. Besides his exceptionally quick wit and gifted athleticism, he had a certain intangible confidence. He brought a lot to the table. But his weaknesses were of the glaring and potentially trip-ruining variety. His most recent nickname was *Double Digits*. He had earned this moniker through his mastery of the art of losing cell phones, thirteen being the most recent count.

That well-ingrained habit was obviously not a big problem on this particular trip. However, it did mean that I would have to carry his passport and money at all times. My main concern was simply to not lose *him*. Especially in this steep section here in the Pyrenees.

We began chatting with a middle-aged Frenchman who didn't speak a word of English. Gavin was holding up his end of the conversation admirably, and the Frenchman appeared very friendly. Of course, in that respect, both of them were fading national stereotypes. I tried participating in their conversation, but these two *Francophones* gave me the cold shoulder. Meanwhile, we had a 4,300 foot climb ahead of us, which is equal to the longest climb on the entire Appalachian Trail.

Gavin's interlocutor had that certain provincial look and gait of a local mountaineer. Slowly, the two of them began pulling away from me as we wound our way up the mountain. A few minutes later they disappeared around a corner. I wouldn't see them again the rest of the day. Gavin, of course, didn't have any money or identification. Quickly, I took on a low-grade worry, which would become only more insidious the higher I climbed without seeing him.

***

"Good morning," she said in lightly-accented English.
"Bonjour," I replied in heavily-accented French.
"Where are you from?" she asked.

"United States."

"I studied English in Vermont," she proudly reported.

"Good choice," I joked. "That is probably our most French state."

"My name is Claire," she introduced herself.

"Bill."

Claire was a bit on the heavy side. But it was French style pleasantly overweight, as opposed to American-style you-know-what. I was able to maintain her pace, and chat at the same time.

"What part of France are you from?" I asked.

"Paris."

"Did you take the train down to St. Jean's?"

"No," she replied. "I started in Paris."

"Is there a trail the whole way?"

"Yes, but it's hard to follow."

"Did you ever get lost?"

"Almost every day."

Then I popped *the question*—the one we would all come to hate more than any other.

"What made you decide to do El Camino?"

Claire answered more decisively than most. "I got a divorce, and wanted to go away."

"Hey, good idea," I said. "In America, everybody goes to psychiatrists after their divorce. A long pilgrimage sounds like a better idea."

"Yes, I've already found a boyfriend," she beamed.

"Really," I exclaimed. "What nationality?"

"He is French."

"Did he hike down from Paris, also?"

"No, we met *yesterday* in St. Jeans."

I was enjoying chatting with Claire. But this seemed like a good time to cut out. Plus I needed to speed up to wherever Gavin was waiting on me.

"Okay Claire, I'll see you in Roncesvalles tonight."

"If you see my boyfriend up ahead, please tell him I miss him."

"What does he look like?"

"He is thin, blonde hair, and wears framed glasses."

"What is his name?"

"Benedict."

"I'll tell him, if I catch him."

We would see this exact pattern repeatedly over the next few hundred kilometers—Benedict galloping ahead of Claire all day, only to re-emerge at strategic points in the evening.

***

If there was one day on the entire Camino where you would really want a weather break, it would be right here. We got it. The steady, bone-shaking rain of yesterday diminished to a small drizzle. The fog thinned out, and there was even a hint of weak sunshine. Fabulous vistas of the yawning Pyrenees presented themselves.

Pyrenees separating France and Spain

What an advantage to have such a natural boundary between two major countries. In time-honored European fashion, two neighbors like this would have normally fought a dozen or more major wars. But I could only find a record of two medium-intensity conflicts between the two countries—one in the 9th century, and the other in the 19th century (Napoleon).

It was the skirmish in the 9thcentury that is most relevant to the Camino. Does the name *Charlemagne* ring a bell? If a certain dread sets in because you could never remember on high school history texts exactly where he fit in the endless European wars, you've got company. All I remembered was that his name came up more than other ancient figures with distinctive names, like

Pepin the Short, Briny the Elder, or Richard the Lionhearted. So he must have been important. He was—unusually so.

Charlemagne was the single most powerful strongman on the entire blood-soaked European Continent. He personally led battles against any and all takers. But his greatest triumph occurred right in this immediate area, when he led his army over the Pyrenees and struck a fierce counter-blow to the invading Moors. In fact, this would prove to be the high water mark to the 800 year Muslim occupation of Spain.

After the victory, on their exit out of Spain, Charlemagne's dashing young nephew Roland valiantly insisted on protecting the rear flank from Moorish counter-attackers. Alas, he was ambushed and killed. Legend has it that upon hearing the news, Charlemagne was so devastated that he let loose a cry of anguish that can still be heard reverberating in the wind today. Fittingly, an epic poem, *The Chanson de Roland,* was penned to mark fallen Roland's heroism. It was to become the most widely known musical work during the entire Middle Ages.

Of course, we all know that the tidy history handed down to schoolchildren and *what actually happened* have been known to differ significantly. In reality, some old-fashioned Shakespearean-style intrigue apparently gripped Charlemagne's ranks. One of Charlemagne's veteran soldiers became concerned that too much glory would be bestowed on dashing young Roland. He proceeded to tip off the Basques—whose women Charlemagne's soldiers had taken certain liberties with—as to just exactly where Charlemagne's army was traveling. They proceeded to smash Roland's rear ranks in a decidedly Basque fashion, killing young Roland in the process. But the tale of Roland being killed by the infidel Moors makes for a much more heroic epic.

Nonetheless, Charlemagne is considered by some to be the first pilgrim on El Camino de Santiago, and the path we were now following was roughly the same route as his 1,200 years ago.

***

The good weather break could only hold up to a certain elevation. As I reached the highest elevations, the elements again became socked in. It was getting colder and the precipitation was picking up. After crossing back over the Spanish border, I was relieved to see a little wooden hut that I remembered from yesterday. I decided to pop in, and try to warm up. Better yet, maybe Gavin would be in there. But when I opened the door, I couldn't believe my eyes.

It looked like every pilgrim on the mountain was huddled up in there. Anxiously, I looked for my wayward nephew. But to no avail. I had to leave my backpack outside, just to squeeze in there. The impressive thing was that I had seen many of these pilgrims leaving St. Jean Pied de Port this morning, about a half-hour ahead of us. Personally, I had been hiking as fast as I could the whole day. Yet, I had just caught up with them. Many were in their late middle-aged years, with accompanying physiques—quite similar to the pilgrims we had admiringly witnessed climbing in the steady rain yesterday. This was the first break many of them had taken in about 13 miles of steady uphill climbing. They had their game faces on.

Because we had done this section in reverse yesterday, I decided to break through the tension. I announced in Spanish and English to the hut full of foreigners, "You are very near the top. Then it is downhill straight to Roncesvalles."

"How many kilometers to the summit?" a frail-looking lady of indeterminate age asked in a softly intense voice.

"Not over two," I answered reassuringly, although that might have been a bit optimistic.

"Downhill, steep?" someone else asked in broken English.

A spate of questions followed. Then I tried describing my nephew, and asked if anybody had seen him. Nobody knew of him. A certain fear passed over me. *Did I inadvertently pass him, somewhere?* He could conceivably be waiting way back down the mountain for me. I cut out of there. I knew from past experience that on days like this it was best to keep moving and not let my body temperature begin to fall.

I soon reached the summit, and then started down. Quickly I came upon the junction in the trail, featuring different approaches to Roncesvalles. Gavin and I had come up the face of the mountain yesterday by mistake. A couple pilgrims were standing there in the fog trying to figure out which way to go. "This way," they said to me, pointing to the trail running off to the right. But I decided to stick with the steeper route that I already knew from yesterday. Within a half-hour, I emerged from the woods back into tiny Roncesvalles. The first person I saw was my ultra-cool nephew. His hands were open, and a look of dismay was on his face.

"Bill, where have you been?"

My sister had warned me that Gavin's motif is to stay on the offensive at all times.

"I was busy practicing my French with a big group," was the only reply I could muster.

Gavin had one of the lowest boredom thresholds of any human I'd ever seen. Up until five minutes before we had left his house in northern Virginia, he had considered strapping his vaunted skateboard onto his backpack. Getting through the Camino without some trip-endangering blunder was going to be a protracted struggle.

Chapter 7

Medieval Attitudes *Redux*

If there was a single place on the entire Camino that best captured the medieval feel, it was the old pilgrim's bunkhouse in Roncesvalles. Dark, dank, and mysterious, with a strange hospitaleiro to boot, it is just the right atmosphere for about the late-tenth century. One could almost imagine cries of help emanating from down in the dungeon, along with sounds of belts lashing, charges of heresy, spies, intrigue, escape attempts, waterboarding, deathbed conversions, sacred chants, and even a profound hush.

Perhaps the medieval ambience was too much for the group in front of us. As modern tourists are wont to do, they pulled out their cameras and started snapping away. Almost immediately, a graying hospitaleiro, with a panicked look on his face rushed over. "No, no," he shrieked in broken English. "Terrible. Terrible. Out. Get out."

To Gavin's and my amazement, they all left obediently, with sheepish looks on their face. This meant shelling out over 100 Euros to stay at the only hotel in the village. Meanwhile, the hospitaleiro rushed away.

When he returned, it was my turn to cause confusion. The 130 or so bunks crammed into the modest-sized room looked like they had been designed for the North Korean gymnastics team.

Worse yet, they had footboards at the end of them. If you happen to be in the neighborhood of 6'11", footboards at the end of a bed are the bane of your existence. While living in Latin America, I had rushed into many a motel and asked dumbstruck desk clerks whether the beds had footboards at the end of them. So I remembered the vocabulary of footboards.

"*Todas las camas tienen las espaldas a los fines de las camas* (Do all the beds have footboards at the end)?" I asked the hospitaleiro. But he looked bewildered by my request. So I asked, "*Podria poner mi colchon en el piso* (May I put my mattress on the floor)?"

"*Que?,*" he answered.

I repeated again, but to no avail. Gavin tried French, but that didn't work any better. I then spoke slowly in English. Forget it.

"Bill, try pig Latin," Gavin suggested, which drew hoots from the people behind us. But that only confused the poor man even more. He anxiously rushed away again.

"Oh great," Gavin said. "He's probably calling the Vatican."

The man came back and tensely asked, "Bed?" Stupidly, I again tried to talk with him in Spanish and English. But nothing worked. Finally, I just pulled out 10 Euros for two beds, and he let us in. And that's when the real controversy started.

***

First, I heard loud footsteps. Then there was even louder knocking on the door of the bathroom stall I was occupying.

"Occupied," I said quietly.

"Ten," came the hospitaleiro's voice in broken English, presumably referring to the time.

"Yes, just a few minutes."

"Bed," he said urgently. "Bed."

"I'm using the toilet."

"Out," came back an increasingly frantic voice. He began steadily pounding on the door.

"I have the right to use the bathroom," I fired back, using an American language of rights. Of course, that only guaranteed a culture clash, given that this man appeared nostalgic for the Church culture of the mid-11th century.

"Bed," he kept repeating.

"I've got to use the bathroom," I protested from my squatted position.

"Now," he said and began hammering away at the door. It felt like a storm trooper outside was on the verge of kicking the door down and straight into my lap or head.

"Shut up," I finally yelled back.

"One minute," he finally said.

However, my small victory was Pyrrhic. By tensing me up, he had also tightened up my sphincter muscles. I called uncle in my toileting effort, and burst out of the stall. The hospitaleiro blanketed me with tight coverage as I walked back to the bunk room, in shame and humiliation. When I reached my bunk, 129 other pilgrims lay in various states of repose.

However, one pilgrim (Avi, the Israeli mentioned earlier) lay there in a state of amazement. In the bunk next to Avi's, Claire, my acquaintance from that morning, had just mounted her "boyfriend" that she had met yesterday. Unwittingly, my downstairs bathroom drama had served as a decoy for their assignation. And perhaps thank God. Had this particular hospitaleiro spotted such an act of rank hedonism, we might have had a true international incident, featuring waterboarding and the works.

I reached down next to my bunk and began grabbing things from my backpack when the hospitaleiro started shoving me toward my bunk.

"Bed," he demanded and grabbed my arm.

"No, go away." I jerked my arm away. He finally walked off in disgust. I went to bed wondering whether this eerie place was a harbinger of things to come on the Camino.

Chapter 8

The Basque Region

"It doesn't matter to us if Spain is big or small, strong or weak, rich or poor. They have enslaved our country and this is enough for us to hate them with all our soul."

Sabino Arana, Founding Father of Basque Nationalism

"Are you ready for the World Cup match tonight?" I asked the young *Spanish* couple walking along with us.

"No, we don't care," the petite girl plainly said. That seemed like an abrupt answer considering how polite these two young Basques had been up to this point.

"Do you even hope Spain wins?" I couldn't resist inquiring further.

"*Somos Basques,*" the girl's soft-spoken partner replied. "We don't care."

That was that. But when we got out of earshot, Gavin asked, "Do you really think they don't care if Spain wins?"

"I have trouble believing it," I said. "I bet we hear muffled cheers tonight coming out of some of these homes."

We had spent most of the day walking 28 kilometers (17 miles) to Larrasoana, where we hoped to watch Spain's match. As we had gotten further away from the Pyrenees, the cold, damp conditions had lifted, replaced by beautiful summertime weather. Gavin and I had joined up with a predominantly French and Israeli contingent (mentioned earlier). At one point, I had gotten carried away crossing a low stone bridge and decided to high-step through the current just below. "*Oh my God*," I had suddenly screamed. The current was much stronger than I had expected, and had carried me into the deeper water. I had been very lucky to make it to the far shore without completely capsizing. At least the group all seemed to get a charge out of it.

"Damn, I've got to change socks and everything," I said. "I'll catch up with everybody."

"Bill, why did you do that?" Gavin asked in a tone of utter bewilderment.

"I'll give you a hint," I answered. "I didn't do it to impress you." It's a bit sobering to think an 18 year-old isn't as big of a showoff as his 49 year-old uncle.

The Basque region through which we now were trooping under a wide azul sky was especially pleasant looking, without having the dramatic scenery of the Pyrenees. In the small towns that we passed through, people went about their business without paying much attention to us. The homes were modest-sized, made of immaculate white stone and red-tiled roofs. I had been living in Florida, where all the properties looked as if they were built by speculators hoping to "flip" them for a quick profit. These sturdy homes couldn't have been more different. They looked like they were built by people planning on staying right here for another 2,500 years.

We had been warned by other Spaniards about this region. But actually, the Basque region is the perfect place for the Camino. They have a long tradition of allowing outsiders to peacefully pass through—as long as they don't stay too long. This was no coincidence, as a brief look at Basque history shows.

***

In the mid-eleventh century, three Frenchmen were riding their horses through the Basque Navarrese region on their way to Santiago de Compostela. One hot afternoon they arrived at the banks of the *Salty River.* Two Basque Navarrese happened to be sitting along the river sharpening their knives. The Frenchmen asked them if the water was fit to be drunk. The two Navarrese assured them it was, at which point the Frenchmen began to water their mounts. The three horses immediately dropped dead in the river. The Navarrese quickly jumped up and began enthusiastically skinning the horses, in order to sell the meat for a profit.

Unfortunately for the Basques, one of the three Frenchmen in this group was a man named Aymery Picaud. This same Picaud had been commissioned by Pope Calixtinus to write a travel guide on the Santiago pilgrimage. It became known as the *Codex Calixtinus.* In the *Codex,* Picaud lashed out at the Basques:

"The Basques are dark in color, wicked in appearance, depraved, perverted, treacherous, disloyal, false, lustful, drunken, and uncouth. If you saw them eating, you would take them for dogs or pigs the way the whole family eats out of one pot. If they could, they would kill a Frenchman for no more than a coin."

And, of course, he couldn't resist adding:

"They have sex with animals so much that they are required to affix chastity locks to the behinds of their mules and horses, so that no other Basques may have access to them."

Despite the shrill nature of his rants, the *Codex Calixtinus,* was destined to become the most popular travel book in the entire Middle Ages. The number of pilgrims on the Camino ratcheted up sharply upon its publication, despite the fears they had of the Basque region.

***

The Basques are the mystery people of Europe. Exhaustive research over the centuries has left historians virtually clueless as to their origins. The only thing for sure is that they are different in every sense from the Spanish and French people around them.

Their ancient tongue, *Eusketa*, is related to no other language on earth. There are physical distinctions as well. They have distinctly long, straight noses, thick eyebrows, strong chins, and long earlobes. They also have the highest concentration of type O, rH negative blood of any people in the world. But where did they come from? Some think they are far-flung aboriginal people. Others have even speculated they are the lost 13th tribe of Israel. Their thick chests, broad shoulders, and burly frames have led many to believe they are descendants of Cro-Magnon man, who lived until 40,000 years ago. But to this day, nobody knows.

And history sure as heck has shown that the French and Spanish don't understand the Basques.

***

The most famous Spanish painting of the 20th century is Picasso's *Guernica*. It is a vivid depiction of the bombing of the sacred market town of Guernica, where the Basque farmers have sold their produce on Monday mornings since medieval times.

On April 26, 1937 at high market time, low-flying German Lutwaffe planes began bombing Guernica in the middle of market hours. Hitler had lent his fascist brother, Franco, these planes for use in the Spanish Civil War. A total of 1,645 Basque peasants were killed in the three hour attack. Franco ludicrously claimed that the planes under his command didn't even fly that day due to bad weather. At one point, he even tried to say that the Basques had dynamited their own city. When the Vatican pressured him to negotiate, he told them the only possible resolution to the Basque problem was complete annihilation of Basque nationalists.

However, when World War II was over, the United States decided to overlook Franco's atrocities. He soon became our ally in the Cold War. That left the Basques with only one viable strategy—insurgency. This is when *ETA* (*Euskadi Ta Askatasuna*) was started. In 1973 *ETA* pulled off their *magnum opus*—a horrific train attack in Madrid that killed Franco's right-hand man. But like everyone else, *ETA* was unable to bring down Franco. Franco's forty-year rule finally ended with his death in 1975. While the masses in Madrid wore black armbands, the Basque youth were dancing joyously in the streets.

It is worth remembering that the few hundred years of the

European nation-state are only a small part of the Basque history. They aren't loyal to any one country.

***

We followed the flechas over a stone bridge and entered the Basque town of Larrasoana late in the afternoon. Nobody much was out on the street. The signs were in Euskati which we didn't have the least clue about. *Do these people really know anything about El Camino? Will we be able to find an albergue?* This would be the first of many towns where these thoughts crossed my mind upon entry.

Fortunately, we would quickly learn that the Camino never disappoints. No matter how desolate or forlorn a pueblo appeared at first sight, there were always quarters in these small pueblos that welcomed pilgrims. None other than the mayor was running a pilgrim's hostel in Larrasoana. He put Gavin and me in a room with just one other person, which was a nice feint towards privacy.

A group of French women passed by our room. We had already come across them a few times during the day. I had tried various greetings in Spanish and English, and they had painstakingly tried to communicate with me in French. But we hadn't been able to find a common tongue. Nonetheless, I had an immediate affinity for one this one lady who appeared to be about my age. There was something I found endearing about the way she visibly staggered every time she strained to hoist her backpack. Now she appeared relieved that her all-day troop was over.

"How do you say 'very pretty'?" I asked Gavin.

"*Très jolie.*"

"*C'est très jolie,*" I said to the woman, which was at least half-true anyway.

She looked surprised. It was the first thing I had said all day that she had understood. Laughingly, she mouthed off some response in French that completely eluded me. I looked at Gavin.

"She said 'come see me'," he reported.

The lady then headed on with her friend to their room. Again I realized, what I had learned from three years of living in Latin America. It is much easier to not be cowardly in conversations with members of the opposite sex when you barely know what in the world you are saying.

***

"Let's find a restaurant to watch Spain's match," Gavin suggested.

"Yeah, we'd better get there early to get a spot."

We joined up with another group of pilgrims and proceeded to make a tour of the handful of commercial establishments in Larrasoana. But to our disbelief, the match was not being shown in any of them. *"El partido de La Copa* (Tonight's World Cup match)?" I inquired of the bartenders. In each place, my inquiry about tonight's match was greeted with shrugs.

"Maybe if we walk around the town plaza, somebody will invite us in their house to watch the match," Martina suggested seriously.

"We should at least hear some screams coming from around the village," an anxious pilgrim from Madrid said.

We were all slow on the uptake; the reality was that nobody here in the Basque region gave a fig about this match that the rest of Spain was obsessing about.

Chapter 9

Hemingway

"You know, Paris was a happy time. And Key West was quite wonderful. But Spain was much the best."

Ernest Hemingway, *The Moveable Feast*

"I've heard of Pamplona," Gavin said as we entered the town's outskirts. "Is that where they have the running of the bulls?"

"Yeah, what else?" I prompted him.

"Uh, who was it? Wait—don't tell me. Uh, uh, oh, Hemingway. Yeah, Hemingway."

Hemingway. Ernest Hemingway. Chicago, Italy, Paris, Spain, Key West, Africa, Cuba, and, finally, Idaho. These are the main places identified with that legendary American avatar of thought and action, Ernest Hemingway (1899-1961). And of all these places, none did Hemingway fall in love with quite as completely as he did with Spain.

His first great novel, *The Sun Also Rises*, is set in post-First World War Paris. The character modeled on Hemingway, Jake, is locked in a love affair of tragicomic flavor with a British woman. Due to a war injury, he is sexually impotent. Jake takes to drowning his sorrows in Parisian cafes. "You're an expatriate," his traveling companion ribs him. "You've lost touch with the soil.

43

Fake European standards have ruined you. You drink yourself to death. You become obsessed by sex. You spend all your time talking, not working. You're an expatriate, see?" Soon, however, this same 'friend' takes up with Jake's love.

Jake, a prototypical alpha male, is just getting used to this alternative arrangement, when a Jewish boxer that Jake can't stand steals the woman away for a weekend. Acrimony and bitterness follow. He decides to head south to Pamplona, Spain for a bullfight.

It was love at first sight. Flamenco dancing, folk music, bullfighting, and dancing formed the pageantry. "At once we felt at home," he wrote. "It was Spain. The wine was good. The food was abundant. The sun was shining."

Statue of *"The Running of the Bulls"* in Pamplona.
Look at those faces. *Caveat emptor.*

To some people's regret, Hemingway popularized the San Fermin Festival—better known as 'the running of the bulls'—to an unhealthy degree. Every July the people with the very lowest boredom thresholds on earth descend on this medium-sized city at the foot of the Pyrenees, seeking their own brand of thrills. Debauchery and madness often follow in their wake. The highlight of the festival is when six raging bulls are set loose in the streets. The television coverage of the festival focuses almost exclusively on the number of injuries—40 or 50 on an average year—along with the occasional death. But that's not the point, according to those who run with the bulls. Their faith is that honor and virility are bestowed by proximity to the bull. Unfortunately, many figure out too late that there are actually worse things in life than being bored.

"Americans come all the way over here and feel like they need to do something crazy to live up to the festival's reputation," a Spaniard lamented to me. "One guy tried to jump off a balcony onto a bull and broke his neck. He filed a lawsuit against the city."

***

"Now I understand why Hemingway committed suicide," Gavin incisively commented as we passed the low-lying buildings of the commercial district on the way into town.

Fortunately, you can never judge a Spanish town by its outskirts. Rather, they unfold slowly, almost like a puzzle. The central plaza has been the epicenter of European life for the last 2,000 years. One follows the labrynth of aged, cobbled streets and alleys wending their way always towards the center. Pamplona's central square was especially comely, with graceful promenades, fine stores, wrought-iron balconies, and open vistas adorning a large open air space. Over the years this same square has witnessed gory bullfights, even-gorier executions, and brilliant fiestas.

Gavin and I sought out the brand new 130 bed albergue, which lay right in the center of town. In fact, we were to see many more gleaming new albergues dotting the route to Santiago. El Camino de Santiago is one of the largest growth industries in Europe.

Speaking of growth, I had another growth that was worrying me greatly. Every albergue had signs posted warning of 'chinches'. Bedbugs. Sure enough, I already had contracted a large, painful sore where the sun doesn't shine. What really worried me was the signs also mentioned that chinches were attracted to a certain blood type. Indeed, I had been bitten by a bedbug at a hostel on the Appalachian Trail that had required medical treatment. I quickly developed a low-level paranoia. *Was a bedbug going to spend all night traversing a crowded albergue to get to my bunk and a drink of my coveted blood type?*

The signs recommended an ammonia-based cream as a remedy. I rushed off to the pharmacist where other pilgrims were lined up with the same purpose. Then I decided to wash our clothes just in case we were hosting a colony of these critters. A Nordic-looking lady in her mid-thirties stood there between the washing machines.

"*Hay una fila* (Is there a line)?" I asked, even though I knew she wasn't Spanish.

"English, French, or German," she immediately corrected me. That gave her nationality away. Most Europeans study English extensively. Many also study French. Nobody studies German. The only reason a person would speak it is because that's where they grew up. Because they lost the war(s), they have to learn our languages. Sorry.

"Is there a washing machine available?" I asked.

"Yes," she responded in crisp English. "But you must wash at 130 degrees to kill bedbugs." We were both fitting national stereotypes: the American demonstrating easy familiarity with strangers, while the German exhibits greater preparedness. Soon we were in an extended conversation about hiking boots.

You couldn't help but notice that a large number of the German pilgrims were wearing big, heavy hiking boots—stereotypes be damned. But by the same token, a disproportionate share of Germans were becoming hobbled by blisters (*"ampollas"*). Gavin and I found it difficult to not make cracks every time we saw somebody schlepping along in their sandals, with their feet all bandaged up, and a pair of heavy boots strapped onto the back of their backpacks. "Perhaps the Armistice treaty should have outlawed big boots," a British pilgrim wryly remarked. One college-age German girl who was wearing heavy boots had been limping heavily when she had spotted Gavin's light moccasin slippers hanging off his backpack. "Could I try walking in those?" she had asked Gavin. He had shrugged and lofted them over to her. The girl had proceeded to take off like Forrest Gump. In fact, we were not to see her for several days. When we did finally catch up with her after a thirty kilometer day, she had sheepishly returned Gavin's half-demolished slippers.

After washing clothes, I headed off with this German lady to dinner. Her name was Sybil. "I'm European," she said plainly. She had lived in London for the last eleven years, was unmarried, childless, intelligent, working for a multinational company, and moderately happy. Yet there was a palpable look of un-fulfillment about her. In many ways she was a representative face of modern Europe. Perhaps the Camino was a good place for her.

In any event, I never saw her again. She was off at first light the next morning, plenty happy to trek alone.

Chapter 10

Northern Spain

I distinctly remember my last week living in Great Britain. I had decided to take a train trip to Edinborough, Scotland. On the way back to London I sat transfixed, gazing out into the lush English countryside. Rustic village after village passed in and out of view. From my vantage point, they all seemed virtually indistinguishable.

Each village had a staid, brown Anglican church steeple that towered over the landscape. Most of these churches had been built from the 13th through 17th centuries during the so-called *Age of Faith*. It is estimated there was one church for every forty or fifty people. This is especially impressive given that England may now be the most irreligious country in the world. Most of these same churches are now locked, bolted, and neglected.

The northern arc of Spain is also littered with small villages. On a typical day's walk of 25 kilometers (15 miles), we would pass through three or four such pueblos. Their similarities were striking. All were tightly condensed, walled in, and low-lying, but with one great exception—the church. Before

This French pilgrim had a medieval style. HIs stick and sack carried him all the way to Finistierre. He then set foot for India.

leaving for Spain, I had asked several ex-pilgrims if it was easy to get lost on El Camino. "If you get lost," they all said, "just look towards the next town and you'll see the steeple of the church."

It looked like the clock had been turned back several decades in many of these pueblos. Very few cars roamed the streets. Instead of people talking on cell phones, you had old geysers, with an apparent infinitude of time on their hands, sitting on benches chatting. Occasionally, one would get especially animated and begin making stabbing points with his finger.

"What are they arguing about?" Gavin wondered.

"The Spanish Civil War," I responded.

"What did they do around here?" he asked incredulously. "Kill everybody under thirty?"

Sadly, he had a point. The birth rate has plummeted in Spain (especially ironic given the long siesta hour!). But the bigger problem is that the youth have migrated massively to the cosmopolitan centers, leaving these backwater towns looking slightly haunted.

Nonetheless, they retain a certain rustic enchantment, and pilgrims habitually take breaks in the central square. The signs by the water fountain usually said *Agua Potable*. In Puente la Reina, several of us gathered around the fountain deciding whether to risk the water.

"It says it's drinkable," Martina said.

"Yeah, but it makes you glow," Gavin commented.

An elderly lady on a nearby balcony anticipated our discussion.

"El agua esta perfecto," she shouted down at us. *"Tenemos un sistema magnifico."* You couldn't help but notice the hometown pride in her voice.

Gavin, however, was unmoved. "So what's that mean—if you drink it, you won't drop dead until the next town?" However, like everyone else, we got in the habit of drinking the water straight out of the pipe or faucet connected to these fountains.

***

Often in these small towns, I would run into the French lady I had so dramatically and breathtakingly characterized as *tres juliet*. Playfully, I would feign worshiping the ground she walked on, help remove her backpack, and run to fill up her bottles of water. This *pas de deux* created amusement amongst our fellow pilgrims. However, our attempts at communicating continued to be an abysmal failure. I tried speaking slow Spanish, assuming that its similarity with her own Latin-based language would bring on recognition from her. Not even close. English didn't work any better. About all I had been able to figure out was that her name was Rosemary. And this wasn't a case of a stubborn Frenchwoman refusing to speak our language. Rosemary flat out didn't speak a second language. And my attempts at speaking French with her can only be described as execrable.

"Looks like you're ready for prime-time, Bill," Gavin would say in a voice dripping with sarcasm. Eventually, we would join other pilgrims in the shade to take mini-siestas with our backpacks as headrests.

Communication problems arose in all directions. A couple of short, stocky Swiss ladies in their seventies kept angling to have photos made with me. This exact thing has been par for the course for me since I was 17 years old, and went from being merely tall, to extraordinarily tall. I won't pretend that it isn't nice at times to be approached and asked for photos. Perhaps that's what Freud meant by "the narcissism of small differences."

I usually stood there like a circus freak on these occasions, with a feigned smile, as cameras snapped. The minute the photo was developed, people often began shaking my arm and exclaiming, "Look, look, look at this. See how tall you are! Can you believe it?" Okay.

Gavin got a kick out of it at first. The requests were usually nice, and I felt obliged to go along with the whole thing, and even clown it up a bit. But as the same routine played itself out, sometimes several times per day, he developed a teenage wariness of the repetitive nature of these scenes.

"Bill, do you get tired of all that?"

"It depends."

As for the two Swiss German ladies, the only way I knew they were in their seventies (Well okay, I had an idea) was that someone else had told me. They sure hadn't told me themselves; they were seemingly incapable of uttering a single word of either

English or Spanish.

"Man, I honestly can't believe it," I said to Gavin. "How in the world can somebody be from Switzerland and only speak one language?"

"They speak the international language," he chided me.

We were to see these two women all along the way. It was always the same. They would run right up to my tiptoes, both talking German 100 kilometers per hour, while laughing and baying at me. Of course, this gave Gavin ample opportunity to stick the needle in.

"Bill, don't be a heartbreaker."

"Hey, remember. There are two of them."

There was one other issue. These two septuagenarians didn't exactly look like they were long-standing members of the Jane Fonda School of Aerobics for post middle-aged women. Yet practically every time we got to a pueblo after walking 25 kilometers, there they would be. How were they getting there? We would eventually find out.

***

Sometimes, however, the inability to communicate can actually be a good thing. An especially burly, intimidating lady also arrived in Puente de Reina as we lay reposed on our backpacks in the shade. She was, we were to find out, French. Her distinguishing feature was the rusty-looking, pipe-like arms that flowed out of a red tank-top shirt.

We had seen her before, aggressively attempting to familiarize herself with members of the opposite sex. Many pilgrims actually seemed intimidated by this woman. There had even been complaints to hospitaleiros over her supposed exhibitionism. Of course, in a group this large, there was bound to be a bull in the china closet. But that person is almost always a male. Nonetheless, given my garrulous nature, I couldn't help but engage in some verbal intercourse with this woman.

"*Felicidades* (Congratulations)," I said when she walked up to us. "*Lo hiciste* (You made it)."

She didn't speak a word of Spanish, nor any English. But she had finally received encouragement from a male pilgrim. She now hovered directly over Gavin and me, looking like she might behead one of us. Her face could charitably be described as deeply unlovely.

"Don't tell her you speak French," I warned Gavin.

"Bill, you brought this on yourself."

"She may be Andre the Giant's sister."

"Then she's perfect for you."

This lady was soon to become widely known amongst pilgrims as *The Terrorist.* We were destined to see The Terrorist all along the way. Worse yet, she appeared more and more angry each time. Pilgrims of both genders were visibly repelled by her. But you had to give her one thing—she hung in there, despite always appearing in deep angst.

Here in Puente de la Reina, she continued hectoring me from above, despite my giving no indication I understood a word. Gavin and I took this as our cue. We slowly got up, hoisted our backpacks, and left town.

All I can say—and this is the God's honest truth—is that I hope our fellow pilgrims made as much fun of us, as we did of them. And obviously I deserve the brunt of the blame, given I was the adult in the group. Fortunately, the religion we were celebrating is very tolerant of us sinners.

Chapter 11

Apology—Waste of Time

"Insanity in individuals is something rare. But in groups, parties, nations, and epochs, it is the rule."

Friedrich Nietzschke

There is a famous painting in the Alhambra Museum called, *The Expulsion of the Jews*. Tomas Torquemada, the director of the Inquisition, is depicted storming out of a meeting with Queen Isabella and King Ferdinand. The remnants of his shattered crucifix lie at his feet; he is in tears. Ferdinand has just informed him that the Jews will be allowed to remain in Spain. "Judas sold Christ out for 30 pieces of silver," Torquemada raged. "You sell Spain out for 300,000 ducats."

It was 1492 and the Jews had offered King Ferdinand and Queen Isabella 300,000 ducats for the right to remain in Spain. The ever crafty Ferdinand had indicated his willingness to accept such a bribe. However, Torqemada had an ace in the hole — Queen Isabella.

"Isabella always hated the Jews," wrote 16th century biographer, Eliyaho Capsali. "Ever since her marriage she had been asking Ferdinand to exile the Jews of Spain." When, however, she saw that the King was reluctant to take such a step, she screamed, "You no doubt love the Jews, and the reason is that you are of their flesh and blood." Ultimately, Queen Isabella overruled her husband.

The Expulsion Decree read:

"Thus, the great damage caused to Christianity by their partnership and connection with the Jews has been discovered. Since it is clearly demonstrated that they always try to draw away the Christian believers from the Holy Catholic faith, we have ordered the expulsion of all Jews and Jewesses in our kingdom. Never should any of them return."

The Jews, who had resided in Spain for the last 1,200 years, were given four months to accept baptism as Christians or flee the country. In 1492, the Jewish community numbered 700,000, almost 10% of Spain's population. Up to half of the doctors, lawyers, and professors in the major cities were Jewish. Spain had achieved the distinction of being the largest and best home for the Jews of the *Diaspora*. Suddenly, however, this renaissance was over and the night of the Dark Ages had descended over the Iberian Peninsula.

About one-third of the Jews decided to accept Christian baptism; they were allowed to remain. The rest of these *Sephardic* Jews had to flee. Many went to North Africa, Spain's ancient enemy. Whole communities of Jews sprung up there, full of well-educated, capable people.

Until doing research for this book, I had thought that inquisition was a one-time bout of lunacy that had occurred in 1492. But, in fact, it lasted all the way until the 19th century. And after the expulsion of the Jews, the Inquisition extended to Muslims, and then Protestants. Ultimately the biggest loser was Spain itself, as it fell from far and away the world's most powerful nation to also-ran status, a fall from which it never has fully recovered.

***

Gavin and I followed the flechas out of another small town into the dusty Spanish countryside. Trailing along with us were the two Israelis and Martina. We passed under an overhang. *"Judios =*

Nazis," was spray-painted in large black letters. Just beyond it was a sign, marked up with "Netanyahu = Hitler."

Our two Israeli companions, Avi and David, walked past the signs without comment. The silence was pregnant. Israelis are world-class travelers. Whatever far-flung spot around the globe a person visits, one is bound to run into Israelis. They're often not terribly popular. "One Israeli is fine," my British sidekick in Chile had told me. "Two are far too many."

In my many encounters with Israelis over the years, I've noticed that they are very reluctant to discuss international affairs. But given that we were walking through a country where Jews had suffered an unspeakable tragedy, second only to the enormous crime of the Holocaust, I couldn't resist asking Avi and David about the Inquisition.

"What is there to say?" Avi responded plainly to my prompting.

"Well, do you think the Spanish government should issue a formal apology for the Inquisition?"

"No, an apology is a waste of time.'

I couldn't help but notice the difference between the Israeli style, compared to that of American Jews. The latter's discourse is much more likely to be filled with an aggressive language of rights, while the Israelis could be said to adopt British-style stiff upper lips.

David didn't show as much enthusiasm for the historical discussions as his cohort, Avi. Instead, he was single-mindedly focused on keeping up with Martina. That was no easy task, even for an Israeli. Martina cut an impressively athletic physique, which clearly hadn't escaped David's attention. He prostrated himself straining to maintain her pace. Actually, the only person who could consistently keep pace with Martina was my very athletic 18 year-old nephew.

Gavin hadn't known the first thing in the world about El Camino before leaving his home in Leesburg, Virginia, other than it was in Europe. Apparently though, he had thought it was going to be a grueling journey in the Alps. In the run up to our journey, his mother kept reporting to me that Gavin was jogging to school with his backpack attached. Swimming, track, and lacrosse were also part of his regimen.

He was also notable around his neighborhood for having a style all his own. Despite having a car, he preferred to travel by skateboard. The time of day was hardly of any concern. It was impossible for his mother to keep track of his whereabouts, as he often slept at unknown friends' houses. Frequently, girls drove by the house, and timidly knocked on the door to pick *him* up. He had returned from one recent date with his neck so charred that the girl he had been with got dubbed, *Dracula.* Yet unlike so many high school teenagers, he really didn't seem obsessed by carnal matters. But who really knew?

Being perfectly chiseled, Gavin was probably one of the few pilgrims for whom El Camino did not represent a major struggle. He could make the paces—usually about 15 or 16 miles per day—without having to dig too deep. Thus, when he was waiting for other pilgrims—including his uncle—he often took to hitting the hardpan dirt and cranking out pushups, despite the broiling sun beating down on his head. It wasn't done to impress. But none other than Martina seemed just that. In fact, a pattern emerged. She began talking less to David (and to me!), and more to my nephew. Call it Darwin's *natural selection.* In fact, it was so subtle that young Gavin might not have even noticed it himself. But David did. After a few days of a full-court press on Martina, he realized the game was off. He and Avi made a pragmatic decision.

David and Avi decided to take a bus to a different region of Spain. They bid us a hasty farewell and were off. Israelis didn't win all those wars by being overly sentimental.

Fortunately, Martina herself was a realist, as opposed to a stalker, and we didn't have a reprise of *The Graduate.* Instead, Martina met a British doctor who was to obsequiously escort her all the way to Santiago, and then on to the Atlantic Ocean.

But wait a minute. El Camino de Santiago is a religious pilgrimage, not a gigantic European singles bar. Right? So allow me to broach that delicate topic.

Chapter 12

The 'R' Word

"Sorry I missed church. I was busy practicing witchcraft and becoming a lesbian."

Popular sticker in Asheville, North Carolina

I recently moved to the popular counter-culture mecca of Asheville, North Carolina. Mainly I was just curious. All along the Appalachian Trail, I had heard about this modest-sized city in the middle of *red country*, known as the San Francisco of the South. Hikers, artists, musicians, and writers all seemed to be beating the door down to move here. Sure enough, Asheville has proven to be different.

It's a beautiful, medium-sized town of clapboard homes, situated at the foot of the Great Smoky Mountains. What surprised me, though, was that amidst all the white clapboard homes were countless even larger white clapboard churches. Why was I so surprised? Because in Asheville, organized religion is sometimes referred to as the *'r' word*. It's almost as toxic as the 'n' word or 'f' word.

But the bigger story is that Asheville is a microcosm of a larger trend that is playing out amongst a wide stratum of our society, especially our youth. Genuine, practicing Christians are looked down on as virtual 'Flat-Earthers'. In large cities, a Christian is bound to spend as much time apologizing for his faith as actually practicing it. "I'm spiritual, but not religious," is the safe, new fallback position.

A few years ago I was swapping contact information with a hippyish guy in his early twenties that I had met on the Appalachian Trail. His e-mail address was religionkills@hotmail.com. I had greatly enjoyed his company the previous several days. But I wasn't particularly surprised by this e-mail address. On that same hike, another young man in his early twenties had engendered great interest one night at a campsite by confidently stating, "I'm pretty sure I could create my own religion, just like all these others. All it would take is some time to write it out."

In *The God Delusion*, Richard Dawkins describes religious instruction as a form of child abuse. There is an active Christian Taliban in America postulates Sam Harris in *Letter to a Christian Nation*. Christopher Hitchen's provocatively titled tome, *God is Not Great* labels God as a "celestial dictatorship". These trendy atheistic tracts have all sold well into the millions of copies to their devoted followers.

Large swaths of western youth and cosmopolitan elites consider it virtually gospel that religion leads to wars. Indeed, it has done just that on far too many occasions. But what these same people fail to take into account is that history's most savage mass murderers—Hitler, Stalin, Mao, Pol Pot—have been utterly irreligious.

The idea that religion is for backward-looking people who are "poor, uneducated, and easily led," ultimately runs into human nature. Consider Albert Camus' famous novel, *The Stranger.* Camus' absurd hero, Mersault, is completely lacking in any kind of authentic faith. Unable to find any meaning in his existence, he finally begins killing out of a nihilistic sense of boredom.

***

I have been a kind of lukewarm Episcopalian most of my life. My father liked to describe Episcopalians as "Catholics who flunked Latin." When one thinks of the classic Episcopalian, George Herbert Walker Bush immediately comes to mind. His newfound friend, Bill Clinton (a classic Southern Baptist) likes to joke with Bush that Episcopalians are the *frozen chosen*. Indeed, Episcopal Church services have a rigid formality that is almost martial in flavor. Biblical rapture, predestination, end-times theology, and burning bush moments are out. They are replaced by a kind of solemn reluctance.

My role inside the church has been that of a perennial backbencher, even by Episcopalian standards. I've just been a face in the crowd—standing, sitting, kneeling, as we members of the 'frozen chosen' are wont to do. I like a lot of the music and occasionally the sermon, and enjoy chatting afterwards with the other parishioners. Then I head off, rarely thinking much about church again until the next Sunday.

While playing on the junior golf circuit, one of my fellow competitors used to rationalize everything that happened by what God had decided. If he missed a short putt, he would pithily mouth, "The Lord didn't will it." You couldn't blame him. He really believed this.

My view of God was very different. I hope to God that He (She) is concerned with something much more profound than whether or not I make a putt on the golf course. Perhaps God cares more about what I do after I either make or miss the putt. In fact, probably my most profound personal breakthrough has been coming to the conclusion that there is not a single earthly thing in this world worth praying for. I resist the strong temptation to make *petitionary prayers* to God for anything—making money, good health, saving my life, a loved one's life, you name it.

In the spring of 1980, I began a nightly ritual of prayer at bedtime. Perhaps not coincidentally, that was right around the time I got introduced to sex. Sex may be the one human activity which offers up a slight glimpse of heaven. Yet, paradoxically, it also serves to point up the limits of earthly pleasures. In fact, I have resolutely concluded that the absolutely only thing in this world a mortal should pray for is the priceless gift of faith. Yet even after 32 years of steady evening prayer, I have found that terribly elusive. In the Old Testament, a mortal is rebuked with the stern admonition, "Oh ye' of little faith." How true that has so often been of me.

***

In 2007, BBC News did a special program showing the United States of America was the unhappiest nation on earth, with more mental disorders and depression than any other country. Perhaps not so coincidentally, the United States is also the place in which technology has advanced the furthest.

A 2009 Kaiser Foundation study determined that the average American kid spends 53 hours per week connected with electronic media—cellphones, iPods, video games, and computers. I recently heard some technology geek exulting on television, "As far as the internet goes, we are at about the year 1470 right now." For a technophobe like me those are chilling words, indeed. Is it really character building to sit in front of a computer all day watching electronic images coming and going on a screen? My hunch is it is going to make us all more boring, and perhaps give our nation a collective case of ADD. "The continuous innovations in electronic media," writes travel writer, Paul Theroux, "seem to me more like a cross between toy making and chemical warfare."

Finally, there is the big question: What does this technology explosion mean for the future of organized religion? Anything beyond the immediate here and now becomes immediately suspicious. In the face of such spiritual headwinds, going on a long-distance pilgrimage makes more sense than ever. It is worth noting that the great religions—Judaism, Christianity, Islam, and Buddhism, were all preached among people who had been nomads.

"Simplify, simplify, simplify," Thoreau exhorted in his classic, *Walden Pond*. "I say let your affairs be as two or three, and not a hundred or a thousand." The great irony—the profoundly happy fact—is that a difficult journey on foot narrows our options greatly, yet enlarges us at the same time. Perhaps it even holds out the possibility of bringing us just a little bit closer to God.

Chapter 13

Latino Pride

"Let's hope this *paella* is half as good as you claim it is," Gavin said.

"I'm telling you," I countered, "I ate it every night on a trip to Barcelona. I slept like a baby, and was in a good mood every day." What we were discussing was the famed Spanish dish of yellow rice, mixed seafood, and vegetables. Unfortunately, a threesome from Barcelona was trailing along with us.

"They don't know how to cook paella here in La Rioja," Jose said.

"I refuse to eat paella outside of Catalonia (Barcelona's province)," added Gabriela.

"Bill, looks like you didn't do your homework for this trip," Gavin piled on.

We were rushing through the hot, dusty Spanish countryside trying to beat the siesta hour. We already knew from experience how Spanish towns completely shut down around 3:30. Somebody not in the know might protest, "Something's got to be open." Forget it. In these small villages through which El Camino ran, *everything* was boarded up.

As we entered Los Arcos, the welcome sight of a pond greeted us. It was summertime and the pond was filled up with schoolchildren. Gavin immediately tore away to join them, while our Spanish hiking partners continued on to search for an albergue. Gavin attracted his usual attention from the teenage girls. But nowhere near the amount his uncle drew. Yes, you read that correctly. But don't get worried.

Dozens of bikini-clad teenage girls mobbed me, giggling and asking for photographs. While I've been through this drill countless times, Spanish girls in bikinis added a touch of flair. Meanwhile, pilgrims on El Camino and other bystanders were streaming by with amused looks, wondering what the heck was going on. The only person who didn't seem bothered by the whole spectacle was my play-it-cool nephew, Gavin. But I was determined to bring him into the game.

"Gavin," I yelled over to him in the pond, "get over here. I've got some important people for you to meet."

"Yeah, yeah," he grudgingly said, and strode over to where this whole pantomime was playing out.

I pointed at the gaggle of females and said, "Meet your future wife." That brought giggles and excitement, to be sure. But this was all going on in Spanish, which my Francophile nephew didn't yet understand. For once, Gavin seemed flummoxed.

"Always choose the shortest girl," I said to Gavin.

"Bill, speak for yourself."

"Shouldn't you ask one of these girls to dinner?" I suggested.

"Bill, girls ask me."

"With that attitude," I warned, "you're gonna' end up like me—never married."

"Dear God."

These impromptu scenes would play themselves out all across the northern arc of Spain. Fortunately, none of them ever made me uncomfortable. Better yet, they occasionally seemed to throw Gavin off balance.

Gavin at high-school graduation, just weeks before leaving for the Camino.

***

Due to the unexpected delay, we didn't enter the old part of Los Arcos until the late afternoon. You could have heard a pin drop.

"Everybody's asleep," I noted.

"Everybody's dead," Gavin corrected me.

"They must have run out of paella."

"No, it was *ETA* again."

Winston Churchill once proclaimed, "The siesta is the finest invention of the Spanish people." That may be true. But for those unfortunate enough to arrive in town hungry at siesta hour—and this is very often when El Camino pilgrims arrive—it can be a very solemn experience. It felt like we were on a hunger strike.

"It's about time to try this paella you keep raving about, Bill."

"At this point, I'd settle for *roadkill*," I muttered.

"You can forget that," he countered. "Look around, the car hasn't even been discovered in this town yet." Indeed, it's not that uncommon in Spain or many other European countries for adults to not own a car. I actually find that appealing compared to America, where not having a car is the last step before taking to dumpster diving.

We continued wandering through the baking hot, anonymous alleys, bereft of any ideas as to where to go. The town seemed devoid of any type of life. A stray cat suddenly sprung across the street in front of us. "That cat looks like steak," Gavin quickly said.

Finally, we saw a fellow pilgrim in rags also doing reconnaissance for food. Needless to say, he wasn't Spanish, or he would have known better than to even look. He led us to the albergue. One look at the bunkroom showed stuffy quarters, entirely inhospitable to a person close to my height. Fortunately, the very last night before leaving home, I had thrown my tent in my backpack. This was in spite of all the guidebooks saying a tent was unnecessary on the Camino. The hospitaleiro humanely allowed me to pitch my tent behind the albergue.

***

Gavin and I headed out again looking for paella, cat steak, roadkill, or practically anything else. It was after 6:00 now, and some of the bars had begun opening again.

"*Los Americanos son diablos* (devils)"' a man kept shouting ecstatically to his friends. "*Son diablos. Diablos.*" The Spanish was going along at such a rapid clip, that I was just trying to capture the gist of it. The man, who could have been anywhere from thirty to sixty, had facial hair covering up his entire face apart from his eyes and his mouth, which was very, very active. Yet these silver dollar-sized eyes had an alert, even friendly look to them. The subject of anti-Americanism seemed to have brought him to a state of virtual rapture.

"*De donde vosotros?*" he asked us.

In this day and age of virulent anti-Americanism, some traveling Americans have adapted by saying they are from Canada. Others go so far as to wear maple leafs on their backpacks. But while I am sometimes a strong critic of some of my country's actions, I still consider myself a bit of an old-fashioned patriot.

"*Somos de Los Estados Unidos* (We're from the United States)," I answered, looking him dead in the eye. There was a split-second pause, in which you could actually see this earth-shaking realization sink into his eyes. He then proceeded to go absolutely crackers on us.

"*Los Estados Unidos, los Estados Unidos, los Estados Unidos,*" he stood up on a chair and began screaming in exhilaration. "Ha, ha, ha." His companions were taking it all in with great amusement as well. But it was difficult to tell if they were laughing at *him* or *us*. I drew small comfort by noting that the path to the bridge we had walked over—and which would now be our line of retreat— was unimpeded.

"*Cerveza, cerveza* (beer)," he shouted. "*Cual tipo de cerveza? Que? Que?*" But my hunger pains were such that I practically felt like biting my arm off; a beer was the last thing we wanted.

"*No gracias, senor,*" I tried explaining. "*pero tenemos estomagos vacios* (we have empty stomachs)." But my mild protest did no good. This frisky man ran inside and emerged with two ice-cold, frothy mugs of beer.

Unfortunately, the subject turned to politics. I had been rebuked by the administration of a school I had worked at in Paraguay for discussing politics in class. "Politics is a life or death matter in this country," they had lectured me, with the threat of dismissal. Spain was obviously no different as demonstrated by its tragi-glorious history. So, for once in my life, I strove to avoid a political discussion. But it was to no avail. The man kept screaming about the Basques and the Palestinians.

"Why do Americans think they are better than other people?" he asked in a loud, but seemingly authentic display of angst. "Everybody deserves their freedom. Everybody."

"Yes, yes," I agreed. But then one of his colleagues mumbled something to him.

Suddenly, the man's excited expression turned dark. "*Aparte de los Israelitos. Merecen morirse—son cochinos* (They deserve to die; they're pigs)." My forbearance gave out.

"The Israelis are no different than the Basques or Palestinians. They deserve rights also." My interlocutor looked thunderstruck. He immediately launched into a rant about Israelis and Nazis.

"*Los Americans son despetivos, despetivos* (disrespective)," he screamed. He began venting his anger about how only an American would turn down a beer. "*Muy despetivo.*" Then he started brushing his hands away, "*Vayate, vayate,* (Go away, go away)," in a brushing away motion.

"*Solo es una diferencia de opinion,*" I attempted to say in a reconciling manner. But he would have none of it.

"*Vayate, vayate,*" he kept screaming, as if flipping us away.

At least we could all agree that was a good idea. Gavin and I headed back over the stone bridge to look for food.

***

Gavin seemed a bit taken aback by what he had just witnessed. We walked along the river silently.

"I'm really hungry," he finally said softly.

"Hey," I said—my ego perhaps getting the best of me—"this is how hungry you are every night on the Appalachian Trail. But there you're surviving on hiker trash food."

We began to pick up the fumes of grilled meat wafting through the still air of a summer-time Spanish evening. Soon we came upon our fellow pilgrims seated in a spacious outdoor café. A large church loomed on one side and the river flowed by on the other. Everything was perfect. We got seated and waited to order.

"Hey," I said excitedly to Gavin. "See that yellow rice on that guy's plate? That's what paella is served in." For once, my nephew seemed impressed.

"Yeah, that looks pretty good."

Unfortunately, every other pilgrim in town who had waited out the siesta hour was queued up to order ahead of us. I quickly became impatient.

"I'll go inside and order at the counter," I said.

"Use your charm, Bill."

I got the attention of the first person I saw behind the counter and ordered two plates of paella. However, a hesitant look appeared on the waiter's face. A conversation ensued between him and another person behind him. Finally, the man turned to me and—with a truly heartfelt look of sympathy—reported the grave news to me. They had run out of paella for the evening. I moped back to Gavin to break the news to him. This was the third time we had unsuccessfully tried to order paella.

"Bill, I'm beginning to think this food doesn't exist."

"Gosh, I'm telling you," I muttered embarrassed, "Not being able to get paella in Spain is like not being able to get a hamburger in America."

Chapter 14

More Latino Pride

I tiptoed into the bunkroom at 6:30 in the morning to quietly wake up Gavin. Today, we were planning to make it to Logrono, the first major city since Pamplona. It reputedly had an especially nice pilgrim's albergue. We hoped to get there early enough to get a spot. But when I looked into the bunkroom, I couldn't believe my eyes. Every single bunk was empty, but one. Gavin's.

"Where did everybody go?" I asked in disbelief.

"They're all members of *ETA*," he answered. "They were running secret attacks all night."

"Honestly, this is amazing," I responded looking around. But soon we would learn that it was only a precursor of what was to come.

The only pilgrims left in town were Claire and Benedict, who we passed on the way out of town. They were just emerging from their tent right as we passed by. She gave us an enthusiastic, *"Bonjour,"* while Benedict stared at the ground. Claire always looked happy as a lark with Benedict. Unfortunately, he often appeared to be restraining himself from breaking into open flight from Claire.

Once we got underway, we spotted a Spanish pilgrim in the distance. We had met her yesterday when she was also walking alone. Her name was Judith; she was from Barcelona.

"Hey, let's catch up with Judith," I said. Gavin didn't say anything, but he did hasten the pace, which indicated he thought it was a worthwhile goal.

"Is there some reason that Barcelonans are disproportionately represented on El Camino?" I asked Judith when we finally caught up. Of course, the question was a setup.

"Because we're the best," she joked. To be sure, the raven-haired daughters of this northeastern province (Catalonia) are known to be especially alluring, with their lovely, Mediterranean olive skin. They are clearly more cosmopolitan, as well; a city like Barcelona seems more similar culturally to the Mediterranean cities of Marseilles or Naples, than Madrid. However, Catalonia was also the center of the single most gruesome period in modern Spanish history, one which very few people in Spain have forgotten.

***

To this day, writers, intellectuals, and socialists consider the 'Republican' government headquartered in Barcelona from 1936-1939 to be the most enlightened form of living ever organized by human beings. It led the storied revolt against the fascist government in Madrid that resulted in the Spanish Civil War.

"Waiters looked you dead in the eye and called you 'tu', instead of the formal, 'usted'," wrote George Orwell in his classic, *Homage to Catalonia.* "Middle-class habits like wearing ties and giving tips were banned. Shoeshine boys were collectivized."

The fascination extended to the most capitalist country on the planet—the United States of America. A volunteer group called the *Abraham Lincoln Brigade* formed to fight on behalf of this great socialist cause. Perhaps though, the cause was a little less romantic than it was initially trumped up to be.

In Hemingway's great novel, *For Whom the Bell Tolls,* there is a gripping scene when the socialists—the supposedly good guys—take over a town. First, they shoot all members of the police force. Then the town hierarchy is promenaded out in front of the peasants where they are thrown over the cliff into the river. A big landowner is then led out when an evicted tenant strikes a surprise blow at him. The man curls up, as the tenant's drunken friends beat him to death.

Peasants continue pushing the priest and mayor over the cliff. "Let's have another," the peasants scream ravenously. A local womanizer, Don Faustino, an inveterate flirt and hugger of women, is pushed forward. "In my life," a resentful peasant said, "in my life, I've never seen a thing like Don Faustino. There may be negroes and rare beasts from Africa. But for me never, never will there be anything like Don Faustino." Faustino is hurled over the cliff with a stunned look on his face. "Let's have another one," the drunkards scream, as they hand around bottles of cognac they had looted from the fascist-owned bars. Next, a working-class fascist who had joined only to be a snob was led out. He is walking to his death stoically until his wife screams from their apartment window above the square, "Guillermo, Guillermo." He breaks into uncontrollable tears. But it is all in vain as he too is clubbed to death.

However, three days later, the fascists retake the town and carry out even greater atrocities against the Socialists.

After the first year of the war, the Socialists had control of the three largest cities in Spain (Madrid, Barcelona, Toledo). Every government in the world expected them to win. Yet, they managed to blow it. How? They made the same mistake that has been the bane of every failed cause in Spain for the last thousand years. They vastly underestimated the loyalty of the Spanish people to the Catholic Church.

The Socialists began burning down churches—58 alone in Barcelona. Their rationale was that the Church had allied itself with the fascists. Nonetheless, the rank and file Spaniard took great offense at this destruction visited on what they viewed as sacred property. Then the German Lutwaffe, in its preliminary outing under Fuhrer Adolf Hitler, came to the rescue of their fascist comrades in Spain. They took control of the skies over Spain and the fascist regime of *Generalissimo Franco*, was born.

Perhaps the most important point though, is the comparison between the Spanish Civil War and the American Civil War. There was no gentlemanly surrender ceremony between two stately figures, the likes of Ulysses S. Grant and Robert E. Lee. Rather, mass graves were—and occasionally still are—found. Often the fighting seemed to take a backseat to the wanton murder of Spaniard by Spaniard. The viciousness of the conflict goes a long way towards explaining why the central government in Madrid has always had such trouble unifying the country.

***

"Estas sola (alone)?" I asked Judith.

"That is the way I travel," she answered in English. Spaniards tend to stick together on the Camino; they also vie with Americans for the least-talented-in-second languages crown. But this woman was not going to lapse into such an easy comfort zone.

"How is the paella in Catalonia?" Gavin asked mischievously.

"You should not eat it anywhere else," she answered unhesitatingly. "Paella was invented in Barcelona." Countless Catalonians would make this exact claim. In reality though, paella's origins are from further down the Mediterranean coast in Valencia. But trying to convince a Catalonian of that is apparently like telling an American that George Washington never chopped down a cherry tree.

"I'm convinced Spain is going to win the World Cup this year," I said (hint: I wasn't).

"It does not matter to me," Judith said matter-of-factly. "I hope America or Germany wins."

"Sounds like you are a contrarian," I said. Actually, it sounded almost exhibitionist. As we were to see, however, she really did mean what she said about the Germans.

***

We Americans take it for granted that we are the biggest and best in the world, especially in athletics. There is a huge problem with this proposition, though—The World Cup. It is the biggest event in all of sports, but the U.S. has never once even advanced past the quarter finals. Periodically some authority figure steps forward to declare soccer to be the sport of the future in America. But others have sagely remarked, "Soccer will always be the sport of the future in America."

Nonetheless, two nights ago, Landon Donovan had scored a dramatic goal in the 91st minute to move the United States into the quarter finals. It marked the single biggest moment in U.S. soccer history. From what I had been able to glean from the news, the American imagination had finally been captured by soccer. The Spanish papers had photos of former President Clinton jumping up and down at the matches in South Africa, while President Obama was glued to the television back at the White House.

Gavin and I arrived in Logrono in a mood of anticipation for our quarterfinal match. Unfortunately, the main albergue was filled. Our fellow pilgrims' strategy of racing to the albergues had 'worked'. Gavin and I were reduced to moping around town in the oppressive heat of the siesta hour, and fighting off hunger pangs.

"This trip is taking my relationship with food up to the next level," Gavin commented, in a seeming state of awe at his own hunger.

Finally, we found a private albergue for 10 euros per person, which was about double the price that pilgrims usually pay (Important note: The Camino is not just the *best way* to see Europe; it's also the *most economical way*). An elderly hospitaleiro immediately saw I had a problem with the tiny bunks, and assured me she would help me arrange my mattresses on the floor that evening.

Gavin and I then headed off to the magnificent center plaza of Logrono. It was Saturday evening, and the town center was full of locals out doing something the Spanish are very good at— enjoying life. We had two urgent goals—find a place to watch the match and a restaurant that had some paella. Believe it or not, we found both.

"You're never gonna' be the same after this plate of food arrives," I announced to Gavin.

"It's the world's loss."

"Hey, there's Judith," I pointed out our hiking partner of earlier in the day. But with her swift, birdlike gait, she was flitting purposefully through the crowd away from us.

"It's your loss, Bill."

"Apparently."

Perhaps it was a good thing Judith didn't stop by our table though. After all, she and every other Catalonian had staunchly warned us—I thought ridiculously so—that only Catalonians knew how to cook paella. For when the waitress plopped down our plates, we dug in to what was indubitably the worst meal we had the entire journey.

"Bill," Gavin said after a few minutes in which his pace of chewing notably decelerated, "can I ask you a question? Is 'paella' the Spanish word for near-death experience?" The Catalonians had been right, after all. This non-Catalonian paella had been burned. Even the rice had been cooked to such firmness that all flavor had been sucked out of it.

Then the match came on. It wasn't much better. Ivory Coast played purposefully up and down the field, while the U.S. team seemed to lack purpose. "The American players look like they want to pick the ball up like a basketball," an Irish pilgrim standing nearby commented wryly. Our World Cup dream was again aborted with an abysmal defeat. Gavin and I filed out of Logrono plaza, disappointed in the food and match. At this point, things took a decided turn for the *worse*. For when we got back to the albergue about 11:30, the elderly hospitaleiro was anxiously pacing back and forth out front. At first sight of us, she launched into a fiery demonstration of wounded Latino pride.

"Esta despetivo," she fumed. *"Despetivo."* There was that word, 'despetivo' again. Apparently, to be disrespective was the ultimate offense in Spain. I commenced telling her about the World Cup match and my authentic confusion as to whether the pilgrim's curfew applied in a private commercial albergue like this one. *"Rudo, rudo,"* she vented. Then she unleashed another colloquial tirade, of which I only understood one word—'puerta'. That's the Spanish word for door. This worried me. Was she going to lock us out for the night?

But then she said, *"No voy a ayudarte areglar vuestras camas."* She wasn't going to help us to arrange our beds. Her sense of hospitality was so strong that she honestly felt like that was punishment. Suddenly, I went from selfish concerns to feeling guilty—even small. *"Perdanos, perdanos,"* I pleaded. She unlocked the door.

Gavin and I entered the dark, quiet bunk room. Prior to us arriving, our fellow pilgrims had been treated to the hospitaleiro's fit of rage at us. They had probably also been able to hear the harsh dressing down we had just withstood. But suddenly and spontaneously, applause broke out all over the room from our fellow pilgrims.

And once again I had the thought—I really hope Spain wins the World Cup.

Chapter 15

A Glimpse of the Moving Medieval Masses

"The doors are open to all, not only Catholics, but to pagans and Jews and heretics, the idler and the vagabond, the sacred and the profane, and to put it shortly, the good and the wicked."

12ᵗʰ Century Sign at a Pilgrim's Shelter

If a modern-day observer was to get just one glimpse of the High Middle Ages, there might have been no better place than the Tower of St. Jacques (St. James) in the middle of Paris on an April morning in the 10th through 15th centuries. There on the right bank of the Seine, not far from Notre Dame, one would have seen thousands of pilgrims per day setting off for Santiago de Compostela. High royal officials and priests would be on hand to bless the throngs in their pilgrim attire. Musicians would crank up their most inspiring tunes and lead the pilgrims to the outskirts of Paris. French cavalry usually rode along with them the first few days in the countryside.

The majority would have been French. But there would have been a healthy number of Germans, British, and even Scandinavians. Most would have been indigent, illiterate peasants. A sizeable fraction would be actual criminals, having been sent by a judge on a so-called *penitential pilgrimage*. Whole sections of society were more or less permanently on the move: merchants, craftsmen, minstrels, scholars, students, as well as the outcasts—lepers, thieves, beggars, and false priests. In short, all human life was there. It was Catholicism at its most inclusive best.

Most of these pilgrims would have never even left their own village, other than maybe a day trip to a neighboring town's fair. The average lifespan at the time was 35 years, and this pilgrimage was typically done near the end of their lives. Their parishes would have warned them to expect death on the way to Santiago. But this, too, would be considered an honor.

Few carried actual backpacks. Instead, almost all pilgrims wore dashing, full-length capes to protect them from the wind and serve as a blanket. In their hand was a staff for protection, tied to a gourd for carrying water. At their waist was a small satchel for carrying money, knives, and toiletries. This image of the wayfaring pilgrim in trademark apparel was often reflected in medieval paintings, as well as the literary works of Dante and Shakespeare. It was a major theme of the Middle Ages.

Statue of medieval pilgrim in a classic pose.

These legions of hopeful pilgrims would move through the beautiful river valleys south of Paris at a rate of nine or ten miles a day. They stopped frequently to pray at various sanctuaries. Except in the major cities, food would rarely have been plentiful. The majority relied on the alms of hospices and monasteries to fend off outright starvation. Often the villagers in towns through which pilgrims passed were forced to guard their food stores vigilantly.

Unsurprisingly, the institution also had its tawdry side. Pilgrims flirted, gambled, and drank to excess. Such misbehavior sometimes even occurred in the religious shrines being visited. Sexual escapades in dark corners were not uncommon. Danger was much more prevalent for the medieval pilgrim, wolves and bandits being the most frequently mentioned. Hospitals were infrequent and rogues lay in waiting for ambush. It was strictly forbidden for women to travel outside of large parties.

But medieval pilgrims weren't like modern tourists in any way. They anticipated deprivation, and even peril. It was widely believed that "the prayers of the starving fly quicker to heaven." The churches in each one of the villages through which pilgrims passed had members designated with the task of burying those who died within its gates.

Medieval pilgrims had a deep abiding faith in St. James, himself. And they were prepared to struggle mightily to get to his tomb. Once in Santiago, a mass was said at the great cathedral in memory of those who had fallen along the way—"To die walking to Santiago is a Christian comfort."

***

In its heyday, the pilgrimage to Santiago de Compostela was easily more popular than the other two great Christian pilgrimages, Jerusalem and Rome. Estimates consistently show that *500,000 people per year walked the Camino.* The only such sustained movement of humans in history to rival it is the Muslim pilgrimage to Mecca. But that journey from Medina is only 61 miles, and within the same country.

However, after approximately 500 years in the limelight, the pilgrimage to Santiago finally lost its luster. First, the *Black Death* wiped out approximately 25% of the entire population of Europe in a mere three years (1347-1350). This event shook the faith of the European masses in a peculiarly medieval fashion. Europe's population almost universally agreed that the people *deserved* such a catastrophe. Nonetheless, their faith was rocked by the fact that the church hadn't actually *predicted* it.

But perhaps the greatest factor in the decline of the Camino was that the Moorish threat had finally receded from northern Spain. The mass pilgrimage had succeeded dramatically in repopulating northern Spain. Kings and queens began to get suspicious of these vast masses roaming unchecked through their provincial and national borders. In 1489, Charles VIII decided to forbid French participation in the Camino, describing it as *tourist loutism*. Then, early in the next century, one of the most consequential figures in history struck a mortal blow to the mass medieval pilgrimage to Santiago.

"Pilgrimages are a waste," Martin Luther sternly declared—no surprise given his rabid anti-Catholicism. The Camino began to slowly wane into oblivion, not to regain popularity again for almost 500 years.

***

Ironically, it was the colossal tragedy of the Second World War that ultimately revived interest in the Camino de Santiago. The blood-soaked Continent was looking for anything that would help promote the idea of a unified Europe and extinguish the flames of nationalism.

"One could hardly find a phenomenon closer to the very essence of Europe," the European Council declared in 1967. The Council soon developed the yellow arrow system, making the Camino more user-friendly. In 1993, UNESCO declared it a World Heritage site. The number of pilgrims went from 3,501 in 1988, to 30,000 in 1998, to 70,000 in 2002. Fully 200,000 pilgrims were expected in this Holy Year of 2010.

And this may only be the tip of the iceberg. It's already far and away the most popular walking path in Europe. More pilgrims are starting the trip to Santiago from farther-off places like Le Puy, Bern, Munich, and even Rome. Some are even walking out their front doors and improvising their own caminos, until reaching the official Camino. And Americans and Asians are just discovering El Camino de Santiago. Many would disagree. But my attitude towards this surging interest in El Camino is very catholic—the more the better.

Chapter 16

European Youth

"Cultures are not barriers. Borders are barriers."

The European Union

If you really want to know what's going on in a country, you need to get well acquainted with the young people. That can be more difficult than it sounds like.

The Appalachian Trail and Pacific Crest Trail had afforded me great opportunity in my mid- and late-forties for immersion in America's youth culture. A couple things had stuck out. I had learned that today's college students and graduates are nowhere near as materialistic as my generation (the Reagan Generation) had been. They garnered high marks from me on that issue. But I was also forced to give them a significant demerit for addiction to technology, which often seemed to cut down on the number of authentic friendships. El Camino now afforded me a close-up look at European youth.

As we were leaving Logrono, we ran into a young foursome of two Germans and two French. I couldn't help noting the irony. Yes, I'm all too aware that history is for bitter, old men. But heck, history has been pretty bitter between the Germans and French.

I recently read the story of more than 200,000 children born of German soldiers and French women during World War II. They bore the derogatory appellation, *les enfants maudits* (the wretched children). France's quick surrender at the hands of the German blitzkrieg traumatically shamed the nation. Embarrassingly, only a tiny percentage of French joined the Resistance. It became common over time for these bastard children to deny their heritage just to avoid being shunned by French society.

And that was just the Second World War. The fighting in the First World War between France and Germany made the second one look like a picnic. The French would lose over 300,000 men in two weeks. The Germans lost over a million men just in the first five months of the war. Names solemnly recorded in history—*Verdun, The Somme*—were the scenes of a million young men losing their lives.

So Europe has some pretty complex hate matrices to overcome, although it has more often seemed like the Germans actually coveted France, and particularly Paris. But that was then, and this is now.

***

Gavin and I lay on the ground with our heads resting on our backpacks in the town plaza of Navarette. An especially healthy-looking, tall, blond-headed boy about Gavin's age walked up and hovered over us.

"Hello," he said with a smile. "Are you okay?"

"Hallo, guten tag?" I saluted back. I knew to respond with one of my few German phrases. I distinctly remembered seeing this guy at a bar in Logrono. Germany had gone on a tear against archrival England, scoring four straight goals. Each time they had scored, this Teutonic-looking boy had leapt to the air in exultation. That definitely meant he was German for the simple reason every other nationality always wants Germany to lose.

What really struck out, though, was his brand of mindless screaming and fist-pumping. It was the kind of overt celebration a red-blooded American boy takes for granted. However, ever since the war ended 65 years ago, such overt displays of patriotism or jingoism have been taboo for Germans. It reeked too much of Nuremberg nighttime rallies, goose stepping, blitzkrieg, and ultimately ruin. But that was old Germany. This was a new Germany.

Meawes was the German boy's name. Meawes soon began filling Gavin and me in on an incredible journey he was planning. He planned to travel from Mongolia, all the way through Russia, to Hungary.

"You're going to go on foot?" I asked in amazement. "No," he said. "I will buy two horses in Mongolia."

"When are you going to do it?" Gavin quickly asked. I quickly became concerned that *he* might get interested.

"I'm going to work two or three jobs to save up enough money to do it when I'm 21."

"How long will the whole thing take?"

"Two years," he said plainly

One of the pleasures of overseas travel is trying to find new ways to communicate with other foreigners. I'm no great linguist, but am willing to jump in the fray.

Meawes along with his girlfriend, Franzi – faces of modern Germany.

"So it sounds like you are looking for *lebensraum?*" I asked Meawes. In high school, we were taught this German word—meaning 'living space'—that Hitler had used to justify invading Poland and the Soviet Union, and give the German people the additional land they deserved in the vast East. I also managed to work in *anschluss,* the term Hitler had used to justify annexing Austria.

"How do you know these big German words?" Meawes asked confused. Indeed, they stuck out like a sore thumb given my overall lack of German.

"Ah, well, I've just heard them," I said.

"Bill," Gavin whispered to me, "he has to know what you were talking about."

I recently read that only three out of a hundred Germans that went east for the invasion of the Soviet Union ever returned to Germany. For a German boy in the 1940's, *that* was their journey of their lifetime. But the journey Meawes was planning couldn't have been more different. Practically every day, Gavin and I had new questions about this exciting trip he was planning. A young German man traveling peacefully through Russia by horse is a significant step forward for humanity.

When I later got to know Meawes well, I even asked him, "Do you feel at all guilty about Germany's history?"

"No, not at all," he answered plainly. "Every country has a bad history." Point well made. It occurred to me how utterly useless are the stereotypes of Germans so many decades after the war. "The only time it bothers me," said Meawes' girlfriend, Franzi, "is when I go on holiday in another country. Somebody usually gets drunk and starts calling me names like Eva Braun."

Group of Germans queuing up for dinner.

A famous German comedian (now there's a rebuttal of stereotypes!) named Hape Kerkeling walked the Camino and wrote a book, *I'm Off Then*. It has sold over 3 million copies, in Germany alone. For the first time in the thousand year history of the Camino pilgrimage, the Germans have now overtaken the French as the nation most represented on El Camino. Many of them seem more European, than any particular nationality. Better yet, they are, for the most part, model pilgrims.

Chapter 17

Blondine

"The Catholic Church could fill up its seminaries if it forbade God from making women look as fabulous as they do."

Pat Conroy, *Lords of Discipline*

"How far until Santo Domingo de la Calzada?" Gavin asked.

"About 10 kilometers." By El Camino standards, that's actually a long distance between towns.

"Great, that'll get us there right at siesta hour," he muttered.

"Let's try to throw some lunch together right here," I suggested.

One-stop shopping is not the modus-operandi in most European villages. For bread, one goes to the panaderia. Meat is at the butcher shop. Coffee or a beverage is at the coffee shop or a bar. It's not as efficient as going to an American supermarket, to be sure. You have to pay three times. But the God's honest truth is that the distance is sometimes shorter than going from one end of an American box store to another. It can even be a bit of fun, like part of the daily social round. Instead of being served by a single mother in hock from bill collectors and counting the minutes to her next cigarette break, one is likely to be attended to by a cheery local. Never mind that his or her grandparents may have helped fill up some of those mass graves as part of Franco's secret police. Time often seems to stand still here in northern Spain.

Three members of Meawes' group joined us in a park in Azafra, as we lay prostrate under the largest tree in town.

"Where is the French girl?" I inquired."Blondine?"

"Yes, I guess that's her name."

"She went looking for bread."

Blondine soon came along with a long baguette sheathed in thin paper wrapping, and with a brilliant smile. She had a pixyish figure, that along with her pert legs, deep tan, and coltish stride were guaranteed to grab your attention. Her trademark feature was the gloves she wore to protect her hands, while holding her walking staff. They gave her very much the pilgrim's look. And the Frenchwoman.

"What part of France are you from?" I asked.

Blondine cools herself off on a hot day. .

"Paris," Blondine answered.

"I've heard of it," Gavin quickly responded.

"Oh, have you," she said, fortunately with an amused smile.

Paris. Need I say any more? The grandiosity of this great dove-colored, Epicurean city is awe-inspiring, to be sure. Personally, I never had a very good time in Paris. It was all a bit overwhelming. At times it has been like I was almost psyched out by the grandeur of it all. However, the last time I was in Paris, I felt like I had a revelation. I was walking through *the Louvre*, passing about the 13,284[th] painting of the Crucifixion or Resurrection. Suddenly, I turned to my friend and said, "I've got it."

"What?" he asked.

"The French are like us Americans."

"How?"

"There is only one building in the world that you can compare to this one."

"Which is?"

"The largest building in America."

"Got me," he said, sounding slightly peeved.

"The Pentagon."

"Get outta' here."

"No honestly," I protested. "Americans try to overwhelm you with power. The French do the same with grandiosity."

I'm American to the core. So please forgive me if I say some foolish things when I'm overseas. It's my birthright. But that afternoon, we learned that none other than Napoleon Bonaparte had, in fact, lived in and made his headquarters at the Louvre. And we all know *Le Petit Corporal* thought big is better. Sounds kinda' American to me.

Our feeling towards the French often seem based on raw emotion, more than analysis. I was recently chatting with an American lady who has been living in Paris for the last fifteen years.

"So are you a Francophile?" I asked her.

"Sure, I am," she answered. "But that doesn't mean I can't hate the French."

The truth, though, is it's a gross oversimplification to say that Americans hate the French. For starters, Americans just aren't very good haters, compared to our European brethren with their ancient rivalries. Better yet, while the French often find us childlike and amusing, they just aren't afflicted with the need to hate us. They're too busy hating their ancient enemies, Germany and England.

Blondine exuded a certain security and self-possession that both Gavin and I found becoming. She was a nurse-trainee and her budget was tiny. But she didn't let it bother her one bit. She simply went about things in her own way.

That seems to be the French's specialty. Whether it's drinking their cappuccino, walking their poodles, or queuing up for a public service, they rarely seem as hurried as Americans. And they live longer. It's hard to escape the conclusion that, in spite of their Gallic annoyances, the French are a little bit special.

***

The Camino may be the best marked footpath in the entire world. *Flechas* and carnet shells reliably guide pilgrims all along the northern Spanish countryside and through countless pueblos. Nonetheless, pilgrims still managed to get dreadfully off course on occasion.

Gavin and I were traipsing through the stucco-colored Spanish countryside, when we came upon a lone, innocent-looking female in her twenties. "Hi, I'm Sophia," she said, flashing a pretty smile that made me want to ask the name of her dentist. Gavin and I introduced ourselves.

"We're from Germany," *I* said, assuming her accent was German. She threw that right back at me.

"I'm from America," she said.

"Why are you hiking alone?" I asked her. She began to *explain*. She had gotten badly lost yesterday and spent several hours walking around trying to locate the Camino. But she had been unable to find anything familiar. At dark, she had had no choice but to finally just lie down for the evening and hope for the best.

"Were you scared?" I asked.

"Not much," she said plainly. "But I had no idea which direction was the Camino."

"The sun sets pretty reliably in the West these days," Gavin pointed out. Fortunately, Sophia was from eastern Germany where the people are more humble. She took his joke in stride. In fact, she would soon be swooning practically every time he opened his mouth.

"How did you get back to the Camino?" I asked.

"This morning a farmer on a tractor saw me. I don't speak Spanish, and he didn't speak English or German. But he knew where to take me." Luckily, the Camino is not like the horror flicks (or news) you see in America where you take a wrong turn in the woods and some incestuous backwoodsman is there to hack your head off.

"The other day, I was completely lost when I heard some noise," Sophie continued. "I followed it to a dirt road. A young boy on a motorcycle picked me up. I pointed to a town on the map and he took me there."

Sophia's travails would continue, and eventually come to seem like the *Perils of Pauline*. Periodically, she would be seen at train stations, bus terminals, and the like. Jokes circulated among pilgrims. If we saw a helicopter, somebody would crack, "Sophia is really varying up her routine today."

But Sophia maintained her dogged independence, and would periodically seek ever more controversy.

Chapter 18

Pilgrim Weaknesses

"What about this albergue?" Gavin asked as we entered yet another anonymous town on a sweltering hot afternoon. "There's a swimming pool."

"Too exposed," I said. "We've got to find at least a little shade."

Blondine, Meawes, and Francesca dragged along with us. When it's this hot, it becomes all about getting from Point A to Point B. To our surprise, we saw in the mid-day glare a familiar face walking in the opposite direction. It was Ron, a mid-thirties American from Colorado. Ron had clearly chosen to walk El Camino for its *chilling-out* possibilities.

"Wrong way, Ron?" I commented.

"My favorite Austrian pilgrim is back at that place with the swimming pool," he said plainly. Then he took one look at Blondine, and a broad smile broke out on his face. "Wow, you're cute," he said unselfconsciously. For good or for bad, we Americans are prone to wear our gung-ho nature on our sleeves. None more so than Ron.

"Ron has only one weakness," Gavin noted, after he was safely past us. "Ron."

Blondine seemed to take Ron's bare-faced compliment in

stride. The brutal sun and heat dominated everybody's mind. Even the dogs moped and panted around the streets like they could keel over and die any minute now. Pilgrims are easy prey for the worst of it. The walk through the endless orange-walled alleyways seemed like a Rubik's cube.

Finally, Meawes, Blondine, and Francesca located a small building that permitted pilgrims to stay for free. A couple of large, hairy males we hadn't seen before were walking around shirtless. They were speaking an unfamiliar, eastern European-sounding language. Every pilgrim had quickly learned the Spanish word for snorer—*Roncador*. Most feared them, nobody more than I.

"The guidebook says this place used to be a prison," I said.

"It still is," Gavin observed.

"Let's find that other albegue," I said, and we left. Perhaps that was a good thing.

For when our friends lay down to rest, one of these *Neanderthals* soon interrupted Blondine's siesta to tell her he loved her. "It was in this horrible English," she recalled. "He smelled like strong alcohol." Blondine had quickly screamed. At that point, the wiry German teenager, Meawes, had jumped up and backed the man off. Perhaps in medieval times, this same pilgrim might have had a miraculous change of heart, and quickly and movingly repented his misdeed. But no such miracle occurred here. He continued leering menacingly at Blondine with a hideous smile; she would spend the rest of the afternoon and evening afraid of him like a wild animal.

Meanwhile, Gavin and I checked into the larger albergue for what would arguably end up being an even worse experience.

***

We were greeted by Judith from Barcelona. *That*, at least, was an auspicious beginning.

"Your Spanish has improved," she said, as we stood there amiably conversing.

Such a compliment would normally be an ego-boost, especially coming from this ultra-healthy-looking Catalonian. She was unusually chatty today. However, there was one small problem. A muscle-bound, blonde-headed German boy in his early twenties shadowed her every move. When Gavin and I went out to the pool, it quickly became apparent that this young fella's animal spirits had overridden Judith's natural decency. They took on the role of exhibitionists. You couldn't get away from them. In the pool, walking to the shower, at the dinner table, you name it—there they were locked in *coitus* seemingly attempting to devise a way to have sex with their clothes on. She looked embarrassed by it all. He seemed anything but.

What's more, I had a feeling this all was only prologue for later in the evening. I anxiously sidled up to the owner, a thoroughly disagreeable looking middle-aged man.

"I don't fit in the bunks," I asked. "Could I sleep outside?"

Spaniards are some of the most hospitable people on earth. But this man didn't look like he had gotten over Franco's death quite yet. He proceeded to give me a lecture on how damaging a tent would be to his public image, as opposed to, say, a couple of pilgrims having assignations on the lawn.

At curfew time, Judith and her boy-man did away with all the innovation. Amidst all the usual snores, grunts, and sleep apnia was intermingled a more decisive sound—that of a German and Spaniard *scrimmaging.*

***

On the long list of positive Spanish character traits, circumspection has never ranked high. As I lay there for hours unsuccessfully trying to go to sleep, my mind went back to my ex-Spanish girlfriend, Anna. We had met at the airport in Barcelona, but were both living in London at the time. Soon we were steadily dating. Everything had worked wonderfully on 'the way up'. But then the phone began ringing at all hours of the evening checking on my whereabouts. I became worried that events were spinning out of control and decided to give her the type of lecture that a person my age who has never been married becomes accustomed to giving.

"We've been together long enough now," I droned on, "that it's time to either move forwards, or backwards. I'm not ready to move forward at this point, so we need to take a step back." My effort at instilling balance in the relationship was an utter failure. In five minutes, I had turned a passionate, amorous girl into a mortal enemy. A few days later, I saw a friend at on the trading floor in London where I worked.

"Have you seen Brad lately?" I asked, of our mutual friend.

"Yeah, Brad called this morning," he told me. "Some Spanish girl called him up at home last night and asked to come over. He said the girl was wild as hell, screaming at the top of her lungs." I had swallowed deeply listening to this story. My ego was scraped a bit, but I also felt the relief of *guilt absolution*. Other similar reports about Anna soon filtered back to me.

Anna had then started dating an Englishman. Of course, *that* was the ultimate mismatch. As the joke goes, "What do you call a good lover in England? An immigrant." True to stereotype, this English gentleman proceeded to make my own slowdown offense look like Hitler's blitzkrieg. After more than a year of this, he had apparently delivered a speech similar to the one I had given the year before. Finally, Anna had fled England back to Spain, vowing to never date another Anglo-Saxon male again.

So perhaps I shouldn't have been surprised by what was transpiring two bunks over. Like the Polish man's attempt to grope Blondine earlier in the day, these things have been going on in albergues for over a thousand years. One of the very oldest sayings on the Camino is, "*Ir romero, volver ramera* (Start off a pilgrim, return a whore)." Nonetheless, besides being annoyed, I also became paranoid as I lay there. It was hard to see just where the ventilation in this hobbit-sized albergue came from. Surely the conditions didn't match the rancid squalor that the pilgrim masses faced in the 12th century. Back then pilgrims died regularly. But we modern pilgrims have higher expectations.

The scrimmaging tapered off, at which point the German boy seemed to go into an exhaustion coma. He soon began bellowing like a bullfrog, exploding the theory I had been developing that snoring was the exclusive province of the old and fat.

My bunk was nowhere near long enough to even get comfortable, much less sleep. I lay there for hour after hour, with my feelings alternating between self-pity, rage, and helplessness. Finally, I had an idea (Don't worry—nothing to do with Judith).

***

"Gavin, Gavin," I whispered into his ear. The unusual thing was that he actually stirred right to attention. "I picked up the tone of desperation in your voice," he would say later that day.

"Can we please get out of here right this minute?" I pleaded with him.

"Yeah." He got up right away. We packed up our belongings and headed out into the dark.

"We've got to be careful about not getting lost," I said. Almost immediately we were confused as to how to get out of town. Such is the importance of the Camino in Spain that every single time I had asked a Spaniard where the Camino was, they had known exactly. But obviously there was nobody to ask at this hour.

"This is what it (The Camino) usually does in situations like this," Gavin interpolated, and ended up being correct. However, not everybody was so pin-point.

A Brazilian couple had been annoying everyone, including us, with their obsession to always beat everyone to their pueblo of destination and claim two bunks. They were habitually slipping out of albergues at 4:00 in the morning. On this morning, however, their plan backfired. They got badly lost on a wrong route out of town and had to spend two frantic hours trying to correct their mistake in the dark.

We strode through the night, guessing as to when the sun would rear itself. Before we saw it, however, we spotted the silhouetted figures of two women.

"Who is that?" I wondered.

"You know who that is," Gavin said. "Come on."

"Who?" I asked in sincere confusion.

"Your two Swiss admirers."

"Oh yeah," I lit up.

It took a while to catch right up to these two older ladies, even though we were moving along briskly. They both had low centers of gravity and moved along like bowling balls. Finally, we drew even with them.

"Guten morgen," I said to the two elderly ladies in the dark.

"Hallo." For the first and only time of the entire journey, the two of them didn't both come right up on me and start yakking in German at 100 kilometers per hour. Instead, they kept moving at their maximum pace—Teutonic discipline in the early morning hours.

"Well, maybe this is a good chance for us to admit our suspicions were wrong," I said. There had been all kinds of jokes about just how these two ladies kept arriving at the pueblos so early. Now we knew the answer. I didn't like the way people were racing to secure spots in albergues. But there was no denying—this was an impressive effort to watch.

In Villafranca, Gavin and I took a long break as the early morning sunshine cleared the horizon. The two Swiss German ladies came barreling through town, with pleasant looks on their faces, but hardly speaking a word. Right behind them, the lost Brazilian couple arrived with desperate looks on their faces. They quickly related their tale, as if a catastrophe of biblical proportions had struck them. The German word *schadenfreude* immediately came to mind. It was un-Christian of me to take pleasure at their misfortune, to be sure. But I simply couldn't resist.

"No tengan prisa (Don't hurry)," I said. *"Los albergues adelante estan completos* (albergues full ahead)." They looked at each other in alarm.

"How do you know this?" he nervously asked in English.

"That's what they were saying," I nodded over to the side.

But they weren't deterred one bit by my 'tripwire', and quickly hustled out of town, looking extra-determined in their pursuit of a bunk for the evening.

Chapter 19

Miraculous

"Many have made a trade of delusions and false miracles, deceiving the stupid multitudes. Oh wretched mortals, open your eyes."

Leonardo da Vinci

Was Shakespeare ahead of his time when he wrote in the 16th century, "Hell hath no fury like a woman scorned."? Apparently not.

In the 13th century, a German family on the way to Santiago de Compostela stopped off for the evening in Santo Domingo de la Calzada. This town, lying in the middle of the barren plains of northern Spain, was a favorite of half-starved, medieval pilgrims. The family opted for the plush local inn for the evening. Amongst the traveling entourage was their dashing 16 year-old son. The innkeeper's young daughter quickly became enthralled with him. But to this besotted local girl's great chagrin, she was unable to compromise his admirable rectitude.

The scorned girl sought revenge by slipping a silver cup in the boy's pilgrim's pouch. She then reported a 'theft' to the local authorities. As he and his family were leaving Santo Domingo de la Calzada the next morning, the police chased the boy down and apprehended him. He and his family desperately protested his innocence. Alas, he was immediately sentenced to death and hung on a tree outside town, as his parents looked on helplessly.

The disconsolate parents bravely decided to continue on to Santiago in order to partly fulfill their son's pledge. Months later, the family again passed through Santo Domingo de la Calzada on their returning trip from Santiago. As the parents approached town, they noticed a silhouette of a body in the tree where their son had hung. As they got closer, they could even see the body moving. In fact, their son spoke right up, asking help getting down from the tree.

The parents rushed frantically to the town's mayor to report the astounding news. However, the portly bureaucrat was seated over a sumptuous chicken dinner, and didn't fancy being disturbed. But the parents continued begging him to get up and witness what they had just seen. Annoyed at their persistence, the mayor finally shouted, "Your boy can't be any more alive than these chickens on this plate." Of course, the chickens on the plate immediately stirred to life, squawking and dancing all over the table. The stunned mayor rushed out to the tree to cut the boy down. A *miracle* was proclaimed.

***

Christianity is the religion of miracles. To be sure, miracles play a significant role in Judaism, Islam, Buddhism, and Hinduism. But in none of them do they play the central role they do in Christianity. This is at least partly out of necessity.

There are two passing references to Jesus by Roman historians, Tacitus and Josephus. Other than that, almost everything we know about the single most important person in history comes from *the Gospels* (Greek for "good news"), which were composed anywhere from forty to sixty years after the Crucifixion. Further, Mark, Matthew, Luke, and John were writing for very different audiences. At times, they report conflicting facts. For these reasons, Christianity is a religion based more on *faith* than strict ethical codes. As the story above shows, quite a bit of faith is indeed required.

In the Book of Acts, the apostle Peter passes a crippled man who habitually begs at the entrance to the temple. Peter fixes his attention on the man and says, "I have no gold or silver. But what I have I give you in the name of Jesus Christ of Nazareth. Stand up and walk." Needless to say, the man was fully ambulatory within minutes, with strong feet and ankles.

Seen from the perspective of the third millennium, a worldly, cynical eye is wont to find many of these miracle stories quite hokey. "It is impossible to use electric lights and the wireless radio," wrote German theologian Rudolph Bultman a hundred years ago, "and at the same time to believe in the New Testament world of miracles."

However, it's worth remembering perhaps the single most salient fact about Christianity. From the beginning, Christianity was the religion of the masses—the unwashed, the fork-tongued, the hair-lipped, the lame, the despised, the desperately poor, you name it. Few could read well enough to grasp the niceties of the Scriptures. What they had was these stories of saints and their miracles, which functioned almost like a second Bible in medieval times. They often make profound points, as long as they aren't over-analyzed.

***

The Roman Empire was surprisingly tolerant of religious diversity. However, there was one great exception—the Christians.

The Christians refused to worship any of the state or local gods, which gave the Romans ground to label them as *atheists*. Because they met at night, they left themselves open to the charge of holding nocturnal orgiastic rites. Savage reprisals followed, including being tortured on the rack, thrown to wild beasts, or burned alive in front of cheering crowds in the Roman Colosseum. But the heavy-handed tactics backfired. The Roman people began to view these societal outcasts refusal to apostasize, and willingness to accept death, as miraculous.

Hence, martyrdom became the key proof of miracles. Word traveled fast. Churches began constructing shrines and relics to saints who had suffered this ultimate fate. The excited multitudes flocked to them for healings, exorcisms, and the like. Church coffers overflowed with revenues.

But suddenly, everything changed. In the year 313, in one of the most consequential acts in human history, Roman Emperor

Constantine converted to Christianity. Overnight, Christianity became the official religion of the Roman Empire. Martyrdom all but ceased. The churches, however, proved very adaptable.

***

In the hilltop town of Assisi in northern Italy in the 13th century, probably the most influential saint of the Middle Ages was born to a well-to-do family. The boy was named Francis, due to his father's infatuation with everything French. As a teenager, Francis became the leader of a wild crowd who spent their nights carousing relentlessly. Like his father, Francis, "loved the songs of France, the romance of France, and especially the free adventurous troubadours of France who wandered throughout Europe."

At age 25, Francis rode off in expensive new armor as a knight to the Fourth Crusade. However, one day after setting off, Francis was struck by a vision from God that military glory was all wrong. He returned to Assisi, where a derisive mob and an irate father awaited him. His father hauled him in front of the bishop, with the entire town looking on.

Francis showed his flair for the dramatic as he tore off his expensive clothes and walked out of the courtroom, leaving himself in rags. He quickly organized a band of wandering friars who embraced the holy insecurity of beggars. They worked for all their necessities and begged only if they had to. "Francis didn't try to abolish poverty," biographer, Peter Metz, points out. "He tried to make it holy."

In fact, *it was this respect for poverty and disregard for personal gain that most clearly distinguishes pilgrimages from the infamous Crusades*, which were going on at the same time. However, humans being humans, this reverence for poverty soon became a cult. People began bleeding themselves several times a day to purify the sinful flesh. The recorded tales became more and more 'miraculous'.

Just consider the two miracles attributed to St. James. First, was his brave refusal to apostasize in Jerusalem that cost him his head. Few doubt that inspiring tale of bravery. But 800 years later, he had apparently been endowed with supernatural powers that had him killing 60,000 Moors in one day with his giant sword.

The Vatican was forced to appoint an official *devil's advocate* to judge the skyrocketing claim of miracles. They raised the number of miracles required for sainthood to two. But that proved easily surmountable. Like the tulip bulb mania of 16th century Holland, or the NASDAQ and real estate bubbles in 21st century America, human emotions were wildly out of control in this religion of the masses.

Chapter 20

Burgos: Gothic Majesty

Burgos may be the best kept secret in Spain. In fact, if I was going to live in northern Spain, it would almost surely be in Burgos. This is in spite of the fact that pilgrims enter Burgos through a hideous commercial district.

"This makes me homesick for America," Gavin commented caustically about the car dealers, road motels, pawnshops, and concrete sprawl that Camino pilgrims pass on the way into the center of town. It went on for miles, with nowhere to seek shade or take a break.

"Hey, there's a McDonalds," Gavin enthusiastically pointed out. "Big Mac time, baby."

"That blows the whole purpose of the pilgrimage," I protested. But I was being hypocritical. I savored some grease also.

"Can we stop in?" Gavin asked in a way that I could hardly reject without seeming to be an ogre.

"Yeah, but let's check in at the albergue and come back."

Fortunately, the story has a happy ending. Like most Spanish towns, once Burgos began unfolding it had an endless quality. We had heard the albergue was near the large cathedral. Soon we came to a large church. But it ended up being merely a nicely adorned body of worship, and the not the giant cathedral that was our landmark. We continued following the arrows.

"Hey, this town has some flair to it," I said excitely. Northern Spain is chock full of virtues, but a cosmopolitan feel doesn't happen to be one of them. But here in Burgos, culinary delights from around the world presented themselves on the broad avenues. Before long, we were over a mile away from the McDonalds, having survived a 'close call'.

"Hey, how about that Turkish restaurant there?" I suggested. Soon we were feasting on giant kabobs, leavened with healthy vegetables, and topped off with tzatziki sauce. It was a welcome respite from the good, but monolithic, pilgrim's menus. They lifted our spirits, and we continued through town.

"How can there be such a large cathedral in a town with no tall buildings?" I wondered. We began running reconnaissance down side streets, armed with various theories about where the pilgrim's albergue might be. But to no avail. The arrows were difficult to follow in the dense urban center.

Finally, we saw *it*. Better yet, a brand new 170-bed albergue was within a stone's throw of the main plaza. We checked in. Gavin decided to lie down for a siesta, while I did what a nerdy, old tourist does. I went for a tour of Burgos Cathedral.

Burgos Cathedral

Europe is the land of great cathedrals. Chartres and Notre Dame in France are world-class by any conceivable measure. Salisbury Cathedral in England is in a class by itself, despite its remote location. St. Peters in Rome is a mecca, and to a lesser extent Rheims in Germany.

My amateur eye would unhesitatingly add to that hallowed list, Burgos Cathedral here in northern Spain. It is widely considered one of the finest examples of Gothic architecture in Europe. Inspired by the *French cathedralism* of the Middle Ages, it doesn't look Spanish in the least.

Because the cathedral sits in an open, spacious plaza, viewers have an opportunity to take in its full glory. Its most spectacular feature is the brilliant filigree spires which soar spontaneously into the sky. One can only imagine the gasps it induced at first sight from indigent medieval pilgrims passing through on the way to Santiago after the spires were added on in 1291. Curmudgeonly thoughts about whether magnificence is even a desirable trait in a house of worship, as well as the entire lives of peasants spent dedicated to its construction, quickly receded from my mind when gazing at this gem.

Franco's regime had fled here to Burgos from Madrid during the civil war. In fact, Burgos is the one place that may have benefited from an association with the kind dictator, given the Socialist's bad habit of burning down churches. The great cathedral escaped unscathed.

But that's history. The better part of the tour was the gossip offered up by the tour guide. It seems a certain Genoese sailor used to frequent a married woman here in Burgos. Being a highly skilled navigator, this seaman was particularly well-versed in seasonal rhythms. His mistress' husband was in the shipping business, and gone six months a year, allowing the swashbuckling Genoan to swoop in to fill the seasonal vacuum. Like most Genoese, this sailor—*Christopher Columbus*—was attracted to the cosmopolitan flair that Burgos offered.

The guide went on to point out that this same Captain Columbus would later delay his departure for the New World from the Galapagos Islands for over a month, when he fell into the arms of an especially delectable, but married, island woman. I guess I am just naïve. After all, how much of a surprise is it that the world's greatest explorer of all time was also a bit peripatetic when it came to sleeping arrangements.

Chapter 21

Claire *Agonistes*

I suppose it's possible to construct hypothetical circumstances in which you would be happy to find yourself on a scorching July afternoon in Castrojeriz, Spain. It would probably have something to do with a catastrophic nuclear explosion that left Castrojeriz the only remaining habitable place on the planet.

Nonetheless, waves of pilgrims, mostly Germans, hurried to Castrojeriz. Meawes planned to celebrate his 19th birthday here, and desperately wanted to see Germany's quarterfinals match against Argentina. These were two of the top football powerhouses in the world. Adding to the drama was that Argentina had made the unusual selection of former soccer great, Diego Maradona ("The Hand of God"), as its coach.

But this was Castrojeriz, Spain, approximate population 85. A technophobe like me loved that they hadn't yet discovered cell phones here. But neither had cable television made it to these hinterlands. So instead of watching, we listened on the radio. The Germans unleashed the same devastating offense they had *blitzkrieged* England with a few days ago. Thunderous cheers arose all around the pueblo.

"Look at this place," I noted with surprise to Gavin. "There are a lot more Germans than Spanish."

"Don't go soft on us now, Bill."

The Spanish actually looked like *they* were the ones going soft. Their resurgent World Cup juggernaut was scheduled to run into mighty Germany in the semifinals. As Germany ran up the score against Spain's old colony, an uncharacteristic silence descended over the Spanish locals. A Germany-Spain semifinals match promised high drama. But was a slaughter in the making?

***

Castrojeriz was to be the one and only place on the Camino where I was truly bored. A bunch of us sat just off the main dirt road, waiting for siesta hour to end and dinner hour to begin. Inadvertently, this afforded Gavin and me the opportunity to witness a truly poignant scene.

In the late afternoon very few pilgrims are usually still out on the Camino. But sure enough, on this insanely hot afternoon, here came Claire. Poor Claire. As usual, she was trailing behind Benedict. All along the Camino, Benedict had been ahead of Claire. At times it was several meters, other times several kilometers. This was no surprise given his lithe, athletic form, compared to her relatively softer figure. She had gamely toiled on a daily basis to stay with him. Now as they entered Castrojeriz, Claire trailed Benedict by a mere step-and-a-half. That was ironic. For this would be the one time she *never* caught up with him. As they turned the corner onto the main street of Castrojeriz where a large group of pilgrims was gathered, Benedict turned *partly* around and quickly said, *"Au revoir."* He proceeded to shoot through town, never to be seen again.

"Man, that looked pretty cruel," Gavin noted.

"It was outright Darwinian," I agreed.

"Bill, you need to talk with her about nature's cruelty," Gavin said devilishly. "You may be next in line."

"Not," I decisively replied. I did see fit, however, to go over and help her digest the town.

"Claire, are you staying here tonight?"

"Yes, I think so," she replied in a husky voice.

"How far is Benedict going?" I unwisely asked.

"I don't know," she was barely able to utter. I pointed her to the albergue and left this dejected woman alone.

Blondine, the other Frenchwoman in town, had a much more positive experience in Castrojeriz. Because the young nurse trainee had acute budget concerns, she didn't want to have to pay for a bed. "There is an open field just out of town, only 200 meters from here," I pointed out to her. "The locals told me it is okay to sleep there." Blondine gamely took to the task, despite

106

not having a tent. Early the next morning on the way out of town, she passed by my tent, and said, "Bonjour, Bill. Merci." She had achieved liberation. In fact, she was to never sleep in another albergue again, often becoming downright bold in finding stealth camping sites.

I packed up my belongings from the field and went back to retrieve Gavin. My groggy nephew again proved difficult to levitate. After getting some kind of affirmation of consciousness, I yelled back into the bunkroom, "It's gonna' be hot. Let's get goin'."

"No, stop," a harsh voice to my right rebuked me. I turned and looked into the hard, angry face of Claire. "It is early in the morning."

"Everybody is already awake," I mildly protested. But she wasn't mollified.

"It's rude to talk so loud," she berated me in a voice many decibels higher than the one I had committed the original sin in. Claire was clearly going through an existential crisis, so I didn't pursue an argument with her. But I did walk away steaming. At least it served the purpose of stirring Gavin. We got going before 8:00, but were the very last pilgrims to leave town on this Sunday morning.

After a few minutes of walking, we came up on Blondine. She was staring pensively down a dirt road. *"Un hombre me dijo que hay una misa a las once* (A man told me there is a mass at 11:00)," she said. It was the first time I had heard her speak Spanish. Or mention religion, for that matter.

"Donde esta la iglesia (Where is the church)?" I asked.

"No estoy cierto," she said. We stood there with her speculating where a church might be somewhere out in this barren landscape. Finally, she headed down a lonely dirt road, looking for some church she may or may not find.

I liked this girl's brand of Gallic independence. There was something different about her. She seemed to bring the best out of (most) people, as opposed to more base emotions. It was almost like her undeniable beauty belonged to the world, as much as herself. Or maybe that's the kind of fanciful notion a person dreams up on a one-hundred degree day in the merciless Spanish meseta.

***

Soon we came upon another familiar figure lumbering slowly along the canal to our right.

"She's gonna' have to walk faster than that to catch Benedict," I said.

"Bill, let's see if we can pass Claire without you creating another international incident," Gavin advised. We sidled up alongside Claire, and then moved slowly past without saying a word.

"Bill," she called up to me in a panting voice, "Bill."

"Yeah?" I answered gingerly.

"I apologize for getting so mad this morning." Just like that, history was made. A French person had apologized to an American for a *faux pas*. Better yet, it sounded authentic. You could feel her taking on the struggle out here in the meseta. My Christian forgiveness instincts kicked in.

"No worries, Claire. This meseta is getting to all of us."

"I think I am leaving El Camino today," she pronounced.

"Where?"

"I don't know," she said forlornly. "One of these towns."

"But Claire, you've come all the way from Paris. Please don't let one or two bad days ruin it."

"I'm not having a good time anymore." Her face was drenched with sweat and her hair all frizzed up; agony appeared to be the predominant emotion.

Alas, we never saw Claire again. I was genuinely sorry. It had been a roller-coaster ride for her, including getting lost countless times on the thinly marked Camino down from Paris. Yet for a while it appeared her high hopes were being borne out. She had experienced exhilaration. What mortal doesn't find that heady? But now she was finishing on a decidedly sour note, without ever seeing Santiago de Compostela. Nonetheless, Claire's transparently wrenching trials and tribulations made her one of the most memorable pilgrims in this mass human movement.

Chapter 22

Furta Sacra

"Is this the tomb that Jesus lay in?" I asked my tour guide. It was the summer of 1994, and I was with a tour group in the Old City of Jerusalem. We were kneeling over *The Holy Sepulcher.*

"This is the Holy Sepulcher," the tour guide responded to my question.

"But is this the actual tomb?" I clarified.

"This is the tomb of Jesus."

"But this right here—this is the actual tomb he lay in," I continued to bore in.

"Yes, this is the tomb of Jesus," he intoned in a tour guide's informational voice.

For some strange reason though, I walked away unfulfilled. Perhaps I just wasn't convinced it really was THE TOMB. Or maybe I'm just too Episcopalian. Religious fervor bubbles up in me slowly.

***

In the 11th century, at the height of the medieval pilgrimage to Santiago de Compostela, Bishop Geylo was making the long return home to France. One afternoon he passed through the small, deserted village of Aquitaine, and decided to stop for the evening at the local inn. The host offered to take Bishop Geylo to the tomb of *St. Prudentius.* He eagerly accepted. There in the town church, he listened to a moving tale of the virtues and martyrdom of St. Prudentius.

That night Bishop Geylo lay awake restlessly. All he could think about was St. Prudentius, lying alone in the church. He quietly arose and walked across the village into the unattended church. There he began to solemnly chant *Laudes*, a Gregorian requiem. Finally, Bishop Geylo was overcome with despair. "The truth, O Holy Martyr," he said solemnly leaning over the tomb, "is that I would be so happy if you would wish to come with me." Then he decided to do what many other mortals of the age did when confronted with a sacred relic. He stole it.

Bishop Geylo rushed back with the booty to his hometown of Langres. There he was given a hero's welcome by the joyful throngs for his daring heist. Better yet, St. Prudentius justified the town's high expectations by posthumously working many great miracles for the region.

This is one of many such tales told in Patrick Geary's eye-opening book, *Furta Sacra* (Sacred Theft). Of course, it's easy to write off the entire enterprise as more medieval lunacy. Geary offers bizarre accounts of monks creeping into neighboring churches to open tombs and flee with the bodies of long-dead saints. In another case, merchants land on a distant shore fully armed to 'capture' a church and force the guardian to divulge the resting place of the saint within. But in a darkened Europe under the constant threat of war, disease, and even hellfire, the desperate masses really did believe that relics offered salvation.

There was one condition, however—that they had been martyred. Given the entire top echelon of the early Christians had been either crucified or decapitated, there was quite a supply. A kind of *martyrmania* had set in. Saints actually began to fear they might be murdered, because they were worth more dead than alive.

***

When the Crusaders captured Jerusalem in 1099, *relicmania* was reaching full swing. Almost immediately, they began exporting Holy Land relics back to Europe. Towns were prepared to move heaven and earth to get them because of their overwhelming economic benefits. King Louis IX of France bought *the Crown of Thorns* for 135,000 livres, which was roughly half of France's annual budget. The King, his mother, and two brothers assembled at Villeneuve-Archeveque near Sens to await the arrival. There, in imitation of Emperor Heraclius who had done the same 600 years earlier after 'rescuing' the True Cross, King Louis stripped down to his waist and shed his shoes and carried the Crown of Thorns into Notre Dame. King Louis accumulated 7,000 additional relics, including the *Holy Sponge and Holy Lance.* He then commenced the construction of the most magnificent and sumptuous building in all of Europe, the Gothic Cathedral in St. Chapelle, solely for the purpose of displaying the prized relics. Paris had become the new Jerusalem.

Unfortunately, many of these relics were fake. The clues were sometimes breathtakingly simple. One medieval pilgrim traveled to two churches in one day; at each he was shown what was purported to be the head of John the Baptist. Terribly confused, he ventured to ask the authorities at the second church about this. An ingenious monk replied that one was the head of John the Baptist as a young *boy*, while the other was his *adult* head. Meanwhile, enough duplications of *the Holy Cross* surfaced all over Europe to span several football fields. One church in Rome claimed to have vials of the Virgin's milk, leftover pieces of bread from the Last Supper, even samples of Jesus' blood and hair.

Relations between kingdoms were defined by the gifts they gave and received (Similar perhaps to Nixon's historic visit to China, when the Chinese famously gave the United States a panda bear, and the U.S. reciprocated with a Cadillac). To give someone a greater gift than you received from that person put you in a superior societal position. Thus, it made great sense for kings and towns to actually steal relics. It bolstered their gift-giving and, thus, status.

St. Nicolas (Santa Claus) had been a particularly popular saint, due to his jolly habit of leaving coins for children in open shoes that were left out for him. The Venetians were especially fond of him. In 1204 they conducted the heist of the century when they moved in on the Turkish town of Myra and lifted the bones of Saint Nicolas. For decades they basked in the glory of being the town that owned the stolen bones of Santa Claus.

A sea change was needed. It fell to one of the most determined and brilliant theological figures in history to effect the upheaval. By the time Martin Luther died in 1546, nearly half of western Christendom was Protestant. Gone were the statues and stained glass figures of the saints. Gone too were the relics. Luther,

John Calvin, and other Protestant reformers viewed the relics obsession as a form of pagan supernaturalism that needed to be stamped out.

But that was the Protestant world. As El Camino pilgrims, we were traveling through Catholic-as-ever-Spain, a country that retains vast quantities of relics and shrines dedicated to long-ago miracle workers and saints. Some of our fellow pilgrims seemed bound and determined to photograph every single one of them.

"Gosh, I would hate to be one of their friends," I couldn't resist remarking to Gavin on multiple occasions, "and have to look at a thousand photos of all this stuff when they get home."

Chapter 23

Root Canal Phase

"Nueve meses de invierno, tres meses de infierno (Nine months of winter, three months of hell)"

Don Quixote, speaking of the Spanish *meseta*

It was dreadful struggling in the mid-day heat of the *meseta*. For approximately twelve days, pilgrims on the Camino pass through this stark region of deforested plains. Gavin and I followed the dirt trail dutifully through a seemingly endless expanse of wheat fields. Everywhere we looked there was an arid stucco look that only seemed to turn a lighter color of orange as the sun rose higher into the sky. We had entered the *root-canal phase* of the journey.

This was the kind of day back in America where you'd like to go panting into an air-conditioned McDonalds and start unapologetically inhaling high-calorie, greasy fast food with multiple ice-cold drinks. Just this once. But all the Camino offered up was a singular nothingness, other than this ubiquitous parched landscape.

"The thing that surprises me is how few people we've passed," I said.

Schlepping through the meseta.

"What's so surprising about that?" Maybe Gavin was giving me a hint. He intermittently opened up wide leads over me, which was worrying. I'd hiked extensively in the southern California desert, and knew it was the wrong place to get lost. Landmarks are scarce. Fortunately, I would periodically come up on Gavin lying prostrate on his backpack. I'd stop, drink some water, stir him back to life, and we'd press on.

Perhaps the most outstanding aesthetic feature of the meseta was the giant windmills we periodically passed by. Spain is now the second largest producer of wind energy in the world. I thought that was pretty impressive. But not everybody felt the same.

"Those things are ugly," the outspoken Sophia said with great conviction every time she passed by one of these large wind farms. Others fervently agreed. Indeed, they have been creating controversies ever since they were introduced way back in the 1570's. That was twenty years before Miguel Cervantes wrote the fictional story of the unforgettable *Don Quixote*.

"Look at those monster giants—more than 40 of them! I'm going into battle, I'll kill them all," shouted Don Quixote.

"What giants?" his partner, Sancho, asked. "They're windmills."

"You know nothing about it," Don Quixote retorted. "They're

giants. If you're frightened keep away. And say your prayers while I attack." This great Spanish literary character exemplifies a seminal aspect of the Spanish character—the tradition of defending honor at all costs.

Gavin and I, however, were nowhere near so honorable. We continued walking with our heads down and brains in neutral through the sepia-grained landscape, barely paying attention to the gigantic wind farms. Finally, we came to a tiny hamlet.

"That looks like a food concession," I panted. We dutifully walked over.

***

This time of year one can expect the ambience in a Spanish restaurant to feature hot, soupy air and black flies. Like all pilgrims, we had become well accustomed to swatting the flies away from our soup bowls and dinner plates in the evenings. However, this particular restaurant only offered one choice. And that happened to be the one thing in Spanish life a foreigner can never get used to. I speak, of course, of the dreaded *bocadillo*.

'Bocadillo' is the Spanish word for sandwich. The striking thing about bocadillos is how utterly incongruous they are with the rest of Spanish cuisine. I've always had a British-style utilitarian attitude towards food. However, Spanish food offers up such a bounty of delights from Iberian hams, to spicy chorizo sausages, to yellow rice, to hot, buttery potatoes, to deliciously flavored croquettes, to endless varieties of tapas, that I consider dinnertime in Spain to be the seminal hour of the day. Compared to those culinary delights, the bocadillo is like a foreign invader.

In fact, Great Britian—where eating is mostly about damage limitation—did occupy this region of Spain in the late 16th century after defeating the Spanish Armada. Presumably, that is how this execrable item found its way into the Spanish national diet. It is honestly the least imaginable sandwich possible. As best as I can tell, it's just a flavorless piece of meat thrown into a hard, crusty white piece of bread. And the microwave has yet to be invented in northern Spain, so one can expect to sit there dutifully eating one cold cheerless bite after another.

Gavin and I took one look at the bocadillo-dominated blackboard and recoiled.

"It's time to make a sacrifice on behalf of principle this

Sunday," I said. "I'm not eating one of these bloody bocadillos."

"The bigger sacrifice would be *to* eat a bocadillo," Gavin rebutted me. Nonetheless, we filed out of the stuffy room empty-handed, hoping to find some shade.

Soon we found a sheltered area under a portico, where we lay down with our backpacks as headrests. Gavin and I had been practicing our Spanish a lot so I said to him, *"Los bocadillos estan horibles."* A man sitting nearby laughed. I hadn't realized he was Spanish. In England I had learned the hard way about the perils of insulting another person's country (and Queen!) while in their country. Comments like, "They should turn Buckingham Palace into a haunted house," were always vastly underappreciated. Fortunately, this Spaniard wasn't a latter-day disciple of Don Quixote.

"Es verdad," he nodded his head with great conviction.

Gavin and I lay prostrate with our heads on our backpacks for over two hours, wondering where in the world we would be that night.

***

"Disculpame, me gustaria ofrecer un brindis (Excuse me, I would like to offer a toast)." I stood up in the crowded dining room.

Gavin and I had hiked most of the afternoon, in varying states of heat-prostrated morale swings. Finally, we had entered Fromista. This little pueblo had almost nothing in the way of modern accoutrements. However, there had been one important exception—a large ranch house that puts up and feeds pilgrims. We had followed the arrows down a side street and right onto its spacious, green lawn.

"Oh yeah, baby," Gavin had said when he saw the swimming pool on the far side of the yard. He had jumped straight in, while I had gone and checked on their policy for extra-tall people sleeping on their well-manicured lawn.

"We are having a three-course dinner tonight," the hospitaleiro had told me. "Would you like to register?"

"Of course."

We had laughed, joked, eaten, and drunk our way through a three-course dinner in the host's packed dining room. The meat, bread, and red wine had been, as usual, *muy rico*. When I had remarked on this, some man had pointed out in strained English, "Well look at what we walk through all day—grape and wheat fields, with cow manure all over the place." Point well taken.

Drinking red wine in Spain was not a snobbism or sophistication. It was as natural as eating, and apparently as necessary. And the plain fact is that bad wine, or even mediocre wine for that matter, has yet to be invented in this country. I always looked forward to my evening glass; red wine was always included in the pilgrims menus. Gavin habitually took part as well, even though he was only 18. I didn't say anything, as long as he didn't do anything terribly disruptive. It turns out he didn't need to; he had his uncle to do that.

***

My experience is that most toasts tend towards the inane and vacuous. And boring, for that matter. With that in mind, I stood and said in both Spanish and English, "This hospitality, this food, this footpath, this way of life has finally settled a question that I have been wrestling with for years. Spain is definitely my favorite country in Europe." Nothing radical about that. Throughout the centuries, foreign visitors have been swept up by this great Iberian peninsula and its unique people and culture.

"More importantly," I continued, "on Wednesday night it will be everybody's favorite country. Because Spain is going to surprise the world and beat Germany."

I knew there were plenty of Germans in the room. Murmurs rose around the room. Meawes was confused. He didn't speak Spanish, and his English was inconsistent.

"What did you say?" he asked. "Something about Spain?"

I looked directly into his Aryan face and made an assumption that here on El Camino in the year 2010, no dangerous atavisms would emerge. "I just told them the obvious, Meawes. That Spain is definitely going to win on Wednesday night."

"This is not possible," this American-style German patriot said.

"Germany has the best team this year," his girlfriend, Franzi, said sincerely. In reality I agreed with both of them.

Another Anglo-Saxon male on the far end of the long table asked in strained English, "Do you watch much football?"

"I have lately," I said gingerly.

Elsewhere around the room, everybody was speaking softly with each other. But nobody—absolutely nobody—had clapped like I had expected. As others stood to do their toasts, I found out why. There were 23 people seated at the dinner table. Every single one was either German or Austrian, besides Gavin and me.

The rest of the toasts featured rote predictions of an impending German victory. Finally, the waiter shuffled over to me and said softly, "Bueno senor. Yo estoy de acuerdo con tu prediccion." At least I'd won the Spanish waiter over.

Chapter 24

Rigid, Frigid Nuns

Like most people, I've passed nuns on streets and wondered how in the world they can stand walking around in *those costumes.* Stereotypes played out on television and the occasionally idiotic joke constituted the balance of my knowledge of their mystical world.

Nonetheless, Gavin and I hurried to Carrion de los Condes, where we hoped to stay in a monastery that puts up pilgrims. It was a good thing we did because a big queue was already forming by mid-day. Everybody just seemed curious.

Two Sisters in full garb stood at the door politely, but efficiently, checking our pilgrim passports. The older one took us up to the spotless bunkroom, where a dozen or so bunks were occupied by completely new faces. A couple of Sisters walked around offering lemonade and verbal ministrations to them.

"I wonder if these are pilgrims that got injured or something," I commented to Gavin. He shrugged his shoulders.

"*Esta la comida aqui* (Is the food here?)?" one of the men asked me.

"*Cual comida* (What food?)?" I wondered.

"*La comida,*" he began anxiously saying to me.

One of the Sisters came back over and pressed a rag up to his head. In a soothing voice, she began assuring him, "*La comida mas tarde* (Food later)." He seemed temporarily pacified. However, others began calling out in various tones that appeared to be non-sequiturs. I went out to the hallway and asked one of the nuns if they were pilgrims.

"Son patientes mentales (mental patients)," she informed me. *"Interesante."*

She then described their daily activities, including walking on the Camino every weekend. Throughout the afternoon, these nuns hurried in and out of the bunkroom, waking up these patients, and directing their activities. My young nephew, who isn't prone to overt sentimental remarks, commented, "That's really impressive the way they work with those unfortunate people." Indeed, we would soon see that these nuns had all kinds of arrows in their quiver.

***

"Excuse me," I pointed out to one of the Sisters. "I noticed there was a grassy area out back. Is there any way I could set up my tent out there?" I didn't feel good about opting out of the bunkroom. But the nun was the one who appeared to be on the defensive. She apologized copiously for the diminutive size of the bunks.

By the time Meawes and Blondine's group arrived, the albergue was full. "Maybe you can sleep out back in the garden with me," I suggested to them.

"That would be great," Blondine said. "But can you ask the ladies for us?" Now *that* was a great irony. A regular staple of European sidewalk café conversation is about the cultural obtuseness of Americans. Our ineptness in languages comes in for special derision. Again, I asked the nun, and she couldn't have been more hospitable to my friends.

But as I was helping get all the details straightened out, a chunky, bearded guy stormed down the stairs. He stood straight in front of me, and began berating me in some unfamiliar language. *"Habla espanol,"* I replied defensively to him. But he didn't seem to understand. His equally fulsome wife was not far behind and lashed into me as well. Blondine, meanwhile, could barely suppress her laughter. The couple was French.

"They said you interrupted their siesta," she reported to me with amusement.

"Well, we're in Spain, so they should tell me that in Spanish," I asserted.

This same man soon became infamous amongst pilgrims for practically blowing the roof off albergues with his snoring. Yet whenever anybody made the slightest noise that woke him up, he would angrily tell them to shut up in French.

Rigid Frigid Americans

Nuns, it turns out, like to have fun. Don't worry. This isn't a prelude to some kind of sick joke. The smiling Sisters woke everybody up from their siestas, passing around cups of freshly-squeezed lemonade.

"We're going to have a group of singers from each country," they announced.

"Hey, let's stick around for that before we go off for dinner," I said to Gavin.

"Yeah, fine."

We edged our way downstairs where scores of people were packed in the downstairs foyer. One of the Sisters announced that the pilgrims from each country were to form a choral group and sing a national song. I started looking around for other Americans. *Surely, there are some Americans among these people.* But I couldn't find anyone other than Gavin.

The Sister began calling out the pilgrims from the various countries. Poland, Hungary, Romania, Spain, France, Germany, Italy, Japan and on and on. Groups of three or four pilgrims from each country would shuffle nervously up to the front. Hushed, giggly conversations would ensue. However, every group managed to conjure up some beautiful tunes; the nuns and the rest of us pilgrims listened in pure, unfeigned enjoyment. The bit you always hear about German being a guttural language—forget it. It's a beautiful language, and the German and Austrian groups were especially wonderful. Smiles were joyous and broad all around.

I once read a novel by the spiritual writer, Scott Peck, called *In Heaven as on Earth.* In the book, Peck purported to describe what heaven was actually like. The scenario that Peck presented did not include anything quite as exotic as the 49, 72, 99, or however many virgins it is that Osama Bin Laden's disciples had salivated over before heading off for suicide-bombing missions. Nor was the heaven that Peck described full of opulent luxuries and fancy gadgets. Rather, everybody was singing. Better yet, they were all singing in one language. Peck didn't actually recognize the language. All he knew was that it sounded *heavenly.* Now there's a loaded word. But I will step out and say that these joyous songs ringing out from pilgrims had a palpably celestial quality about them.

"Ahora, los Estados Unidos de America," the emcee nun announced and turned to me.

A toast was to precede each country's song. *That* I could handle. Picking up on my previous night's toast, I hailed the hospitality of the Spanish people and particularly the nuns. And for the second night in a row, I predicted victory two nights hence for Spain against Germany in the critical semifinals match of the World Cup. But, once again, there were a lot more Germans in the crowd than Spanish. Good natured jeers followed my toast.

"Are there any other Americans here?" I asked in English. Nobody responded.

"Cual cancion usted prefiere (What song do you prefer)?" the Sister asked.

"Senora, yo necesito otros Americanos," I pleaded. Gavin, meanwhile, had become a *peeping tom.* Every so often I would spot his head ducking strategically in the doorway, only to quickly jerk away when he saw me looking for him. "Can somebody please get Gavin in here," I yelled over to the door. Finally, somebody was able to retrieve him. Perhaps an uncle is supposed to occupy a higher position in the proverbial hierarchy than his nephew. But as the reader may have gleaned, we treated each other more like peers. But now it was time to break the pattern.

"Gavin," I anxiously ordered him. "You know how to sing. Get up here and sing a song."

"Bill," he spread his arms out helplessly, "I can't sing."

"But you can sing something."

"I can't."

"Well, sing the *Star Spangled Banner* then," I said quickly. "You know the words to that."

"I don't," he said breathlessly. Embarrassingly, I wasn't confident I could recite our entire national anthem, either—but give me 49 more years and I should be able to. Few in the crowd understood our rapid-fire English. So they all assumed Gavin and I had come up with a plan. *"Senora, disculpanos,"* I groveled in slow Spanish. "We don't know any songs."

"Nada?" she asked in amazement. *"Por favor, canta algo de cualquier* (please, sing just something)."

I looked at Gavin again. But all eyes were on me. Without

sounding too schmaltzy let me just say, I love my country. But I wasn't about to embarrass it and myself by bellowing something that would give every pilgrim a nightmare.

"*Lo siento* (I'm sorry)," I said mournfully. Then it was time for her to really to really send me on a Catholic guilt trip, without even trying to.

"*No te preoccupies* (Don't worry)," she said. "*Esto siempre pasa con los Americanos* (this always happens with the Americans)." She said it sympathetically. But it was more like the coup de grace.

In the infamous, novel, *The Ugly American,* the authors, Burdick and Lederer, postulate that when Americans go overseas, we quickly become mean, vulgar, and aggressive. Apparently, you can add to these stereotypes, we can't sing. This is especially sad, because singing is one of the things that bring humans together. The Welsh and the Aboriginal people are notorious singers and they both have histories as two of the most peaceful nations in the world.

Gavin and I left the monastery to scope out a café for dinner.

"Man, if you don't like the Catholic Church for that," Gavin sincerely said, "you're never gonna' like it."

"Amen," I added.

A German pilgrim who had been on hand for my toasts each of the previous two evenings came walking by. Gavin had previously dubbed this man, 'Einstein', due to his bulging eyes and unruly grey hair. Fixing a cold stare at me, he said in English, "You full of bullshit. Germany no lose." Up until now, all the Germans had taken my toasts good-naturedly.

"Was he joking?" Gavin asked.

"Didn't look like it."

"I didn't think so." It had been a bad evening in my role as American goodwill ambassador.

Chapter 25

Romanesque or Gothic

*"Twentieth century architects have not been able to
create anything, anywhere, both as elegant and as
powerful as a late medieval steeple."*

Nikolas Resuner, renowned 20th century art historian

The year 1000 was a watershed moment in human history. In the years leading up to the millennium, end times theology had dominated. People had quit working; families had been abandoned; children had quit going to school. Christian Europe had waited in both dread and hope for the end of the world and the *Last Judgment.* Diabolical images of the happenings of hell—wild beasts, the mad calling of sex, damnation, and horrific death had reverberated through medieval society. Humans had been desperate.

But then, like the *Y2K* computer scare a thousand years later, the worst didn't happen. The Devil had failed abysmally. The feeling was that humanity had finally turned the corner. Hope ran high.

Christians could now build churches out in the open, instead of living behind the closed walls of monasteries. The largest church-building spree in history began. El Camino de Santiago was to play a key role in it. Large populations of artists, artisans, craftsman, bishops, and nobles roamed all over southern France and northern Spain. That is where most of the churches were built—approximately 15,000 in all. It became quite common for one parish to sponsor building a church in another village; pilgrims were expected to carry slabs of stone to the new location.

One of the countless Romanesque churches that Camino pilgrims pass in pueblos all along the way.

Soon a recognizable pilgrim's style had evolved of simple, round arches, heavy walls, and thick columns. It was called *Romanesque*, and became the dominant theme of the Camino architecture. Most were built in the 11th and 12th century, right when the Camino was gaining widespread popularity throughout Europe. "Certainly there are simpletons and illiterates in the church who cannot contemplate the Scriptures," proclaimed the Council of Arras in 1025. "And although one does not worship a chunk of wood, the interior of man is excited by the visible image."

Romanesque was the first distinctive style of architecture to spread across Europe since the Roman Empire. Effectively, the Church had made a major contribution to western civilization.

***

Success begot confidence. Confidence begot grandiosity. By the 13th century magnificent *French-style* cathedrals started springing up along the Camino route. International tourists are surely more familiar with these French-style cathedrals than their Romanesque predecessors. The greatest and most famous cathedrals, abbeys, and churches in the world were built in this French style.

The key breakthrough was the pointed arch. This allowed medieval humans to build churches with greater vertical reach and beauty. The stained glass interiors permitted light to enter, as opposed to the darker, cooler Romanesque interiors. Substantively, this signified light had triumphed over darkness. Instead of hunkering down in fear of God, humans were reaching out trying to comprehend God. Indeed, there was reason for confidence.

Humanity's pace was accelerating forward in the 12th, 13th, and first half of the 14th century. 'The Church' had begun major universities in Oxford, Cambridge, Salamanca, and elsewhere. Literacy levels were being ratcheted sharply up. Economic advancement was creating middle classes in the major European countries. Lifespans were increasing rapidly as medical breakthroughs benefited the masses. Church architects and builders had reason for confidence, which was reflected in these soaring cathedrals.

Unfortunately, as has usually been the case in times of such optimism, humanity instead stood on the edge of catastrophe. The Black Death which struck midway through the 14th century (1347-1350) wiped out approximately 25% of Europe's population in three years. Soon, that old middle-European bugaboo, anti-semitism, had surfaced again, followed by religious wars breaking out all over Europe.

'The Church' was never again able to attain the level of unquestioned devotion that it had in the Middle Ages. For that reason, in the 17th century during the *Age of Reason* these French-style cathedrals became known as *Gothic Cathedrals*. It is no accident that a sinister-sounding pejorative such as Gothic was chosen. The Goths and Huns were people of Germanic heritage, who like the Vandals, were infamous for their barbaric behavior.

Nonetheless, the 300 year building period of these majestic French-style Gothic cathedrals still stands as perhaps the greatest-ever age of European architecture. But in my modest opinion, the more humble Romanesque churches that still dot the majority of the pueblos along the Camino more aptly capture the essence of this great pilgrimage of the masses.

One final interesting fact about these great cathedrals: in *The Cathedral Builders,* Jean Gimpel wrote about the dirt poor hovel dwellers who built these immaculate houses of worship. Gimpel had carefully studied the payroll records of monasteries and medieval builders and found something worth knowing. In spite of the obviously sexist leanings of the medieval church, a large share of the critical tasks in these huge construction projects was done by women.

Chapter 26

The Crucible

"A journey is a fragment of hell."

Mohammed

"I'm telling you," I said to Gavin. "This looks almost exactly like the desert."

"You keep saying that."

"It's because you've got to take precautions when the sun is this strong."

"Such as?"

"Stay well-hydrated."

"Thanks for the advice," he said saucily.

The frolicking, chatty groups of the first 200 miles had morphed into solo pilgrims trudging doggedly under the brutal, mid-day sun. Clusters of hikers would be spread apart by 5 or 10 yards all along the dusty path, nobody saying a word.

Gavin had been a hit with all the other pilgrims so far, despite his relatively tender eighteen years. But for all his intelligence and even intellectual maturity, he didn't always play it smart. A pilgrims needs to take care of himself in the desert, or semidesert. Among other things, that includes drinking enough water, and wearing a hat and sunglasses. For the most part, he was drinking enough water, out of the fountain pipes in the pueblos we periodically passed through. However, the floppy hat that would protect Gavin's head lay inside his backpack. Perhaps this budding young Francophile couldn't bear to don anything quite so dorky. Nor was he wearing the sun glasses, which he had predictably lost.

We continued passing through two-street, one-church, fifty-to-one-hundred-people villages with water fountains in the central plaza. The signs indicated, *Agua Potable*. Like most pilgrims, we drank it straight up.

"How does it taste?" I would ask Gavin.

"Like hemlock."

***

"You alright?" I asked Gavin. He was leaned over in the middle of a desolate stretch as I walked by.

"I don't know." The cocksure tone was gone. "I feel a little nauseated."

He looked stricken. But stuck out here in the blazing sun, there was little I could offer. The nearest town was miles away. Our paces reversed themselves. I began hiking a couple hundred yards, then stopping for him to catch up.

"Gavin, can you drink some water?"

"No."

"Here, take some Advil." He slowly gulped them down. But he was looking worse. The mid-day sun beat down on our heads. There was absolutely nowhere to seek refuge.

"Man, please put your hat on," I reasoned with him. "You need the protection." He slowly, but dutifully, did what I suggested. *That* was a sure sign that things really were amiss.

I pulled off my sunglasses, and said, "Here, put on these sunglasses." He grudgingly hoisted his backpack. But he was getting even slower, and I was starting to get nervous. I hadn't started backpacking until my mid-forties, and have been known to panic. I simply lacked that bedrock confidence to fall back on when the inevitable emergencies happened. The prospect of my sister's son being in serious trouble out here rattled me.

"I'll tell you what," I said, "let me run up ahead. If I don't see a

130

town in the distance, you may have to abandon your backpack. I'll come back and get it later." Off I went as fast as I could. It was an article of faith among pilgrims that you could see the next town well ahead, just by looking for the church steeple. But we were in the middle of a 17 kilometer stretch without a town. The map did show we were within a few kilometers of Calzadilla de la Cueva. But all we could see in every direction was more austere, saline landscape.

I started back to get Gavin when a threesome we knew came by, looking alarmed.

"Bill," Javier said, "Gavin is vomiting."

"Is he okay?"

"He was on his feet and told us to go on."

Gavin finally came along at an octogenarian's pace. "Just get rid of the backpack, Gavin," I said. "It can't be far." But he continued pulling 100 or 200 yard stretches, and then bending over with his hands on his knees.

"Hey, I see some buildings up ahead," I said. "Here, give me your backpack." I put out my hands; he unstrapped it, and gave it to me. I began carrying the two backpacks like golf bags, stopping every couple hundred yards for a break.

Finally, we got to the pueblo's lone albergue. A long line of pilgrims was queued up. We jumped to the front. Luckily, they gave us a private room on the second floor. Gavin grabbed the trash can out of the bathroom on the way to his bed. He then commenced *projectile vomiting*. After each round, he would cease, followed by a few minutes of preternatural calm, after which more waves of violent nausea would ensue. I ricocheted around bringing water, Coca-Cola, you name it.

Some things look easy, until you actually try them. But not parenting. It never has even looked easy to me, despite never having been one. And now I was getting a taste of the roller-coaster of emotions a child can put you through. I didn't know what the hell to do.

"Hey, there's Meawes and Blondine's group," I said to Gavin, while looking out of the window. "Blondine is a nurse. I'll get her." The prospect of seeing the stylish Blondine plying her trade quickly boosted our morale—my morale, anyway. By the time I got down to inquire of her, she had already heard. I led her to the second floor, where explosions were still echoing through the hallways.

"He wasn't wearing a hat in the sun," I said, as we hovered over Gavin.

"Why weren't you wearing a hat?" Blondine asked in surprise.

That finally brought some life to Gavin. "No, it was the *water*," he protested.

"No, it was not wearing a hat," I argued. We would periodically scrimmage over this all the way to the end.

The intensity of the vomiting seemed to abate a bit. Blondine and I left him alone. But I was still shaken by what I had seen.

***

A post middle-aged German woman named Heidi was lying out in the front yard in the shade. We had periodically exchanged polite greetings at random places along the way.

If they were going to make just one improvement to El Camino, my suggestion would be for the pilgrims to give each other trail names. On the Appalachian and Pacific Crest Trails, a person's trail name was a major part of their identity. And given the spiritual nature of El Camino, the names would surely be especially vivid.

The name I would have given Heidi would have been *Job*. She was as reliable and patient as the day is long. She had started in Geneva, Switzerland in the spring, which meant she had already done 500 miles before the rest of us had even begun. Heidi began walking every morning promptly at 6:30, and maintained a slow, but steady pace. She rarely took breaks, never hurried, and was in as good of shape as a woman her age could reasonably expect to be in.

"Have you ever hiked?" I asked her.

"Never."

"Did you train for El Camino?"

"Of course."

Good answer.

"Are you married?" I asked.

"No, divorced," she said evenly.

More questions. Gosh, why can't I be as subtle as a European. But I was curious.

"Are you very religious?"

"Yes."

"Glad to hear it," I said.

Suddenly, I heard a familiar voice non-chalantly say, "What's going on?" When I looked over my shoulder, it was Gavin. Better yet, he seemed to have regained some of his insouciant ways.

"Gavin," I exclaimed, "you have risen from the dead like Jesus!"

"No," Heidi immediately interjected. "You can't compare a person to Jesus." Her tone wasn't sharp, but lecturing. She then patted the grass in front of me and said, "Give me ten pushups and tell God you're sorry." There was something I liked about the tone she struck. It was just the right balance between firmness and levity. So I dropped onto the grass and gave her ten.

"Gavin," I corrected myself, "You've risen from the dead like Lazarus."

"That's more like it," Heidi said, regaining her amicable tone.

When I recommend El Camino to various people, they often wearily reply, "I'm not Catholic," or "I don't want to be overwhelmed by a bunch of religious fanatics all day and night." But this modest rebuke was to be the only time on the entire journey I was at theological odds with anybody over anything. The modern Camino is very ecumenical indeed.

Chapter 27

Playing Hurt

The fiery heat of the meseta continued to hold everybody in its steel grip. Droves of pilgrims were now leaving albergues in the pitch black early morning. The few pilgrims who tried to sleep until sunrise started complaining to the hospitaleiros, who resorted to posting signs that pilgrims could not leave the albergue before 6:00 in the morning. But it never worked. People always found a way out into the early morning darkness.

The morning after Gavin's fireworks, we were the last to leave the albergue by over two hours. Of course, this meant naked exposure to more brutal heat. At least 'the new Gavin' was willing to put principle aside and wear his dorky, wide-brimmed hat.

"How are you feeling?"

"I'll make it." We were out of crisis mode. But he was visibly weakened. His heretofore confident stride had been replaced by a zombie-like gait. It ended up taking double the normal time to get to the first town, Sahagun. The first person we saw was

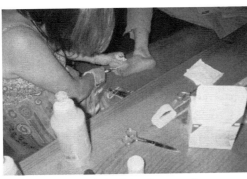

Hospitaleiro injecting needle to drain my blister. I had to wait in a line for this invaluable service.

Emily. She was a French Canadian girl we had come across a few times in the meseta. Yes, I said French. Not that Gavin started breakdancing, when we saw her. But he did bolster up a little bit. Just slightly. However, he was frequently critical of the French Canadian accent.

"You won't believe how different it sounds," he kept exclaiming distastefully.

"For God's sake, you sound like the British," I said. "They claim we don't even speak the same language."

Gavin wasn't impressed by my analogy. But he did seem impressed with this 18 year-old provincial Canadian girl, who was traveling with her older cousin, Jean Francoise. I had even noticed that he occasionally veered away from his offhanded, Fonzie-like style when around Emily, who was his exact age.

"How far are you and Jean Francoise going today?" I asked.

"We're feeling bad and planning to stay here," she said. "Many people are sick."

"Not a big surprise the way we're packed in these stuffy refugios," I commented.

"Bill," Gavin said, "this might be a good place to stay and watch the match tonight."

"Well, okay." We had only gone 8 kilometers.

Unfortunately, Emily's older cousin, Jean Francoise, was a *planner*. He saw to it that they washed clothes every day (Gavin and I were lucky to do it once a week), ate dinner and got to bed early, and were out at first light every morning. You could debate whether such a regimented style was in the spirit of pilgrimage. But it sure didn't leave much room for spontaneity and give-and-take, which happened to be my nephew's forte. We did have the pivotal Spain-Germany semi-final match to look forward to. Unlike us older Americans, Gavin's age group does understand soccer. But Gavin proved he really had been playing hurt. He remained in bed for most of the next 20 hours.

While Gavin was sleeping that afternoon, I went out and found a pair of sunglasses for him in the local market. The heat was murderous. I ran into the peripatetic German girl, Sophia.

"Where are you going to watch the match tonight?" I asked her.

"In El Burgos de Ranera."

"Can you make it there in time?" I asked perplexed.

"I'm taking the train," she said unselfconsciously.

"Hey, Meawes is supposed to be there," I said. "How about giving him this note?"

"Sure," she said dubiously. In reality, she and Meawes weren't on speaking terms. This iconoclastic eastern German girl had spoken repeatedly about how horrible the German striker,

Miroslav Klose (who was the third leading scorer in World Cup history), was. "This girl is stupid," Meawes had kept muttering. I had thought their internal warfare was kind of funny, if for no other reason than it disproved the stereotype of the monolithic German. I handed her the note I had written to Meawes predicting a Spanish victory. She took it with amusement, and headed on to the train station.

Just before game time that evening, I entered a restaurant. The first two people I ran into were Rosere and Anna, a delightful twosome from Barcelona. Being Catalonian, they had a nonchalant attitude towards the match. But Spain had never even been to the semifinals and the whole town was tensed up around television sets. Palpably ingrained in their stoic faces is a country that knows disappointment is often right around the corner. But in the 85th minute, a Spanish striker fired the ball past a stunned German goalie. All hell proceeded to break loose. Resounding cheers reverberated for several minutes all over the village. I could even hear them down in the basement where *I* was vomiting loudly and repeatedly. I returned upstairs and sheepishly apologized to the girls and the bartender. Fortunately, the cheers had muffled my loud exertions.

But that night back at the albergue, there was no drowning out my further thunderous explosions. They echoed throughout the 100 bed sleeping quarters. From my kneeling position in the bathroom, I could hear speculation coming from the pilgrims' bunks, as to just who the lucky person happened to be. The next couple days, a few people even sidled up next to me to timidly ask, "Was that you the other night?" I silently nodded, and they took the point. I didn't have a *martyr's complex*. Bleeding myself, or otherwise inducing suffering, wasn't for this particular pilgrim. Vomiting would have to do as my Camino sacrifice, matching Gavin's offering of a couple days before.

My surprise bout did provide ammunition to Gavin's argument that it was the water that was laying people low. In any event, a contagion was spreading through the pilgrim community. Many were now choosing to take a train to get them through the meseta region (Imagine the atmosphere on board such a train).

The Camino was proving a bit more demanding than I had expected. On the Appalachian and Pacific Crest Trails, if you fell ill while in a trail town, you would simply take the next day or two off. Not on El Camino. Because a new wave of pilgrims arrived at the albergues each day, we had to keep going.

***

"Are you alright, Bill?"

"We'll see," I responded softly. His 20 hour siesta had given him his mojo back. Now, I was the problem.

I hugged some bushes to the left on the way out of Sahagun, trying to fit in with their shadow. But most of the time we were sitting ducks. All I could do was tilt my big hat in the direction of the sun, and keep my head down. After 8 kilometers, we came to our first town. It wasn't even siesta hour, yet the blazing sun had already chased everyone inside. The shimmering heat was visibly rising from the sidewalk.

"Here," I said quietly to Gavin and pointed down a side street. A long building had created a narrow strip of shade. Soon we were both horizontal on the pavement with our backpacks as pillows. I was at least out of pain. Finally, after the better part of an hour, Gavin asked, "Is this it?"

"It would be dangerous to go back out there," I sighed. "I'm worried about getting dizzy in that heat," He wanted to keep going and catch up with Jean Francoise and Emily. I was the goat.

We found the town's only albergue—a converted monastery in an otherwise non-descript town. Unfortunately, it didn't look like they had updated the bunks since medieval times. Worse yet, a handful of people occupying these crib-sized bunks were already snoring hugely and helplessly. I went down to the hospitaleiro and laid out my sob story. "Is there anywhere on the floor I could sleep?" He fell for it.

"Would you like to sleep in the chapel?"

"That would be great."

At bedtime Gavin and I walked into the chapel to lay out our sleeping mats and sleeping bags. A bald headed, athletic-looking Italian and a Polish woman in their thirties were doing the same thing.

"*Eres un sacerdote?*" the Polish woman asked me, in what will surely be the one and only time in my life I'll ever be asked if I was a priest.

"*Ya no* (No longer)," I answered to her eternal confusion.

"At least the baldheaded guy's in good shape," I whispered to Gavin. "We should be okay."

The man then proceeded to blow holes through my theory that snoring was the exclusive domain of the rotund. A horrible malfunctioning motorboat sound ensued for eight straight hours. I lay there helpless at first. Then, I proceeded to make a total ass out of myself.

It's his fault. It's not fair because he's gonna' feel great tomorrow, and I'm gonna' feel horrible. This is how a *snoree* thinks. I commenced trying to puncture his snoring by banging my shoe on the floor and yelling, "Stop snoring." But he had this long rhythm with a particularly breathtaking hesitation strategically placed in the middle. Several time I temporarily blunted his noise emissions. But ultimately he was like the Chocataws that did Custer in at Little Bighorn. He kept on coming. At first light, he bounced up, got his things ready, and cheerfully headed off. Meanwhile, I lay there sullen and tired, wondering if I was too ill to hike in the heat.

After gathering all our things, I told the hospitaleiro (as if hospitaleiros haven't been hearing this exact complaint since the 9th Century) about the awful snoring.

"The Polish lady said that some American was yelling half the night," she responded. But a split-second after making that revelation, her expression suddenly changed, when she realized who she was talking to—the jackass himself. Of course, it had selfishly eluded me that the poor Polish lady had been sandwiched between my bleating and the Italian's chainsawing.

Gavin, for his part, thought the whole thing was funny. He had slept like a baby. That was a good thing, at least for him. For we had the longest and most exhausting day on the entire pilgrimage ahead of us today.

Chapter 28

The Longest Day

"A pilgrim ought to torment his own depraved and lusting flesh with hunger and thirst, with great abstinence, with cold and destitution, with punishment and hard labor."

12th century Catholic Missal

Today was a day to have my game face on. I simply didn't want to disappoint Gavin again by having to stop early, like yesterday. But I was plenty sleepy. A viral feeling lingered.

"Bill," Gavin asked, "why did you let that guy bother you so much last night?" I had no answer. For once, I kept my mouth shut and we walked. Gavin actually seemed to morph seamlessly from his vaunted wise-guy role into a mini-caretaker. He refrained from opening up a wide gap ahead of me. Instead, we walked one in front of the other. Silently.

"How long would it take to learn to speak a language fluently, change my name, everything?" Gavin had asked me at the start of the trip?

"Let's see, changing your name won't take much time at all," I had told him. "But learning to speak the language is gonna' take some work."

"Would you be willing to teach me?" he had asked, seemingly sincerely.

"Why not?"

We had thus made a resolution to practice at least one hour a day. *Yeah, right.* That's the kind of resolution that's made to be broken.

"Americans expect everybody to speak their language," is a commonly heard complaint. Indeed, we have great faith that if we repeat our English loud enough and slow enough, then the listener will be able to understand us—no matter where in the world we happen to be. Another bad habit is when we are around both English and non-English speakers, we're off to the races in the colloquial English of a family reunion, leaving the non-native speakers bewildered.

The French, who consider their language like a museum masterpiece, have the same bad habit. While living in Paraguay, I had separately made several French friends. I decided to get everybody together one night at one of these friends hotel for introductions. That ended up being a mistake. They yakked in French all night, leaving me high and dry.

My experience with the Japanese was completely different. In Mexico City I had two Japanese roommates. One was a bulging sumo wrestler who habitually stuffed himself with a pack of Oreo cookies every morning at the breakfast table. The other was a tiny, soft-spoken ballet student. But any time the three of us were together, they were careful to speak nothing but Spanish.

I was intent on emulating the Japanese. Believe it or not, Gavin and I more than kept our resolution of an hour of daily practice. When isolated from other pilgrims, he would often ask, "Bill, could we practice some more of the past tense?" or "Could we review some of those verbs from yesterday?" When I was that age, I would have thought anybody willingly practicing a foreign language, other than maybe at gunpoint from a parent or teacher, was a hopeless nerd. But practice was only logical. It simply made his trip better. Other pilgrims often heard this going on between us and eagerly jumped in to participate.

But today was a day to conserve every morsel of energy. Languages were out today. This was all about walking and forward progress.

***

Gavin and I arrived in Reliegos after 25 kilometers. It was mid-afternoon; we had been walking steadily for five hours. I was pooped. There were few signs of life, as the heat maintained its iron grip. Nonetheless, morale was high as is always the case after reaching a destination on foot.

"Hey, look at that place over there," I pointed out. "Elvis Presley's bar. Whaddya' say for lunch?"

"Why not," Gavin replied. "He was famous for his food, right?"

We walked in where a middle-aged man with a handlebar moustache greeted us effusively.

"*Elvis, No se ha cambiado nada* (You haven't changed a bit)," I joked.

"*Todos dicen esto* (Everybody says it)," he confirmed.

Unfortunately, the greeting was about the best thing going for this particular restaurant—except for maybe the waitress. When we sat down, a short, petite girl shot over and quickly began placing silverware on the table. Besides her slender frame, her most notable feature was her dark eyes. They were very, very dark, almost bewitching. I threw my usual banter out to her.

"*Como te llamas?*"

"Christina."

"*Eres de Reliegos?*" I asked her.

"No, Leon."

Cristina seemed shy, almost fearful. However, it began to seem like she had bigger concerns than merely flirtatious customers. A disagreeable look had come over Elvis' face, just since Christina had visited our table.

"I'm telling you," Gavin whispered in a conspiratorial tone, "this place is an obvious *ETA* hideout."

"Maybe you're on to something," I went along. Meanwhile, the waitress scurried around, trying to be as unobtrusive as possible. A couple of middle-aged males came in and began quietly chatting with Elvis. That goaded Gavin on further.

"See, look at those two guys," he bore in. "They fit the profile of *ETA* the way a fat Frenchman does a snorer." Taking Gavin along on this trip had at least stimulated his imagination.

Christina brought the food. Immediately, I realized that I had made a big mistake. "Look at this," I moaned to Gavin. "They barely threw any pasta into all this tomato sauce."

"Good idea, Bill," Gavin countered, "ordering pasta with meat sauce on a 110 degree day."

"Christina," I waved her back over, *"la comida esta horrible en este restaurant."* She peered back towards Elvis. When the coast was clear, she commenced giggling. We may have been the first customers in this small pueblo to tell her directly what we thought about the food. Spaniards are not prone to challenge authority.

Of course, Gavin couldn't resist. *"El,"* he said motioning back to Elvis. *"Es ETA?"* Christina's dark eyes flashed recognition at Gavin's remark, and she began giggling uncontrollably.

"Por que tu trabajas (Why do you work) *en este restaurant?"* I asked.

"Yo no se (I don't know)," she meekly said, again looking down at the floor.

Women rights are nowhere near as advanced in Latin countries as the United States. I distinctly remember a language institute in San Luis Potosi, Mexico where I had taught several years back. The women teachers from the United States, Canada, and England habitually raved at teacher's meetings about how great their Mexican boyfriends were. But soon these girls found out there was a different side of the story. Whenever a woman's assertiveness interfered in the slightest way with a Latin male's point of honor, the night of the Dark Ages would descend on these macho males.

Gavin was probably right in one sense. There really did seem to be more than meets the eye in this restaurant. I exchanged e-mail addresses with Christina, and we left. Upon returning to the United States, I received an e-mail from her. First, she told me how much of a kick she had gotten out of my comments about how horrible the food was. She was no longer working there. As for why, she wrote simply, *"En Espana, los empleados exigen mucho mas que una muchacha pueda entregar* (In Spain, the employers demand much more than a girl can deliver)."

***

You've got to trust your gut. This haunted village with a sketchy eating establishment had been our destination for the day. But we both wanted to hike. So we followed the arrows of the Camino out of town and back into the blazing hot Spanish countryside.

"A la izquierda, a la izquierda (to the left, to the left)", we soon heard several voices yelling. Several bicyclists in tight bike-racer

suits came flying by, leaving trails of dust in their wake.

"Why do all these bicyclists always seem so egocentric?" I wondered.

"Because they're Italian," Gavin immediately replied.

Statistics show that 18% of pilgrims do the Camino by bicycle. In the afternoons, however, bicyclists are probably more than half the pilgrims on the trail. Albergues don't even permit bicyclists to check in until 7:00. For that reason, biking pilgrims tend to be younger, fitter, more dashing, and, yes, more Italian than the rest of the pilgrim population. Good for them. However, in my greatly biased opinion El Camino is better covered on foot. These bicyclists don't immerse themselves in the Camino culture or get to know the personalities the way we were able to do on foot.

Carnet shells, along with yellow flechas (arrows) make the Camino the best marked footpath in the world.

Gavin and I continued along a dreadfully boring, flat stretch that paralleled a major highway. A van came riding by. The driver made a point of yelling hello to us.

"Wait." Gavin stopped suddenly in his tracks. "Did you hear that?"

"What?"

"I heard scallop shells clanging in the back of that van," he said.

"Oh yeah," I laughed in recognition. Gavin was theorizing that pilgrims were hiding on the floorboard of the van. But the scallop shells that pilgrims hang on their backpacks were banging against each other, thus giving them away.

"Let's see," he smiled deliciously, "Sophia's hiding down there for sure."

"And Felipe and Shakespeare," I surmised. "That's how they always beat us to the towns." We were just being facetious, of course. But this exact kind of thing surely does happen. I had seen such bouts of "yellow-blazing (catching a ride along the yellow-blaze of the highway)," periodically break out along the Appalachian and Pacific Crest Trails. Humans will be humans.

Actually though, the Camino offers a service that is quite legitimate. For the price of seven Euros, a van will come by the albergue in the morning, pick up your backpack, and drop it off at an albergue in whatever pueblo a pilgrim designates. Because of age, infirmity, or whatever reason, they might not otherwise be able to complete the Camino. More power to them.

***

"Bill, have you got any water?"

"Yes," I said, looking at his empty water bottle, "but don't be too bold."

A kilometer later, Gavin asked, "Have you got any more wipes? I've got to perform a *roadside bombing*."

"How bout' let's put this on the list," I said handing him our last wipe. "Before leaving pueblos, you take a crap and fill your water bottles."

"Bill, we were lucky to get out of that place alive back there. It was an obvious *ETA* hangout." My perspicacious nephew had all the answers today.

We both seemed to be carried by an unspoken impetus this afternoon. It lay in the back of my mind, and I could tell his as well. But neither of us wanted to say it. *Leon*. Leon is the biggest city on El Camino. It's storied history, dating back to medieval times, figures large in the Spanish epic. Among other things, it was reputed to have the finest Gothic Cathedral in Spain.

Yes, it would be nice to say that we hankered for Leon for such high-minded cultural reasons. The truth, however, was at least partly more basic. Gavin knew Emily and Jean Francoise—well,

Emily—were planning to stay there. And I knew that Meawes, Franzi, and Blondine—well okay, Blondine—might be there. Leon was still almost 20 kilometers away, and it was nearly 6:00. But one of the superior pleasures of life is the strong urge to keep moving, and, better yet, having the freedom to accede to that urge. We gave license to this impulse, and kept walking.

Coming into Villarente at twilight, we straddled the shoulder of a long bridge. Mack Trucks blew by in both directions, making us feel like tiny specks. "Man, this is the most dangerous place on the entire Camino," I said half-seriously.

"Heavy trucks are on old *ETA* tactic," Gavin said knowingly.

We stopped on a bench for some Nutella (a Gavin favorite) and crackers, and I pulled out the map. "I reckon it's probably 7 or 8 o' clock," I observed. "Leon is 13 kilometers away."

"Look at this town," Gavin observed. "I wouldn't play this joke on my worst enemy." He had a point, although it didn't look terribly different from your standard one traffic light, two street layout of many small American towns. Gavin also had a purpose. He wanted to get out of here and on to Leon. But he knew I was recovering from a virus and dog-tired. I wanted to go also, but wasn't sure of my capability. Without stating our purpose, I simply said, "You ready?" We got up and started walking through town. Most Spanish pueblos eventually redeem themselves. Not this one. At least not until I saw Rosere and Anna.

"Hey, there is Rosere," I said.

"Oh great," Gavin muttered. "There goes thirty minutes." He was right.

"Isn't it about time I found a wife at 49?"

"Good luck."

They—Rosere, particularly—had been shadowed from the beginning by a middle-aged Spaniard named Javier. Indeed, this fortyish woman from Barcelona was a bit hard to take your eyes off, with her long shiny limbs, jet black hair, and eyes of a deer. Better yet, both girls had delightful personalities to match. Perhaps it was one of history's misfortunes that these Catalonians had lost their civil war. But they seem to have won in every other way.

"*Ustedes siguen caminando* (You continue walking)?" Rosere asked in surprise, noting the late hour. Of course, if you give a male a chance, he's going to tell you about his adventure. In my case, vomiting, Italian snorers, Elvis, and now our long day, all featured prominently in the report I rendered to them.

"Donde esta Javier?" I asked, referring to the Spanish pilgrim that had been shadowing them since we had first met. There was a long, pregnant pause.

"He no longer with us," Rosere answered in broken English. I remembered thinking while living in England that they were the world's best at *exclusionary tactics*—the fine art of freezing you out through ice-cold. However, my instincts told me these Barcelonan girls had probably rejected this unwanted suitor more through fire, than ice. By the way, do I sound like an expert on the subject of rejection?

Gavin stood by watching our conversation, at turns, looking amused and bored. His body language said, let's go. I wanted to stay here, but I also wanted to continue our long day. We went. All I can say is that we humans aren't terribly rational creatures. Perhaps we should thank God for that.

***

It started getting dark. That always quickens the paces. Soon we cleared a hilltop and began seeing lights in the distance. Slowly, Leon's impressive skyline appeared down in the distant valley. It was Friday night.

"This could be tough finding a pilgrim's albergue at night in a big city."

"You'll figure it out, Bill," my peerless companion said in a voice that was only 50% sarcastic. We thought we were close, but the trip through the city blocks had an endless quality to it. As has been known to happen when walking around a foreign city, nature was calling.

"Man, I've got to take the worst leak," I muttered.

"Watch me," Gavin said decisively. He found a bush off to the left of the sidewalk, hit his left knee as if tying his shoe, and proceeded to urinate—all while people shuffled by without paying any attention.

"Wow, I've never seen that technique," I said impressed.

"Welcome to the 21st century, Bill." My only viable response was to quickly hit my left knee also.

It was now completely dark. We had walked 45 kilometers (30 miles). At least one of us was dead tired. We were in the very center of Leon, and anxious to find the pilgrim's albergue we had heard about. We commenced taking turns dropping our backpacks and doing reconnaissance missions down various side streets, while the other guarded the backpacks. But to no avail. All we could do was ask reputable-looking citizens of this metropolis if they had any idea where the pilgrim's albergue was. After several head fakes taking us in different directions, one guy really did seem to know what he was talking about. Better yet, it took us up the narrow-cobblestone streets of the Old City.

***

As is the wont of most Europeans on weekend nights, people were out walking around town in the happy state of deciding where to have dinner. Bystanders like us could feel the ripple of conversation, the joy of laughter, and love of ideas that are the European style. Americans on these occasions tend to be in our cars, heading to specific destinations. Hopefully without sounding too priggish, this is one area we might do quite well to emulate our European cousins. Everybody all around looked pretty content.

"Even if we find it," I said, "what are the odds they let us in at this hour?"

"Wait til' they find out who it is," Gavin assured me.

I kept asking strangers about a pilgrim's albergue; it was clear we were getting warm. My grasping style seemed a little too American for my Europhile nephew, who was content to just go with the flow. But I badly wanted to get this backpack off my back.

Finally, we arrived. The hospitaleiros were beginning to shut the big wooden-crate doors that are so common off main walking streets in big European cities.

"*Disculpame, somos peregrinos* (We're pilgrims)," I said. "*Podriamos entrar?*"

"*Desafortunadamente, todo esta completo,*" he said softly.

"It's full," I said dejectedly to Gavin.

"Use your charm, Bill."

I tried a sob story about how far we had walked, and that we were meeting friends in this albergue. "*Esta possible dormirnos en el piso* (Is it possible to sleep on the floor?)," I groveled. The man was actually sympathetic, but said all 160 beds were full. There was no space available even on the floor. I then asked about other pilgrim albergues. He gave us vague directions to an albergue on the other side of town.

Normally this time of night, we would just stealth camp absolutely anywhere we could find. But we were in an all-concrete area in the very densest part of a major city. We slowly began threading our way back through the alleys we had just passed through with such hope.

Gavin's paternal grandfather is an immigrant from Ireland. Perhaps this is what helped him to adopt a stiff upper lip and get on with it. We dutifully wound our way a few kilometers all the way back to the side of town we had entered. It was after midnight. We found an albergue that was still accepting pilgrims. But *that* made it suspect in our eyes, considering the hour. Worse yet, it was unbearably stuffy, given that we had been in the intense heat all day. As for the beds, forget it.

"I can't stay here," I quickly said. "I'll get you a bunk though, and find somewhere outside."

"No, I'll go with you," Gavin said softly. We headed outside and started down another side street, where there was a fenced-in soccer field.

"How about in there?" Gavin suggested.

"Yeah," I said skeptically, "but I don't think I can get over the fence."

"Let's look for the gate." We walked to the end of the field and came upon a locked gate.

"We can jump over here," Gavin said. I experimented with stepping up on a bar to catapult me over. But it honestly looked like a potentially leg-breaking, trip-ruining leap over.

"You can sleep in there, man," I said exasperated. "I'm gonna' have to look for somewhere else."

"No, that's okay."

We found a small plot of dirt just off a sidewalk.

"There's a bit of glass here," I pointed out with my headlamp. We quickly started brushing that away. I then set up my tent and got in, while he lay down on his pad in his sleeping bag to *cowboy camp*.

So there was no French nurse name Blondine, or any French Canadians cheerleading our long day's hike and late arrival. But it had been a great day anyway. We had seen a lot of Spain. Better yet, we had done it on foot. Most importantly of all, we had gotten a taste of that feeling *non-pareil* that true pilgrims have found so tantalizing through the ages—the fulfillment of all-out effort.

Meanwhile, in the pilgrim's refugio that we had struggled so hard all day to make it to, but missed by a hair, pilgrims lay awake throughout the night listening to other pilgrims violently barfing.

Chapter 29

Too Knowledgeable about Clowns

"Safety is a crime no writer should ever commit, unless after academic tenure or praise."

Pat Conroy, *My Reading Life*

It had all the makings of a magical moment. In fact, it *was* a magical moment. Unfortunately, a fairly large asterisk is also necessary.

The sun—and fortunately not the police—had roused Gavin and me from our urban campsite this morning. We had then commenced another cross-town hoof across Leon. I didn't feel capable of heading straight back out into the meseta and starting the struggle all over again in the intense heat. So when we passed by the large albergue, I said, "Let's check in."

"Whatever," Gavin had replied. Normally, taking a day off on El Camino is a no-go. But since we hadn't stayed there the night before, they allowed us to check in.

The building appeared castle-like from the outside. But the minute we walked in the bunkroom it felt like we had entered the land of the hobbits. It looked like they had chopped off the 160 bunks to cut down on pilgrim living space. Even though it was mid-day, pilgrims had already begun high-pitched vomiting. Perhaps it was just endemic to this albergue. Leon, itself, had been a center of Jewish commerce in the Middle Ages. It had probably seen its share of torture racks and hysterical screams.

Gavin and I had then gone for an amble around town, to escape the oppressive atmosphere. We had soon come up on what many people consider the most gorgeous edifice on the entire Camino—the famous Gothic Cathedral of Leon. The Northern European architectural influence was striking, in an otherwise typically low-lying, sun-drenched Spanish landscape. To the naked eye, the building actually seemed to have more stained glass than stone.

"Good God, the upkeep on this place has to be horrific," I had commented.

"That's beside the point," Gavin had rebutted.

"But I can't believe they let everybody in for free."

"It's a miracle," he had said. Yes it was.

The perennial debate among pilgrims was whether the

What medieval humans were capable of: the Gothic majesty of Leon.

cathedral in Burgos, Leon, or Santiago was more beautiful. *That* really was beside the point. Nonetheless, I will say the Cathedral here in Leon may well have the most breathtakingly gorgeous interior of any building I ever had the privilege to enter. The stained glass windows were so richly embroidered, they almost seemed liquid.

Gavin and I had then eaten lunch in an outdoor café under a portico, before heading back to the albergue in the scalding mid-day heat.

The building had already begun to feel uncomfortably stuffy as it filled up. It wasn't difficult to imagine this evening that there would be more bleating pilgrims emptying their insides out with ever-greater decibels.

"Gavin," I had said in a confidential voice to my nephew who was in the bunk right above me, "how about if we lie here for another couple hours and then get out of town about six? We can find either a small village or some small place out in the countryside with fresh air for us to sleep."

"Yeah, whatever," my one-quarter Irish nephew had again answered.

Immediately, it had felt like we had made the right decision. The fiery intensity of the sun had begun to wane a bit just as we had left town. As always, the fresh air and movement were supreme tonics. And our behavior had been predictable. We passed a couple of small villages with music, merriment, and smoke wafting out of packed pubs. It was Saturday night.

"We could find a place to stay here?" I had offered.

"It's up to you, Bill," Gavin had responded in a neutered voice. Of course, this had all been *pro-forma*. Deep down we had probably been thinking the same thing. We could turn this twilight surge into a full day. That would mean making it 25 kilometers to Villadagos del Parano, and hopefully some familiar faces. We had continued moving. Again, darkness had descended on us as we were moving at endorphin-fed full speed. But this time, we didn't have the cosmopolitan glow of Leon to guide us home.

"The best thing about trying to find this place is supposedly there's nothing else around," I had said hopefully.

"That's contrarian reasoning."

But sure enough we had been following a path along a highway when a comely little building nestled up on a hill on the other side of the highway had come into view. It had been the albergue.

"We might end up getting bounced around like last night," I had muttered as we were crossing the highway. But instead, as we walked up the hill to the albergue, two females were sitting at a picnic table. They immediately proceeded to give us a standing ovation, and jokingly chanted, *"Ole, ole, ole."* Our adoring audience was none other than the two Barcelonan girls, Rosere and Anna. Our triumphant arrival had finally come, a night late.

"Do you mind if I talk with them this time?" I jibed at Gavin, after he had been so impatient the previous day.

"Bill, show me how to do it."

Feeling was good all around. Rosera and Anna had walked 37 kilometers today, from where we had seen them at twilight yesterday, and had just arrived 45 minutes earlier themselves. *The Camino brings the best out of people.* That horribly banal cliché—that you never know what you can do until you try—really is true.

But there is something about long days and campsite

conversations. Hikers, trekkers, and pilgrims have completed their daily tasks and are finally *worry free.* Probably not coincidentally, this is when they tend to venture into otherwise prohibited topics. I vividly remember a girl on the Pacific Crest Trail shocking her fellow campers one night with excruciating details of her boyfriend's depredations on her own friends. On the Appalachian Trail, a fellow hiker had brought a hush over a packed shelter one night with his breathtaking knowledge of cannibals. (He quickly picked up the trail name, *Cannibal*). And now, here on a pain-free night surrounded by the most enjoyable company, and with great anticipation of Spain playing in the World Cup finals tomorrow, I got started on the subject of clowns. The story I began telling was about the *second* most famous clown in history. I refer, of course, to the now deceased upon state execution, John Wayne Gacy.

***

Storytelling is a great tradition in my native South, dating back to the illiteracy of slave times. And the way I uncorked this tale with all the perfect vocabulary, etc., it was clear I had told it in Spanish before.

It is rare for a storyteller to have an audience in such rapt attention as I did on this occasion. Rosere and Anna's dark Catalonian eyes hung on every word.

"*Now,* everybody get a good night's sleep," I joked upon finally finishing the story.

"*Disfrutaremos los pesadillos* (We will enjoy the nightmares)," Rosere commented.

Gavin and I poked around the albergue amongst the prostrate bodies of exhausted pilgrims. The stuffy air again conjured up the specter of sick pilgrims heaving loudly all night.

"How 'bout if we go camp in that soccer field across the street?" I suggested.

"Sure." This time we were able to find a way inside the fence, and walked to the far side of the field. I pitched my tent and Gavin threw down his sleeping pad and bag.

Gavin had half-seriously remarked on a prior occasion that Rosere was the female pilgrim that best fit the profile of a potential partner for me. Now, right as I was crawling into the vestibule of my tent, he said softly, "Bill, don't you think you showed a little too comprehensive of knowledge about Gacy tonight to Rosere?"

His tone actually carried a trace of uncustomary concern. "Yeah," I finally said very reluctantly, "I guess I got carried away."

About all I can say is that I found his concern for my welfare very, very touching, indeed.

Chapter 30

The Big Day

Most Americans aren't aware of this for obvious reasons, but the Sunday of the World Cup finals is a big day around the globe.

I had been living in Brazil in 2002 when they won the Cup for the fifth time. Once Brazil had secured victory in the final match (held in Tokyo), the whole town where I was living had emptied onto the streets at 4 o'clock in the morning. A non-stop pandemonium was maintained all day and through the next night. Then just when it had looked like normalcy might return, the team had returned from Japan to a hero's welcome. The fans, drunks, hookers, and looters all had caught their second wind. The whole thing had made me uneasy, and I had been relieved when stability had finally returned to the streets.

Gavin and I were now trying to make it to the picturesque village of Astorga to watch the pivotal match. It was a routine 26 kilometers away. We had walked until around midnight the previous two nights, and got going later than most this morning. But we still had plenty of time.

"Man, I'm feeling weak again," I said after less than a kilometer. "I've gotta take a rest." I walked over to a shady spot under a tree and lay down. The Camino was abuzz with World Cup chatter, and I sensed Gavin's impatience. So I unenthusiastically hoisted my backpack to continue. But I was feeling lightheaded. Exerting great energy in such intense heat was potentially dangerous. I soon pulled off the Camino again into the shade.

"What's the problem, Bill?" This was embarrassing. I had

been touted by my mother and Gavin's mother as the expert in the group, who would guide my nephew to the Promised Land. Now I was proving to be his millstone.

"Here," I said handing him some bills of euros. "I'll meet you in Astorga. But if I don't make it there today, under no circumstances leave Astorga. I'll be there tomorrow."

"Yeah, yeah." He hurried off to Astorga as fast as he could. It was our first separation since leaving the United States. I would later learn that he had gone 200 meters, before accelerating up the right fork of a trail junction, at which point he had ended up three or four kilometers off The Camino.

Meanwhile, I was in the bucket. I had found on my previous long-distance hikes, that on days like this it's best to be in a state of virtual communion with yourself. One step at a time. I slowly passed through the scenic village of Hospital de Orbigo, and luxuriated in having a cold drink in the shade. On the way out of town, I saw two female pilgrims hanging out in the doorway of an albergue. They were Dutch (Holland was Spain's opponent tonight).

"Don't even consider watching the game," I joked with them. "Your only concern should be your personal safety. Not victory."

"You're just a jealous American," they said half-truthfully. We chatted briefly with a standoffish British lady, which dampened my frolicking mood a bit.

"Thank God, England's not playing tonight," I said to the Dutch girls. "You would have to seek a hideout." They laughed knowingly about their ancient enemy.

"The Dutch are everybody's favorite travelers," my roommate in a backpackers hostel in Lima, Peru once observed. Indeed, it was hard not to feel comfortable around them. And their cleverness ("going Dutch") is undeniable. How many countries are practical enough to change their name—in this case from the repulsive-sounding *Netherlands* to the more fetching name of Holland? Better yet, the people are given a third name, the Dutch.

"I would stay here and watch the match with you," I said sincerely to these two Dutch girls, "but my nephew is waiting." I headed off, but they had restored my good mood (We would see a lot more of them). This was a great atmosphere. There honestly wasn't anywhere else in the entire world that I would rather have been on this day.

However, I was soon exhausted again and felt myself becoming dangerously overheated. I needed to get off out of the intense heat. Fortunately, after a few kilometers, I came to another small pueblo, Valdez Loria. I anxiously looked around for a place to let me inside and off my feet. But it was siesta hour. Luckily, it was also Sunday which meant the bars were still open (You figure that one out). I entered a smoke-filled bar where a timeless Spanish scene presented itself—pleasant-looking, middle-class men in their Sunday best, occupying the bar. Yet it is this same scene that in its own way represents Spain's Achilles heel. There really is something about the Spanish character that is gloriously tragic.

Every Spaniard thinks his country is the best, his region is the best, his pueblo is the best. It's the old obsession with honor. Incidentally, it was from tiny pueblos like this that the likes of Cortez, Magellan, Balboa, and the other great Spanish conquistadores came from. It is the supreme irony that in this land of such far-flung explorers and adventurers, the people are so irreparably provincial.

I ordered an empanada and a Coke, and went over to the corner to try to just cool off. I never go to this kind of place back in the United States. Yet I loved this particular scene, even if it was smoke-filled. You can't have everything. The waitress soon brought me a complimentary cup of soup. What a nice touch. Her style was an unhurried modesty, as opposed to the hustling, tip-obsessed waitress of an American franchise chain. It is worth noting, though, that the Spanish are great *stoics.* They put up brave fronts, but you never really know what's going on back home. All Spanish homes have well-tended gardens and beautiful facades. But reputedly many are empty boxes within. Nonetheless, after a brief flirtation with the Dutch earlier in the afternoon, I was foursquare back in Spain's camp tonight.

I slowly walked out into the blazing sun and followed the arrows out of town. Almost always my feeling leaving these tiny pueblitos was the same. The people are as authentic as the day is long. But, dear God, thanks for not making me spend the rest of my life here.

***

The meseta was decidedly hellish. And this seemed like the very most infernal part of it right here, on this World Cup Sunday. There was more than one fork in the trail where it wasn't clear where to go. For a couple hours, I ambled westward in the face of the fireball-shaped sun, wondering if I was off track. There was no shade anywhere to rest. I worried about my legs becoming shaky. On days like this when your body is emitting so few endorphins, you rely on sheer willpower. Finally, I got what looked like a break. I came upon a major highway. Better yet, there was a bus stop with a canopy right in front of me. I did a beeline to gain shade under the canopy, and immediately sat down next to a naked lady. Neither one of us could have cared less.

She was probably in her sixties and had been in the middle of a change of clothes when I had walked up.

"*Como lejos hasta Astorga* (How far)?" I quickly asked.

"*Tres kilometres,*" she answered softly.

"*Tres kilometres?*" I responded in disbelief.

She was Romanian, and looked like she was in the struggle of her life. Let me honestly say, I was absolutely blown away by the way so many post middle-aged women laid it all on the line on The Camino. I loved it. To me, it represented a truly fabulous aspect of the Camino. This particular lady looked like she was in the middle of her own existential crisis, struggling like hell and probably also feeling a bit shaky in this terrible heat. I was still a bit worried about making it to Astorga myself, tonight. Her situation seemed especially dicey.

Gosh, I hope she's right about the distance. About the time she got her pants on, I stood up to go.

"*Cual direccion?*" I asked.

"*Por alla,*" she pointed straight ahead. But when I started for 'alla', it led nowhere. *This is the wrong day and the wrong weather to get lost in.* A car came by and I held out my hand for him to stop, which he promptly did. A middle-aged man jumped out of his car, and animatedly gave me extensive directions of how El Camino led into Astorga—all furthering my allegiance to Espana tonight.

"*Como lejos* (How far)?" I asked.

"*Ocho o diez,*" he said.

Oh, wow. I thought about going back to deliver the bad news to my Romanian colleague, but decided against it. I did, however, see her again the next morning, when Gavin and I passed her. She had walked until dark and then gotten out early in the morning. This daily pattern would repeat itself all the way to the end. She gets my nomination for pilgrim of the year.

Chapter 31

Viva Espana

"It occurred to me there are certain things some nations do better than everyone else, and other things for worse. It is difficult not to wonder, why?"

Bill Bryson, *Notes from a Small Island*

"This place combines the best of *German charm* and *British efficiency*," my American friends and I used to joke, while living in London. Obviously we were being droll, for the simple reason that most people would consider just the opposite to be the elixir. But it really is striking just how endlessly different some countries can be in the most fundamental ways.

The British are confounded by instant American amiability. But when they finally do warm up, their senses of humor are brilliant. The Germans often seem flummoxed by humor. But they are good, if not great, at almost everything else. The French are downright left-footed when it comes to business, but pretty much wrote the book on high culture. Italian governments have traditionally been laughingstocks; yet this same country is almost everybody's favorite foreign destination. The Greeks seek to perfect themselves, while doing just the opposite for their country. And on and on.

By my lights this is all a historically happy fact. Honestly, wouldn't it be great to learn from each other? But because of national ego, mythologies, and outright cant, we are habitually blinded to this great possibility. Regrettably, we Americans seem to be especially weak in this department.

The Spanish were getting ready to give us pilgrims a demonstration on how to watch an athletic event. It was actually very simple. They all watch together. Better yet, they do it in the most accessible place possible, the central plaza.

The night of July 13, 2010 saw a feel-good, carnival-like atmosphere in the very typical Spanish pueblo of Astorga. Two large screens were set up, giving access to all. Food, drink, laughter, friendliness, and asking really tall Americans to have your picture taken with your group were in. The economic crisis, financial worries, and class hierarchies were out. It was time to make history.

An old-fashioned defensive donnybrook ensued. Like most Americans, I have trouble fathoming the excitement and drama of scoreless athletic contests. But every Spaniard in the packed square looked as if the match hinged on each body check, pirouette, pass, and kick. Their enthusiasm was contagious, and I watched closely. The only negative vibe I got all evening was when a young Spaniard jumped up to the screen and thrust his middle finger at the head of a Dutch player. The match went into overtime.

Suddenly, in the 93d minute, Andres Iniesta, from a tiny Spanish pueblo similar to the one we were now watching from, fired the ball past the leaping Dutch goalie. It ricocheted off the left crossbar and into the net, at which point the largest celebration since the Spanish Civil War erupted. The last few minutes, a steady roar of 'ole, ole, ole,' splayed all over the square. Victory came, followed by fireworks. Even the most hard-bitten soul had to be happy for this storied country and its unmatchable people.

Gavin had watched the match with Sophia, Shakespeare, and Felipe up on the front row. I immediately went looking for him afterwards. But everybody had chaotically dispersed.

I simply couldn't get my mind off my formal experience in a soccer-mad country. In the 1996 European Cup in London, England had lost a shootout to Germany. Sporadic riots had broken out all over central London. In the midst of it all, a tall Russian was overheard speaking his native language while walking through Trafalgar Square. A British hooligan proceeded to *stab* the Russian. When the police later asked him *why* he had done it, the hooligan replied in a logical voice: "I thought he was speaking German."

That story stayed with me throughout my years in England, and I always tried to avoid the subways and other public spots on Saturday evenings during soccer season. But there was another issue that was at the front of my mind as I searched for my absent nephew in the chaotic masses. Surveys consistently show the Dutch are the tallest people in the world. If some hooligan did feel compelled to improve his self-esteem with a cheap act of violence, I'd make a pretty prestigious target. I was already a bit uncomfortable as a few shouts came my way.

I arrived expectantly at the albergue, and anxiously looked for Gavin. No dice.

"A que hora usted cierra el albergue, senor (What time do you close)?" I asked the hospitaleiro.

"Cinco minutos," the elderly man said firmly.

"Please let me get my nephew. I'll be back."

He didn't respond.

I rushed all over the small village, checking anywhere it sounded like fireworks were exploding. *That*, incidentally, was just the opposite of what I'd normally be doing in a situation like this. But my search yielded nothing. So I rushed back to the albergue to not be locked out. Gavin still had not arrived. The hospitaliero, whose only real disappointment in life seemed to be that he was not born in Hitler's Germany, was giving lip to another pilgrim who was trying to get him to keep the albergue open for a friend. This guy was impervious to patriotic spirit. The only arrow that I could find in my quiver was to tell him a flat-out lie.

"Senor," I said solemnly. *"My sobrino tiene catorce anos de edad. Estoy desesperado. Por favor, da me poco mas tiempo* (Mr., my nephew is fourteen. I'm desperate. Please give me more time)?"

He grunted. I again took to my heels out into the fireworks. Soon I came upon Gavin walking nonchalantly back to the albergue, with Sophia clinging to his side.

"Hurry up," I said. "I've been begging the guy to not lock you out."

"He's just *ETA*," Gavin responded lackadaisically. "They're mad Spain won."

We got inside at which point the hospitaleiro locked the door behind us. He did have *his* moment though. The next morning found pilgrims sprawled on the front steps. And while one of the biggest celebrations in Spanish history unfolded, we were lying horizontal on mats in a packed, quiet room as explosion after explosion rocked the town.

Chapter 32

Tragic Glory

"History is little more than a register of the crimes, follies, and misfortunes of mankind."

Edward Gibbon

The Rise and Fall of the Roman Empire

The future queen, Isabella, was getting anxious. Now 22 years of age, and not yet having found the proper suitor, she was beginning to hear that *ticking sound*. It was time to take bold, decisive action. Isabella dispatched her most trusted associate, Alanus, to secretly go east from Castile into the province of Aragon. There Alanus was to seek out Prince Ferdinand, and inform him that a certain young lady awaited his attention.

Ferdinand was only sixteen years old. But he had already fought in two wars, as well as fathered two bastard children. He fancied himself as a man of action. He accepted immediately and made his way to Castile in disguise, as one of a gaggle of eight strolling minstrels. The secret assignation was scheduled to take place in the Castilian town of Duena.

Isabella and Ferdinand were actually cousins, but had never met. Nonetheless, the minute Isabella laid eyes on the group she is reported to have picked Ferdinand out among his traveling companions. *"Esto es, esto es,"* she cried out in joy. Ferdinand, on the other hand, may not have been as excited. Isabella's face was described by contemporaries as "too round and plain, with a slightly pouting mouth and wide nose."

Nonetheless, this encounter and the subsequent marriage was to be one of the most consequential unions in human annals. It would lead at turns to the most glorious, yet most tragic, moments in Spanish history.

***

Isabella and Ferdinand's great obsession was a unified Catholic country. Despite the fact that the Moors had been in Spain for almost 800 years, Ferdinand and Isabella still considered them occupiers. In January 1492, Spanish troops entered the gates of Granada and put an end once and for all to the Muslim presence in Spain. Within a few years, they were burning Muslim manuscripts in what many still consider a major crime against history.

To finance the military operations against the Muslims, Queen Isabella and Prince Ferdinand had borrowed money from the Genoese and their ancient community of Jewish financiers. But once the war was successfully completed, Isabella and Ferdinand turned on their creditors with a vengeance (Inquisition). This made them extremely popular in Spain. The Genoese and Jews were loathed by all classes in Spain as rich, clannish foreigners. These two actions in 1492—expelling the Moors and the Jews— gave Castillian Spain unity over the country's various regions for the first time in its history.

In that same year of 1492, a Genoese sea captain began seeking a royal audience with Ferdinand and Isabella. This particular captain was known to have vast maritime experience, having already sailed to Tunis, Iceland, and Africa. On the side, he did a lucrative trade in new maps and travel books of the day. Now he had a daring proposal for the two royals.

For good or for bad, Ferdinand and Isabella were risk takers. Captain Christopher Columbus was able to gain their support (Portugal, France and England had already turned him down) for perhaps the greatest adventure in history.

In reality, Christopher Columbus had a truly noble vision. He wanted to launch this historic ocean-crossing in *Genoese style*. That meant setting up trading colonies with the natives they found along the way. The possibilities were tantalizing. Imagine

European goods being traded in return for the native artifacts of the Aztecs, Mayans, and Incas. Alas, the royals had more base motives—the old imperial model of exploitation. Columbus fell loyally in line with royal prerogatives in order to preserve the mission.

***

A popular book of the time by Sir John Mandeville of England (a country no stranger to imperial ambitions itself) depicted native peoples as "one-eyed, dog-nosed, and prone to cannibalism." The meticulous journals that Christopher Columbus took clearly indicate that he was familiar with this book. Worse yet, this philosophy gave him and his crew license to treat the natives in sub-human fashion. Thus the old joke, oft-repeated, about the two Indians standing on the beach. Up walks none other than Christopher Columbus. One Indian turns to the other and mutters, "Oh shit, there goes the neighborhood."

Columbus and subsequent Spanish conquistadores expropriated gold in massive quantities for import back into Spain. This created an immediate booming effect on the Spanish economy. No nation in history had ever won so much wealth for itself in so little time. Spain reached the most powerful position a political entity had attained since the Roman Empire some 1,500 years before. But these same actions ultimately led to its downfall.

The huge amounts of gold meant there was more money chasing a limited number of goods. Ruinous inflation—the iron law of history—was the end result. Spain had become a victim of its own greed. Within a century the Dutch, who were by their very nature brilliant traders, had replaced Spain at the pinnacle of European power.

The actions taken by Ferdinand and Isabella over 500 years ago still cripple this wondrous, yet ill-fated, country.

Chapter 33

Going Up

"Is that snow?" I asked hesitantly.

"No," Gavin answered.

I didn't argue. It seemed so improbable. For the last couple weeks, it had seemed like the harshness of the meseta would never end. But things had changed immediately after leaving Astorga. We had been climbing steadily, and were back in the mountains. None too soon.

The previous day Gavin and I had stopped off at a café in a small mountain village. The television had shown the victorious Spanish team arriving to a hero's welcome at the airport in Madrid, after an all-night flight from South Africa. Rafael Nadal, the recent Wimbledon winner, and Pau Gasol, the Spanish center of the world champion Los Angeles Lakers, had been on hand to greet them. This national unity was all the more moving in light of the fact that in time-honored fashion, the Spanish government had once again completely screwed everything up. The Spanish debt crisis ("el crisis") was having reverberations in financial markets around the world, and the Spanish economy was moribund. But their athletes had gained some redemption through brilliant performances.

We had spent the rest of the afternoon climbing, and then slept on some mats in the steeply inclined mountain hamlet of

Rabanal del Camino. This morning we had commenced climbing again. Steep, rocky mountain faces enveloped us on both sides. We were heading through a mountain pass.

"This is the highest point on El Camino up ahead," our new hiking companion, Eva, said.

"Not higher than the Pyrenees," I contested her.

"Yes, it is."

Indeed it was. And those glistening white patches on the side of rocks were actual redoubts of snow and ice.

"How long are we in the mountains?" I wondered.

"A Spanish man in the village last night told me it was mountainous like this all the way to the end," Eva said. This news seemed to give everybody a little extra bounce in their steps. We soon came upon a ramshackled hamlet of not more than a few dozen people, with livestock milling around on the banks of the village. "If there's not any food in this town," Gavin said, "those livestock might be in play."

Fortunately, there was a restaurant serving breakfast. Better yet, it said, *'Todo lo que Pueda Comer'* (all you can eat). I had thought 'all you can eat' was one of those only-in-America concepts, where our nationwide obesity rate is 21%. How many times have I heard (and said), "Boy, I'm gonna' make them regret they ever saw me," while entering an all-you-can eat restaurant, only to walk out an hour-and-a-half later with a distended stomach and the owners as equally unhappy as me.

The man and woman running the restaurant looked like they probably lived in this humble abode. *"Dos comidas completas,"* I ordered. She pointed over to the modest spread that lay on a modest-sized wooden table. A couple of the bowls were already empty.

"Will they give me the *Oliver Twist* treatment, if we ask for some more granola?" Gavin wondered. "It's a judgment call," I opined. "Personally, I'm thinking I might save my political capital for a toilet paper request." Indeed, when I entered the bathroom, I had to pop out, brace myself, and ask for toilet paper. Nonetheless, we were able to leave this modest restaurant in this tiny village with all the critical tasks accomplished, and our stomachs mostly full, without committing an American-style atrocity at the buffet.

We kept climbing. Finally, we arrived at the famous *Cruz del Ferro,* marking the very highest point on El Camino. A 50 foot tall wooden pole with a cross was sticking out of a pile of stones

In the *Gospel of Matthew*, Jesus says, "Own no gold. Carry nothing." Meekness is revered; pride is damned. A pilgrimage on foot definitely fits within that humble philosophy. But what about a 50 foot pole with a large cross on it? Or was it garish? It's honestly not for me to say.

Gavin and I didn't tarry long. It was going to be a 33 kilometer day to Ponferrada. Fortunately, it included a 3,200 foot descent for much of the afternoon.

"You're gonna' like this downward glide," I exulted.

"No, I feel less Catholic on these downhills," my nephew, who-should-have-been-my-uncle, replied.

***

The long, stagy robes were impressive. Most albergues were run by ex-pilgrims. However, the man in charge here in Ponferrada was a priest.

Gavin and I had arrived at this huge new 180 bed albergue in Ponferrada after our long descent in the late afternoon. Surely, we thought, there would be a couple beds available. "Dos camas," I requested, as I pulled out our pilgrim passports to be stamped.

"Todo completo," the priest responded.

"Dios mio," I reacted. But then I remembered. Ponferrada was a popular El Camino junction and starting point. Indeed, we saw many new faces milling around the ample lawn of the albergue. A lot of them were speaking German.

"De donde usted es?" I asked the priest.

"Brazil," he responded. In fact, we were to learn that more and more of the El Camino clerical support was coming from Latin America, where the populations are bursting at the seams with practicing Catholics. This also brings up a delicious historical irony. Europe, the incubator of western civilization and Christian missions around the world for centuries, has become a missionary destination. Priests now have to come all the way from Latin America to the Old Continent to preach the gospel to the uncomprehending European pagan masses!

Chapter 34

Friday the 13th

*"Th' abuse of greatness is when
power disjoins from remorse."*

William Shakespeare, *Julius Caesar*

We've all heard the phrase, "Only in America." It is usually some European wryly commenting on our eccentricities, if not outright idiocies. But I submit that there are certain tales that are just as irredeemably European in character. And the story behind the castle overlooking Ponferrada—*the Castillo de los Templarinos*—is one of the most dramatic of the entire Middle Ages. It is a splendid Shakespearean drama of intrigue, betrayal, gold, castles, popes, kings, mysterious knights, crusades, and ultimately tragedy.

Its roots go back to the fourth century when Constantine's mother, Helena, set off on a pilgrimage to the Holy Land, upon her son's historic conversion to Christianity. Helena's goal was none other than to find the *Holy Sepulcher*. Lo and behold, she did just that. Unlike my experience (mentioned earlier) 1,600 years later when I had hovered in doubt over the Holy Sepulcher, Helena was afflicted with no such skepticism. She had returned back to Rome gushing with glorious tales about her pilgrimage.

The floodgates soon opened. For the next 700 years Christians from all over Europe traipsed on their journey of a lifetime to the Holy Land. In 1065, one group alone of Germans numbered 7,000 pilgrims.

However, this was all to change in 1075, when a group of fanatical new converts to Islam, the Seljuk Turks, began harassing Christian pilgrims traveling to the Holy Land. Tales of this mistreatment of pilgrims soon made its way back to Europe. The combustible Christian masses quickly became inflamed.

"They overturn and desecrate our altars," proclaimed Pope Urban II. "They will take a Christian and cut open his stomach and tie his intestine to a stake." The Pope offered a simple and straightforward solution. "The noble race of the Franks must come to the aid of their fellow Christians in the East," Urban exhorted. "All should go, rich and poor alike. God will lead them."

Thus the First Crusade was proclaimed.

***

Pyschologists and historians have long debated what motivates those who answer 'the call'. Was it religion? This was the Age of Faith and the main respondents were illiterate peasants. So religious beliefs probably were a major factor. But given the human love of action, adventure was surely a factor, as well.

In any event, the nearly 200 year period of the Crusades (1096-1291) was the most dramatic expression of Europe on the offensive in the High Middle Ages. Morale was sky high as the legions of peasants marched down from Europe towards the Holy Land, singing, "*Onward Marching Christian Soldiers.*" However, their enthusiasm soon enough ran into grim reality.

In his Camino narrative, *Off the Road,* Jack Hitt reports that after one unsuccessful siege of a Muslim castle, the crusaders were stranded without water. The men "were so terribly afflicted by thirst that they bled their horses and asses and drank the blood; others dug up damp earth, piling the earth upon their chests."

In modern times, we are accustomed to the Muslims being more willing to resort to fanatical tactics than Christians. The Crusaders, however, weren't inhibited by any such enthusiasm gap. They well knew the Muslims would make slaves out of the healthy crusaders and execute the rest of them. When the infidels launched charges at them in open fields, the crusaders gallantly repelled them. These European peasants were none too gentlemanly to then decapitate the heads of Muslim prisoners, place them in slings, and fling them over the fortress walls. It 'worked'.

Soon the crusaders had breached the walls of Jerusalem. The band of victors then proceeded to wantonly slaughter whatever Muslims and Jews they could find, to finish the job. "If you would hear how we treated our enemies at Jerusalem," gloated one Crusader, "know that in the portico of Solomon and the Temple our men rode through the unclean blood of the Saracens (Muslims), which came up to the knees of their horses." It was the first time a Christian military force had entered Jerusalem in almost 500 years.

***

A group of nine knights had played an especially critical role in the savage fighting. Traditionally, brutal military actions have been followed up with a fare of rape, pillage, and plunder. However, these knights were true believers. Their mission became one of the most sacred in Christianity—protection of pilgrims visiting the Holy Land. They became known as the *Knights Templar.*

The Muslim world was aflame with rage as stories began circulating of crusader atrocities committed while capturing the Holy City. They vowed *jihad* in revenge. "This place is dreadful and dangerous," one contemporary historian wrote. "The Saracens sally forth and kill travelers on the roads." The Knights Templar vowed solemnly to kill any Muslim who so much as 'dissed' a pilgrim traveling to the Holy Land.

The Knights Templar were an unusual breed, by any measure. They are universally described in medieval manuscripts as bestial, compact, and squat, with thick, bushy beards. Parts of their heads were shaved and they went about their daily activities in felt dressing gowns. Hunting and jousting were strictly forbidden, and sexual relations were completely off limits. Dedication to their task was absolute. Youth from all over Europe dreamt of gaining induction into this highly secret order.

Kings and queens all over Europe were falling all over themselves to patronize this *holy army*. They began bequeathing estates across Scotland, England, France, Spain, and Portugal to the Templar. The Spanish nobles proved to be especially generous; after all, the Knights Templar were not only fighting the Moors, but protecting the pilgrims walking to Santiago.

In perhaps their most lasting achievement, the Templars set up what many consider to be the forerunner to the modern banking system. Pilgrims walking to Jerusalem or Santiago could deposit cash with the Knights Templar. For their deposit they received a specially-coded chit, which could be redeemed at any of the numerous Templar branches around Europe and the Middle East. It was an amazingly effective way for people to travel at the time.

By the end of the 12th century, the Knights Templar had become the most powerful force in the Middle East, with a total of 3,500 castles spread all over Europe and the Mediterranean. They were exempted from local taxes and tithing, and crossed international borders at will. That dreadfully familiar term in European history, *plenary powers,* had effectively been granted to them.

Religion, politics, and money. This was all bound to end badly. It did. Nonetheless, the airtight secrecy of the covert action that ensued still boggles the modern imagination.

Friday the 13th

Phillip le Bel (Phillip the Beautiful), the King of France, was considered an especially handsome man. Add to that, vain. He was known to spend several hours per day in front of a mirror grooming himself.

Like most sovereigns, Phillip didn't fancy sharing power. The Knights Templar, with their mysterious cachet and rock star appeal, loomed ominously in his mind as a threat. Worse yet, he had been forced to borrow money from them to finance his reckless spending. Phillip well knew the iron law of history— power passes from the debtor to the creditor. What to do?

In 1306, he opted for the oldest trick in the book. He seized all the Jewish property in France, and expelled all the Jews from the country. Phillip then tried raising prices, debasing the currency, and, of course, borrowing more. But none of his desperation strategies worked. Now he began to cast a covetous eye at some bigger fish.

The irresistible parlor game in medieval Europe was

speculating on just how much gold the Knights Templar had secretly stashed away in treasure trunks. Phillip soon became obsessed with the idea of shutting them down. But the Knights Templar was far and away the most formidable militia force in his entire kingdom. This called for an especially deft power play. I personally find it charming that most Americans (including myself) are congenitally incapable of keeping a secret for more than ten minutes. That's why Phillip's power play was an 'only in Europe' event. It demanded secrecy on a breathtaking scale.

In September of 1307, Phillip mass mailed a set of sealed orders to every lawmaking official in his kingdom. The functionaries were forbidden, under penalty of death, to open the papers before Thursday, the 12th of October, at midnight. There were 15,000 Knights Templar in France alone, so one small leak would fatally compromise Phillip's planned crackdown.

The next morning, *Friday the 13th* of October, waves of lawmaking officials and royal agents all over France swooped down on every Knights Templar stronghold in France to suddenly arrest them. By nightfall, several thousand Knights Templar had been arrested. Scores of wild charges were hurled at the Templars, including homosexuality, sodomy, devil worshipping, Christian hating, defecating on the Cross, saying the mass backwards, and sorcery. The knights who had seemed virtually omnipotent, were now helpless. The church's motto, strictly followed for a thousand years, had always been, *'La Ecclesia non novit sanguine'*—The Church does not shed blood. In order to not alienate the Church, Phillip chose to burn the Templars. The noxious stench of Templar flesh could be smelled wafting all around the country.

The two Templar *Grand Masters*, Jacques de Molay and Geoffrey de Charnay, were imprisoned and badly tortured. Nevertheless, they managed to hold out through seven years of daily beatings, before finally signing public confessions. On March 18, 1314, the Archbishop of Sens, convened a mass public meeting at Notre Dame in Paris to report the confessions. Jacques de Molay, now in his seventies and having already endured seven years of daily torture, asked to speak. The bishops assumed that de Molay wished to publicly confess, and thus granted him the stage. He spoke these words:

> I acknowledge, to my eternal shame, that I
> have committed the greatest of crimes. I made

the contrary declaration to the truth only to
suspend the excessive pains of torture. The life
offered me on such infamous terms I abandon
without regret.

De Molay's courageous speech is considered one of the
highest points of drama in the entire Middle Ages. Geoffrey de
Charnay moved over and stood beside his Grandmaster as a sign
of support for his statement. The proceedings were immediately
suspended, and the two Templar leaders were sentenced to be
burned that night. A gradual, smokeless fire was prepared to
ensure that their agony would be prolonged. They were slowly
cooked to death.

The decapitation of the Knights Templar was so ghastly, Friday
the 13th's reputation has not recovered to this day.

* * *

The sheer size of *Castillo de los Templarinos* overlooking
Ponferrada is astounding—fully the length of twelve football
fields. Considered on eof the best ruins of the Middle Ages,
modern pilgrim ricochet all arund it, snapping innumerable
photos.

But imagine being a medieval peasant and looking up at this
architectural monstrosity with its magnificent pointed turrets and
drawbridge. It was probably inevitable that rumors would run
rampant about the mysterious workings and deep secrets within.

In *The DaVinci Code,* Dan Brown insinuated that the primary
mission of the Knights Templar may not have been protection
of pilgrims after all. Acccording to Brown, they might have been
encharged with the Holy Grail. Further yet, Brown postulates that
the Holy Grail might have been something much more important
than a wine chalice—perhaps Jesus' body. Easy for him to say.

Personally, I looked up at that handsome palace with the
penants waving gallantly in the wind, and found it hard not to
get a little sad about the tragic fate of these long-ago knights.
History books are replete with examples of powerful military
forces finally getting their comeuppance. But the Knights Templar
really were different from your classic medieval despoilers and
booty hunters. They valiantly protected the medieval tradition of
pilgrimages to Jerusalem and Santiago de Compostela. Given all

the perils a medieval pilgrim faced, I sure would have liked having them around. Their likes have never been seen again.

Chapter 35

Evil?

"This thing of darkness, I acknowledge mine."

William Shakespeare, *The Tempest*

Over the last 25 years the number of female pilgrims has drawn roughly even with male pilgrims. Given that women represent the fastest growing segment of adventure travel, El Camino de Santiago has an especially bright future. Many of these women travel solo. They often revel in bouncing from one group to another—*nomadotopia.* One college-age girl kept telling me about some creep who liked to spy on her in her sleep. But stories of outright harassment were few and far between.

A great exception to this trend of solo pilgrims is set by Dr. Kip Reddick (mentioned earlier) of Christopher Newport University. Kip annually leads student groups on the Camino, for which they receive university credit hours. He habitually left the albergues early in the mornings and walked at full speed to their destination, attempting to make a block reservation for all 20 students. However, many albergues didn't permit this, which meant the whole class had to hustle. Every night at 6:00, the group had a theology class and discussed the events of the day. It was all very impressive. But humans being humans, there were various levels of devotion to the ideals Kip set.

One of his students, Darla, required special attention. And she was prepared to go out of her way to get it. Unlike the more modest Europeans, Darla dressed as scarcely as was at all seemly for a spiritual pilgrimage. This was magnified by the fact that she had the damndest figure you ever saw. I honestly don't say that in a prurient sense. But describing her any other way would be like somebody trying to describe me without using the word 'tall'.

Gavin and I ran into Darla on a steep alternate route, while leaving Villafranca del Bierzo. She was standing there alone, which we later learned was no coincidence. Immediately, she was Chatty Cathy. We started walking with her and she quickly filled us in on the group's scurrilous gossip. The impressive thing, though, was how everyone was very happy with Kip's leadership. As for me, I hadn't had any 'burning bush moments' yet on El Camino. And Lord knows, Darla seemed like an unlikely source of one.

In a perfect world—or rather a perfectly imperfect world— Darla would have developed a juvenile crush on me, pursuant to throwing herself at my mercy. In a *Pavlovian* reaction, I would have readied to enthusiastically ply her mysteries. But then, suddenly, I would be seized by some heretofore unknown angel. All the temptation would just as suddenly drain out of me. I would decide that such an action was unacceptable for a very simple reason. It was morally wrong.

Neither that, nor anything like that, happened. Instead, events followed what was perhaps a more ordinary human course. Gavin, Darla, and I, along with the two Barcelonan girls, Rosere and Anna, were schlepping along at a modest clip, a couple kilometers shy of Las Herreras. We were speaking mostly Spanish, but with a little English (*spanglish*) thrown in.

We stopped for a break and sat on a low-lying stone wall running along a creek. The geography had taken a notable turn for the better since we had gotten into the mountains. It continuously amazes me how much things like running water boost the morale of human beings.

As we sat there, a couple of big-talking, swashbuckling guys in their late twenties approached. Their eyes visibly lit up when they spotted Darla—all very human and understandable. The shorter, fiery one's modus operandi was easy to synthesize—use of large quantities of four-letter words delivered with a clipped military bark. He had just returned from Iraq and seemed to be taking the battle for freedom of speech a bit too literally. In any event, my first surprise was that Darla was not repelled—if not outright frightened—by these two marauders, who Gavin immediately dubbed as 'The Pirates'. Actually, she seemed to greatly enjoy their attention.

With our group, Darla had been treated as an equal and forced to struggle to participate in a foreign language. She was on a level footing. But 'the pirates' showered her with much craved for attention with their manly use of the vaunted 'f' word. They asked her to go to an albergue in La Faba with them. Sheepishly, she turned to tell us she was headed off with them.

***

"Laziness is the root of all evil," Scott Peck wrote in his all-time bestseller, *The Road Less Traveled.* I have often thought back to that one line, in the fifteen or so years since reading it. *What did he mean?* The two eminent psychiatrists of the 20th century, Freud and Jung, both ascribed evil to an unwillingness to meet the shadow. Perhaps, that, too, is laziness.

Hitler looks anything but lazy in the newsreels of his fuming rants at Nuremberg. But did he ever take the trouble to consider the views of the Jews, Slavs, gypsies, and countless others he slaughtered? Hardly. Rather, he preferred giving patriotic speeches paying homage to the German fatherland and the Aryan peoples. He and the audience all look ecstatic during these harangues. Having to take into account the aspirations of other people would have would have been more complex. The Fuhrer was too lazy to make the painstaking effort.

Hannah Arendt famously coined the phrase "the banality of evil." She had flown to Jerusalem to witness the war crimes trial of Adolf Eichmann. Eichmann had been head of the infamous SS, which had overseen the concentration camps at Auschwitz, Treblinka, etc. He had once infamously said, "I will jump happily into my grave knowing that millions of massacred Jews will have gone there before me."

Arendt had sat there in the courtroom in Jerusalem anticipating the proverbial devil in red undershorts, with horns sticking out of his head to walk in the room. Instead, what was paraded in front of the judge was a balding, bespectacled civil servant. He had been so anonymous looking that he had wandered the streets of Buenos Aires freely for almost twenty years, despite a worldwide manhunt for him. Eichmann, of course, pleaded that he was just following orders. There was probably a good deal of truth to that. But by refusing to consider what those orders were, he had refused to meet the shadow.

Now let me offer my apologies to poor Darla, right here and now, for even the presumption of mentioning her in the same vein as these historical blackbeards. Shame on me. She was simply following the path of least resistance—doing the easy, maybe lazy thing. And I certainly didn't know these other two big talkers well enough to make a summary judgment of them.

Nonetheless, when the two 'Pirates' and Darla walked away, I said to Gavin, "You know. I think I've just had my El Camino epiphany."

"Hold on Bill," he promptly replied. "Let me get my pen out."

"I've been in all kinds of situations with people using that kind of vulgar, egotistical language," I said sincerely. "I've even talked that way myself, at times. But that whole scene was a turnoff."

Gavin didn't rebut me, which was a form of consent. At that point, we had walked almost 400 miles. Some might say that's a pretty modest epiphany for 400 miles of slogging. But hey, I'll take real change whenever I can get it.

The Appalachian and Pacific Crest Trails had been extraordinarily positive journeys, to be sure. But there were all too many hikers prone to bouts of machoism, foul language, aggressive pursuit of women, and bragging about the big miles they had hiked. But there had been very few overt examples of this on El Camino. The discourse had seemed more civilized. A spiritual pilgrimage really is a different type of journey.

Chapter 36

Pilgrim Potpourri

Gavin and I strategically allowed some distance to open up between us and 'the Pirates' and Darla. At dusk, we were passing through another anonymous town, with an albergue up on a rocky hillside.

"Here?" I asked quietly.

Gavin shrugged his shoulders, presumably meaning assent. We walked up the hill and checked in. Right away, I didn't like what I saw. A couple of pot-bellied, *orca-framed* Frenchmen with ominously large noses were wandering around. "Man, those guys look like some true bombers," I muttered to Gavin.

"Yeah, that one on the left looks like he's got the athletic ability of Picasso or Einstein," he observed, which was about the most devastating critique imaginable. Immediately, I began scanning the vicinity for anywhere to throw down my tent out of 'bombing distance' from these potential *Roncadores*. But there was nowhere remotely satisfactory on this hillside. The sleeping area was a concrete holding room with small dividers between each sleeping pad. A sense of doom came over me.

In all seriousness, snoring is more than just a minor irritant on the Camino. I remember arriving at a state-of-the-art new albergue in Santo Domingo Calzada. It had two sections: Roncadores and non-Roncadores. Many of us had raved at the ingeniousness of the idea. However, at dark in the *non*-Roncadores room a Spanish pilgrim had begun this awful snorting sound. The German girl, Sophia, had immediately snapped at him, "You are a snorer. You are supposed to be in the Roncador room." But the Spaniard didn't speak English. A comical argument had ensued between the two of them in which neither of them had any idea what the other was saying. But that didn't stop both of them from becoming passionately angry. By the time we had wearily trudged out of town the next morning, we had been less impressed with that new albergue.

In another albergue, a Spanish girl had kicked this hulking beast in the bunk right next to hers with her bare feet. She got away with it for the simple reason that he didn't wake up.

But the person who had suffered the worst fate when it came to snoring was probably Michael. He was a theology student from Boston who got along well with everyone. However, his customary good nature was overridden on occasion by daytime mutterings about this or that snorer ("You just wouldn't believe..."). Finally, a local Spaniard had given him an idea that was going to be his silver bullet—waxed earplugs. Michael had purchased them at a local pharmacy and slept like a baby that evening. But the next morning he couldn't get them out. Several pilgrims and a hospitaleiro had valiantly tried to remove them as well, but to no avail. Finally, he had gone to the emergency room. After 45 harrowing minutes, a Spanish doctor had successfully extracted them. The story had a happy ending, however.

"How much did the emergency room cost you?" I had asked.

"Nothing," he had said, in the amazed tone of someone familiar with the U.S. health care system. I was to hear the same thing from several other pilgrims who required medical care along the way. The thousand year-old Camino tradition of free medical treatment of pilgrims is still intact. Unfortunately, so is the snoring tradition.

Tonight, the minute the lights were out, these two rotund Frenchmen commenced this awful, phlegm-larynxed, sinus-dredging sound. In packed shelters on the Appalachian Trail, it was common for hikers to try toning down snorers by making *chick-chick* sounds at key points in the snorer's rhythm. I began doing this, and other pilgrims joined in with a chorus of chick-chicking. Unfortunately, these two beached whales had been eating pasta and drinking red wine. They proved to be utterly chick-chick proof.

I began to feel sorry for myself. We had the steepest climb since the Pyrenees ahead of us tomorrow morning. All I could think about was how bad I was going to feel, and how good these two *culprits* were going to feel. By definition, a snorer is sleeping wonderfully. So I took it a step further and began banging my shoe on the ground and yelling, "Stop snoring." One of them would temporarily stop, before regaining his inexorable rhythm.

The main response my theatrics got was uncontrollable giggles from two Belgian girls who lay just on the far side of these hulking beasts. In fact, they were to derive hysterical pleasure the next few days by imitating my heroic efforts to shut down these two Roncadores.

"Gavin," I said suddenly the next morning. "That's it. No more albergues. We're sleeping outside."

On the way out though, a young French pilgrim that we had seen all along the way handed me a lone feather. I had unsuccessfully tried communicating with this guy countless times. Now I stood there holding a lone feather, wondering what his purpose was. He then took another feather out of his backpack and rubbed it up against his nose and said, "Roncadores."

"Oh yeah," I laughed. "Why didn't I think of that." He, too, had been in the melee of snoring and shoe banging last night. Now he was suggesting that I rub this feather under a snorer's nose to disrupt their breathing. Soon this feather was to become one of my most important belongings, next to perhaps my wallet.

***

"Man, this is the toughest climb since the Pyrenees," I said between gasps.

"Would you like to turn around?" Gavin asked unsympathetically.

"I'm sleep deprived," I panted. "Take it easy on me."

White rapids rushed at us from the opposite direction on the steep climb up to Cebreiro. At turns, we walked through open green pastures and a green tunnel of oak and chestnut trees. Despite having left the meseta only a couple days before, it now seemed like ages.

Just before reaching the summit, we officially entered *Galicia*. This was portentous. As with almost all pilgrims, it was to be our favorite section. For starters, the region is a dead ringer for Ireland. Anthropologists universally agree the people are of Celtic origin. White, pasty, freckled skin and reddish hair are much more commonly seen than tan, shiny skin and jet-black hair of the

Iberian peninsula. Better yet, the moss-filled stone walls, stone houses, and stone quarries of the Irish countryside, also dot the Galician landscape.

One of life's pleasures – walking through Galicia.

The summit town of O Cebreiro is a picturesque stone village with cobblestone streets and striking views out into the Galician hills. However, Irish weather had pervaded the mountain. The elements were completely socked in. It was Sunday and we entered a packed church for a pilgrims mass, truth be told as much to get warm as to achieve salvation. Then we took a tour of the *chocolaterias*, gingerbread houses, and ice cream parlors that saturate this mountainous village.

"I'm cold man," I said. "Let's go check in the albergue."

However, as we headed over to queue up for the albergue, I stopped dead in my tracks.

"Look," I said, pointing at two large, middle-aged males already lined up for the albergue. "Is that those two beasts from last night?"

"Bill, snorers are like ETA terrorists," Gavin lectured me. "They all begin to look alike after a while."

"How about let's just get out of here?"

"Fine."

We high-tailed it down the mountain. After a few miles, we were back in the crystal clear sun. Better yet, it wasn't the bullying, furnace-like sun of the meseta. Instead, it was a crystal-clear glow that magnified the ethereal majesty of the Galician mountains. We were entering the *Valley of Silence*. The arrows took us through one small village that seemed to literally cling to the side of this mountainous spine. In another village, the small albergue was full. So we continued walking. The fresh mountain air, healthy sunshine, and modest difficulty of the trail made it all blissful.

Finally, in late afternoon we arrived in the mountainous hamlet of Biduelo. To our surprise, the two Catalonian girls, Rosere and Anna, were just arriving. We checked into the albergue with them. Soon, the two Belgian girls from last night arrived as well. They were still laughing hysterically about my anti-snoring tactics of the previous evening.

All of us immediately commenced the comically serious process of trying to identify any potential snorers, and juxtapose the mattresses that lay on the floor to open up a margin of safety between us and *them*. Alas, a dyed-in-the-wool snorer won't be denied. A man on the other side of the room quickly put me in misery again, when the lights were turned out. In the middle of the night, I ended up hauling my mattress into the adjoining dining room, which startled the arriving cook early the next morning.

***

If you were asking what the perfect night would be like on a European vacation, it might look something like our night spent in Biduelo.

Rosere and Anna had joined up with a Polish-French pilgrim in her mid-twenties, named Eva. Everything about her bespoke European and cosmopolitan. Eva had lived and studied in several countries and was adamant that we speak any language other than her native French or Polish.

"You should become an interpreter for the United Nations," I suggested.

"Yes, perhaps." We males and our damn ideas.

The two Catalonian girls, Rosere and Anna, were willing to speak slow Castilian Spanish. Gavin was able to pick up on most of the Spanish, as well as talk French to the two Belgian girls, as well as Eva, who finally relented and spoke her native language. I had thrown in my lot with Spanish years ago, and stuck to that. It was all a veritable babble of languages and cultural interchange. What could be better?

In the midst of all this, the two 'pirates' strode confidently into the room. They immediately drew a bead on our female-dominated table. *"Dios mio, alla son los dos Americanos* (My God, there are those two American guys)," Eva whispered to Rosere. Apparently, they had already had dodged some testosterone-laden verbal sorties from these two Americans on the make.

"What's going on?" the lead 'pirate' asked the girls. Gavin and I had yet to ever speak a word to the two of them.

"We eatin'," Rosere answered in broken English.

"We're trying to decide whether to go 50 kilometers tomorrow all the way to Sarria," the short one rattled off in clipped english. "And get this. We're gonna' drink a beer in every pueblo we go through." Nobody responded, which he took as a green light. "We used to pull those in the Army all the time, so why not out here." More tales of derring-do followed. Silence. An annoyed look flashed across his face, when he didn't get the fawning reception he surely deserved.

I strongly believe eccentric behavior should be tolerated up to a point. However, this guy was busting my—and everybody else's—bubble for the second straight day. Further, this was just the type of crude behavior that has given us Americans such an ambivalent reputation abroad. Rule number one in a foreign country is to try to speak the language of the country, no matter how awful it may sound. Most Americans can get out a few phrases in Spanish. But, if you absolutely have to, English should be spoken with due modesty, not braggadocio. After all, your interlocutor is doing you a favor speaking your language in *their* country.

So for these reasons (and if you suspect some pettiness on my part, perhaps you're right), I used exclusionary tactics. I immediately started rifling questions to everyone in the group in Spanish, eliciting responses in Spanish. The Pirates stood hovering over us, chafing. The others took their cue from me. Finally, the Pirates receded.

The next day I noticed that Eva and Rosere proved very effective in blunting the advances of these two misplaced marauders. We may not have done Dr. Kip Reddick any favors, though. The Pirates soon embedded themselves in Kip's group and were to shadow them the entire rest of the way. Kip, though, had a better way to handle them that effectively incorporated his Christian beliefs. I, for one, was to come to admire it.

Chapter 37

Point of No-Return

"*Aqui, aqui* (Here, here)."

"*Que* (What)?"

"*Mira, mira* (Look, look)," he excitedly pointed inside his house.

"*Que?*"

"*Habitacion* (Room)," he screamed.

"*Cuanto cuesta* (How much)?" I asked.

"*Gratis* (Free)," he yelled, and again attempted to summon us with wild whirlwind motions.

"Why would he rent it for free?" Gavin asked.

"You're asking the right question," I said wearily.

Gavin and I were entering the pilgrim crossroads town of Sarria, the point of no-return on the Camino. The man's offer may have been perfectly legitimate. But you have to trust your gut. We just naturally continued on up a steep hill to the cobblestoned center of town. We were immediately taken aback. Long lines spilled out of the various albergues.

Sarria is the last town that is at least 100 kilometers away from Santiago de Compostela. From here on out, a pilgrim needed to get their pilgrim's passport stamped twice a day in order to receive a Compostela. Up until now, the number of pilgrims from foreign countries had clearly outnumbered Spanish pilgrims. But now multitudes of Spanish-speaking pilgrims roamed the streets. A Compostela certificate was actually valuable for many

Spaniards, getting them deep discounts on domestic bus and airplane tickets. Many even sought the Compostela for its value on their resume.

And to be quite honest, the more I had listened to locals along the way, the more vibes I had picked up that Spaniards really do feel a deep kinship with St. James, himself. *"Jesus es por todo (everybody),"* one Spaniard had told me with great sincerity. *"Jaime es por Espana."*

Gavin and I stood in the center of Sarria, taking in the whole scene.

"Well, this is it," I said to Gavin.

"What, are you converting to Catholicism?"

"There are worse things a person could do."

"Like waiting in line for an albergue," he said.

"We're on the same page," I agreed. "But we're not going back down the hill to that man's place."

"We're on the same page," Gavin agreed.

The mid-day sun made it exceedingly unpleasant to tarry for long. The only thing we could do was find some café where we could hang out until it got cooler.

"Kip said we could go to his theology class at 6 tonight," I suggested. "You up for it?"

"Yeah."

"Then, when it's over, we can just leave town and hike until dark."

"Sure, why not?"

Gavin's mother back in Leesburg, Virginia would have been shocked at how agreeable her tempestuous 18 year old son could be. But that's one of the purposes of El Camino, or any other long-distance journey on foot. As a person faces greater demands with less options, he or she is bound to become more magnanimous . Perhaps that's one reason people spend half the rest of their lives reliving these adventures.

***

"The Bible says you must taste the evil spirits," Kip said in a voice mixed with amusement and conviction. "I was in my late twenties. I had just started a commune in northern California, and was growing pot to support it. One night I'm hiking in the mountains and come upon Mount Shasta. There's this gorgeous white-capped peak lit up by the moon. I immediately fell to the ground and started screaming, crying, bawling. Finally, the only thing I could do is start praying to God."

We were sitting in a park in Sarria, Spain in the late afternoon. In the audience were Kip's nineteen students, along with the two 'pirates', Gavin, and myself. Kip's conversion story seemed to genuinely impress everyone for the unadulterated joy he reaped in telling it.

"Pilgrimages," he continued, "were a way for the medieval peasants and serfs to 'get a life', so to speak. For that one long season of pilgrimage, these peasants and illiterate workers were effectively the nobles of society. This whole network of support lay ahead for them. It broadened their socialization beyond the village serfdom—a kind of once-in-a-lifetime liberation."

"The churches also sponsored a lot of prisoners on penitential pilgrimages," Kip added. "It was a neat bargain. The pilgrims were asked to carry rocks and quarry to build other churches."

"Wow," Gavin said in what may have been *his* El Camino epiphany. "You have to think you're building more than a McDonalds to do that."

The pirates had been respectfully sitting there taking this all in with the rest of us. But asking them to remain completely in the saddle was too much.

"No government or king could have told me where I could or couldn't travel," one of them said. Both of them laughed loudly and repeatedly, when they themselves were talking. I was wondering how Kip would handle these overt attempts to impress his mostly female students. A lot of teachers would have strictly quarantined characters such as these off from their students, possibly creating ill will and dissension. Kip, however, opted for a completely different tack. He chose to engage them. He had already built instant camaraderie by telling of his own tastes of evil spirits earlier in his life.

Kip's approach seemed to have a civilizing effect on everyone, including the Pirates. It was respectful and inclusive. Perhaps it could even be described as loving. So often it has been the *teachers* that prove to be the most valuable members of our society.

Meanwhile, Gavin and I gathered our belongings and headed out of town at dusk to hike until dark.

Chapter 38

Galician Liberation

"Night, sleep, death, and the stars. Perfect love will change you."

Walt Whitman, *Leaves of Grass*

The hills were a lush green. The aroma of cabbage and herbs wafted through the air. The grass crushed under the feet. Fields, gardens, and thatched roof *gingerbread homes* in the distance looked perfectly manicured. The air was crystal clear. Everything was perfect.

"Hey, this is very Christian," I exulted. "First, the hellish suffering in the meseta—now, this Galician utopia."

We loped at a brisk pace as the air got cooler and the sun sunk below the hills. The sound of our footsteps—the loveliest of sounds to me—struck a crisp din. Gavin and I were only planning to hike a few kilometers. But that quickly went by the wayside. Periodically, we would hear bells ringing. Soon, a Galician shepherd with his herd of cows with bells attached to their necks would come in a broad path down a stone road. Gavin and I would jump on stone walls to give them safe passage and avoid stepping in fresh manure.

"Hey, there's the *home team*," I said cheerfully when we turned a bend in the trail. It was Brittany, Anna, and Stacy, three American girls who were doing the Camino for purely religious reasons. For this reason, they had been staying in as many church-run hostels as they could find. Often they had to alter their mileage, or even stay in a less comfortable facility.

I had been messianically preaching the virtues of camping out to our fellow pilgrims, as the daily onslaught to albergues had begun to reach maddening levels. Some had finally begun to listen. Amongst my unlikely disciples was this threesome.

"We were thinking about staying right here," Brittany said. "What do you think, Bill?"

"Yeah," I answered skeptically to Brittany. "That might do." They were in generally flat spots, but right next to a creek. It looked damp. *Snakes?*

"We're hearing lots of bells ringing," Anna said. "Our big worry is cows walking through here."

"That's a tough call," I said. "We're gonna' go *a little further.* You're welcome to come along with us."

They chatted a little bit, before deciding to stay put. Gavin and I headed on. Fifteen minutes later, we found a nice, open field on the approach to the small Galician village of Mouzos.

"This doesn't look bad, here," I said.

"Yeah," Gavin said lukewarmly.

"Whaddya' think?"

"It's up to you, Bill."

"Well, we could walk up to the top of the hill, and if there's nothing just come back down here."

"Yeah."

This exchange set a pattern that would prevail all the way to Santiago, and then continue all the way to the sea. If in doubt, go.

We got to the top of the hill and nothing but more hills revealed themselves. Of course, neither of us said anything about turning back. We accelerated. It was virtually rhapsodic walking through Galicia this time of evening.

"Next decent spot, we've gotta' take," I said.

"Whatever," Gavin responded. There were plenty of green, open spaces that would make suitable camping spots. But they were all located within these slate stone walls that dot the Galician landscape. Stone has long been both the eternal curse and glory of Galicia. The region has undoubtedly the best stone masons in all of Europe. Long, thin, beautifully cut slabs of stone from deep stone quarries form finely-chiseled stone barns and homes.

"How about right in there?" I asked Gavin, when we came to an especially inviting field. We made our way over the low stone wall, and into the pasture.

"Yeah, but this is somebody's property," Gavin said. "What if they let the cows loose early in the morning?"

"Maybe," I sighed. "Hey, see that guy over there? I'll go ask him." An elderly man was locking a gate, after putting up some animals. But as I walked up he froze, looking at me like I was a wild animal—perhaps a giraffe--that had escaped from the local zoo.

"Sir, excuse me," I addressed him in formal Spanish. "We're looking for a place to sleep for the evening. Would it be okay to sleep in the field within your walls?" I received nothing but a blank stare. So after a long pause, I repeated my question. Again, I got a bewildered look. Finally, I simply asked if this was his property. However, that drew no response either, positive or negative. Twice more, I slowly repeated my request for Gavin and me to sleep in his field. But he continued looking at me like I was asking for directions to Antarctica.

"*Gracias, senor,*" I finally said, and we moved on.

"Bill, did that guy speak Spanish?" Gavin asked in amazement.

"Man, if he did, my Spanish is in big trouble." I would soon hear there was a good chance that this shepherd did not speak Castillian Spanish. Many elderly Galicians speaking nothing but Galician.

We resumed walking at full speed, with darkness now closing in. Of course, walking was what we really wanted to be doing anyway—as long as something turned up at just the right time. But we were disregarding my father's oft-stated axiom: Be a pig. But don't be a hog.

Soon we came to another flattish field inside a stone wall. "We could go here," I said stepping over the wall.

"Do you prefer sheep or cow maggots?" Gavin accurately observed.

"Yeah," I said, "and those people in that house over there may be readying their sawed-off shotguns."

"We're not in America," my nephew pointed out. Nonetheless, Gavin's body language said get outta' here. I wasn't wholly in disagreement. After all, we had a good six or seven minutes of dim light remaining. It was simply exhilarating galloping through these green hills in the chilly air. That trumped everything. Quickly, a full curtain of Galician darkness descended over us.

"Let's get the headlamps out," I said.

We dutifully reached into our backpacks and pulled out the coal-miner headlamps that we hikers strap around our heads.

"Let's stay close together to maximize the light," I suggested, and he heeded. Even Gavin respected darkness as a formidable reality. Mostly, anyway.

"Hey, I see light ahead," I said.

"Those are a wolf's eyes," he corrected me.

It appeared to be some sort of tavern just off to the right of the Camino. I walked up and tried to enter, but the door was locked. I decided to knock. A non-descript middle-aged man wearily opened the door. He reported that not only was the tavern full, but their backyard was full of pilgrims. *"Ellos llegaron hace diez horas* (They arrived ten hours ago)," he reported. Point well taken.

He did say that if we walked just a couple hundred meters more, there would be a field where we could possibly camp. We hurried off expectantly. "Hey, this looks perfect," I enthused when the outline of a large field revealed itself. But the minute we cleared the trees and entered the wide-open expanse, a cold wind began bullying us. My heart sank.

"Man, this is gonna' be really bad for you without a tent," I said. Gavin didn't reply.

"Honestly, you're going to be totally exposed." Gavin again said nothing.

However, when I suggested, "Hey, let's go back there and see if there's anywhere we can stay," he readily agreed. We walked back towards the tavern. But there was simply nowhere at all suitable for camping. So we turned around and headed back to the field. As we neared the edge of the field, we saw another tent.

"Hey," I said, "I'll set my tent up right next to that person. The two tents together can make a wind shield. You can sleep right behind us." But the minute I started to throw down the tent, it flailed all over the place like three sheets to the wind.

"Man, that wind feels like it's coming through a gunshot pass," I agonized. "Hold this part and keep it right here," I instructed Gavin, while I tried snapping the parts together. Finally, I got it set up and staked down. That's when the *gentleman* in the other tent began loudly stirring.

A bespectacled middle-aged man, with a particularly unfriendly look on his face, poked his head out from one of the flaps. Unpleasant-sounding words came spewing out of his mouth. I heard the word *'permiso'*, but didn't know what language he was speaking.

"*Si, ya tenemos permiso acampar aqui* (Yes, we have permission to camp here)," I responded, which was halfway true, anyway.

"No, Bill," Gavin said. "He's French. He's saying he didn't give you permission to camp right next to him."

"I wish just one of these French that blesses me out, would do it in English or Spanish," I fumed again. I'd be damned if I was going to move my bloody tent in a public field.

"You're gonna' sleep in the tent," I told Gavin.

"No Bill," Gavin replied evenly. "I'll be fine."

My offer was mostly pro-forma because I knew he would reject it. But I was worried. I really was.

Gavin at age 16 on a Christian mission in Liberia.

"Man, these clear nights are the coldest." I agonized, "Here, take these long-johns and balaklava." I thanked my lucky stars for stuffing them in my backpack at the last minute before leaving home. Gavin quickly put them on. Meanwhile, I began hauling the hay that lay to our side over to construct further fortifications for Gavin. Gavin jumped in the fray and we soon had something that would hopefully hold up better than the *Maginot Line*. Oops. One tent over from me, that analogy—the Maginot Line—would be another sore subject.

Gavin got in his sleeping bag with a towel I gave him to wrap around his head. Then, I got into my tent. But I quickly felt guilt pangs. So I got out and carted more hay over to our straw fortification. *He should be alright.* It was a beautiful, cold, starry night in the Galician mountains.

***

I slept a little, and worried a lot. After a few hours of listening to the dominant moan of wind bullying the flaps of my tent, I couldn't stand it any longer. Needless to say, I would be the all-time goat if my 18 year-old nephew died of exposure, while I lay in the snugness of my tent. I decided to get out and check on Gavin.

I walked over to where Gavin lay and hovered over his inert body. His head was almost entirely covered by the balaklava and towel. He was completely still, which made me paranoid. I shined my headlamp on his pupils, which shone through the balaklava. One way or another, he seemed completely at peace.

"You alright, Gavin?"

No answer. I got back in my tent in an uneasy frame of mind. Never have I been so happy to hear a teenager's attitude-drenched voice as when Gavin said, "Bill, did you just wake me up?"

"Yes," I said. "It's too cold out there. You've been exposed too long. We're switching." I meant it, too. I wasn't gonna' be able to get relaxed, otherwise.

"Bill," he fired back. "There is no way I'm going in that tent. No matter what you say." It was a strong enough answer to at least allow me to lay there with some degree of comfort the rest of the evening.

At first light, I heard the footsteps of pilgrims marching by on the nearby trail. The nearest town was fifteen kilometers back. That meant most of these people had started hours before the sun had even shown its first glimmer.

Gavin and I took our time packing up. I looked over to where the other tent had been. "Look at what that CAD did," I said in disgust. A banana peel lay there.

"You're lucky he didn't leave a bowel movement," our French expert said.

"Oh is that another aspect of French culture that eludes us obtuse Americans?"

"No, it's human culture," Gavin educated me.

Chapter 39

Eternal Human Dilemna: How to Travel

"Min' be th' travaille. Thin be the glories."

Geoffrey Chaucer, *The Canterbury Tales*

With adrenaline hangovers from the previous evening's surge, it was a good day for a cakewalk. That's what we got. The Camino pleasantly lost 1,000 feet in elevation. Soon we crossed the Mino River, where Gavin would be swimming later that afternoon. We ascended up a steep flight of stairs and into the center of yet another charming pueblo, Portomarin. Lines the length of two city blocks snaked out from two different albergues.

"Look at this," I said in awe. "Worse than medieval times."

"It's definitely starting to feel *penitential*," Gavin responded, which showed he was picking up on some of the Camino history.

"Hey," I said. "There's that girl with the short hair. Let's see what's going on." Gavin would never admit his fondness for anything. But I noticed when I made suggestions like this, he quickly closed ranks.

"Laura, is this all one line?" I asked.

"Yes, most people left this morning at four," she said in amazement. "These new pilgrims don't have any etiquette." That refrain would become increasingly common as we closed in on Santiago de Compostela; pilgrims were now openly racing each other to secure beds. In the meseta, pilgrims had used the intense heat as an excuse to start walking before the sun came up. But that justification was now moot; Galician mornings are cold and misty.

Schoolgroups are part of the expanding mosaic of the Camino.

Speaking of cold, Laura's mother was right next to her. She sat there stony-faced, as Gavin and I chatted with her daughter. When I learned they were from rural eastern Germany, my mind went back to the days after the fall of the Berlin Wall in 1989. "It's going to be good for the younger people, but difficult for the older people," many had commented. That seemed to be the case here. Laura's mother had been saving up money for this trip for a couple years. Her more modish daughter was determined to strut out her English and meet people.

"There are the two Belgian girls," I pointed out to Gavin. A bit more reluctantly, Gavin followed me over; he wasn't enjoying this as much as me. But give him thirty years, and then we'll see.

Delphine and Anna were habitually late risers. That had worked fine in the early parts of the Camino. But these mad early morning dashes to the albergues had severely cramped their style. Reluctantly, they had been forced to join in the rat race.

"Nobody is even talking to each other in the albergues," Delphine reported in a state of seeming awe. "And people don't even say 'hello' anymore on the Camino."

"Sounds obsessive," I said.

"Sounds Catholic," Gavin commented.

"Yes, it is," Delphine laughed. "We're number 64 in this line. But we don't know if we are going to get a bed."

"How many beds are there in the albergue?" I asked.

"We don't know."

"Well shouldn't they come out and tell the people beyond a certain number, they aren't going to get a bed so they don't needlessly suffer."

"Bill," Gavin popped in again. "You obviously don't understand the Catholic religion. The person who waits the longest in line and *doesn't* get a bed is the big winner." That solved that. They eventually did get a bunk. But not everybody did. The town ended up setting aside some park space for pilgrims to sleep out in the open.

While everybody stayed queued up waiting to be tapped for *bedhood,* Gavin and I went off to eat a Galician lunch, a little bit proud of ourselves (always a dangerous feeling) for our independence. The first course in every meal in Galicia is invariably 'Caldo Gallego'. It's a rich, steaming broth full of veggies and chunks of meat. Then they brought us some filete terneras (steak), French fries, French bread and olive oil, along with beverages and red wine.

Life didn't suck.

$$* * *$$

"The pleasures of travel consist of the obstacles, the fatigue, even the danger," wrote French poet, Theodore Gaultier. "What charm can anyone find in an excursion, when he is always sure of reaching his destination, of having horses waiting for him, a soft bed, an excellent supper, and all the ease and comfort of his own home? One of the great misfortunes of modern life is the wont of any sudden surprise."

Gaultier wrote that in the 19th century. One wonders what he would have thought of today's travel industry, replete with sanitized tour packages and hand-held trips. Since the earliest human peregrinations, the question has always been how to travel more fulfillingly, more fruitfully, more enjoyably. Interestingly, the word travel is derived from the word *'travails'*, which connotes beleagurement. That brings up a great irony. In this age of supersonic jets and instantaneous communication, it has become harder to travel well.

Modern tourism so often seems to be all about destination. One can often subtly hear the frustrations of travelers who return from their long journeys. Deep in their sub-conscious seems to be the subtle occurrence, "Is that all?" The hope of the sublime, life-changing encounters somewhere along the road usually proves elusive.

Pilgrimages, however, are much more about transformation. Incidentally, a person does not have to travel to distant locales to achieve this. The year after I got out of commodities trading after fourteen years, I took a position as a coordinator of a welfare-reform program in Texas. Far and away my favorite part of the job was going into welfare case centers in South Texas and trying to convince welfare recipients—95% who were single mothers who had had horrific experiences with males—to join the program. There was something about these grungy case centers I found *deeply real*—much more so than the more lavish arenas of the London International Financial Futures Exchange or the Chicago Board of Trade.

It is this innate human desire for the deeply real, I believe, that is what has made pilgrimages so popular throughout the ages. On the Camino everybody walks an average of 15 or 16 miles, day after day. Pilgrims sleep in compact bunkrooms full of 100 or more strangers, not exactly the Ritz Carlton Hotel. Queueing up for showers, toilet use, and laundry machines are part of the drill. Even without trying, a person is forced out of their comfort zone. It feels real.

Gavin and I felt like we had found just the right balance for us. After our delicious lunch, he went and jumped in the river bordering the town, while a fellow pilgrim snuck me into his albergue to take a shower. Gavin and I then took a siesta in a local park. We got up about 5:30, and swung by the local supermarket to purchase cold cuts, milk, and chocolates for a late night and early morning snack.

On the way out of town, we ran into Francesca, an always good-natured, middle-aged Austrian divorcee. "Why in the world would somebody ever want to divorce her?" I had remarked to

Gavin on a couple occasions.

"You just don't understand," my worldly nephew had explained to me.

But today her sunny presence was for once overshadowed.

"Oh gosh," she moaned. "The man who is going to be in the bunk next to me tonight is a beast. You should see the thick black hair all over him?"

"What country is he from?"

"I don't know," she answered fretfully. "But I know he's going to be a terrible snorer."

"Come walk with us," I suggested. She thought about it, but I think she sensed the question was pro-forma. It was a good thing because Gavin and I both knew what we were gonna' do.

Chapter 40

Galician Mysteries

The Galician hills may be one of the best kept secrets in the world. Without actually being dramatic like the Alps or the Rockies, they nonetheless have a beautiful sense of proportion to them. Little wonder the Galician autonomy movement is so strong.

Even amongst the Spanish people, the region represents something of an enigma, the mystical green hinterlands behind the mountains. Galician folklore is full of tales of witches, ghosts, and goblins, probably because of the frequent wet, foggy weather. Perhaps most mysterious of all is the Galician seaport of *Finistierre*, which Europeans for centuries considered to be the geographical End of the World.

The people are highly provincial. Because they have rarely been able to support themselves economically, the men have traditionally had to head off in pursuit of economic opportunity. This has left the women in charge of running the villages and farms. Their garb is often black, and it can be difficult to tell if you are talking to a 30 or 60 year-old. But they are known to be especially chatty to strangers, often voicing an encouraging *"Adelante* (Forward)," to passing pilgrims from their stone porches.

***

Galicia's fairy tale beauty was on full display at twilight as

The Camino is the best way I've ever found to travel.
Just the right amount of everything.

Gavin and I cleared the steep shelf leaving Portomarin. We were immensely enjoying ourselves again, gliding in cool air at maximum speed through the dark forests. We were learning, however, that this consistently hilly terrain didn't present much of anything in the way of camping spots.

"Wow, you can't take five straight steps on flat ground around here," I remarked.

"A normal person could," Gavin corrected me.

Gavin's mischievous dig aside, we weren't seeing anything at all suitable as night approached. The Appalachian and Pacific Crest Trails had inoculated me against most fears. But I still could get worried. "We're gonna' have to quit shooting our mouths off about what a no-brainer it is to camp out," I said.

"Take that to heart, Bill."

We continued climbing up to the tiny village of Naron. "We've gotta' stay somewhere around here," I said. "This map says there's nowhere flat for the next 50 kilometers. Unfortunately, this one-street town looked like a promontory. It featured a fall-off down to the valley on our left and a steep hillside on our right; as far as we could tell, there wasn't anywhere that offered the possibility of camping. "Wow, they could put an airport runway here," Gavin commented. In this case, his sarcasm was well founded. "No kidding," I joined in. "It must have been one of the old Vatican 'Flat-Earthers' that drew up these maps."

We did the predictable thing and kept moving. After all, it wouldn't be completely pitch-black for another five or ten minutes. Soon we found ourselves on a ridge descending slowly towards a river in a full-fledged night hike. Such a thing should not be overdramatized. After all, you're basically doing the same thing as in the day. But it's much more difficult because you have to focus on every step, as opposed to walking along aimlessly.

"Honestly, we should slow the pace down a little," I said. "We might have to sustain this awhile." My fleet-footed nephew heeded my suggestion, without actually acknowledging it. We settled into a quieter nighttime trek. Soon we saw a lone light in the distance.

Soon, we saw a lone light in the distance.

There was a long building over to the left of the Camino, with nightlights shining. "Hey, this is an albergue," I said. "We might have to break principles and stay here, if they'll let us in." I knocked on the door, despite it being 11:00. An annoyed-looking Spanish man opened the door. I tried to explain what we were doing.

"*Estamos cerrados* (closed)," he said. "*Abrimos manana a la uno.*"

"They'll be open at one tomorrow afternoon," I reported to Gavin.

"Gee, did you get us reservations?"

We both looked up at the steep hill just above the albergue, with a stone picnic table at the foot of the incline.

"I'm sleeping on that picnic table," Gavin immediately announced.

"How are you gonna' keep from falling off?" I contested.

"Your body adjusts," he said. I had no idea if this was really true. But I was tired and trudged all the way to the top of the hill looking for somewhere to pitch my tent. Finally I found a small area that was slightly less steep than an amusement park slide. I threw down my tent and settled in for a restless evening. Unbeknownst to me until the next morning, I was situated right next to a dead cat.

If the point of travel was to stick your neck out and create some human moments, we seemed to be on the right track.

Chapter 41

The Modern Washed Masses

"Did you hear who is going to be in Santiago for the 25th?" Darla asked.

It was 8:00 in the morning. Despite the fact that we had camped out 17 kilometers ahead of Kip's group, they were again passing us. They all got great delight in coming over and viewing my comatose nephew lying on the picnic table.

"St. James," I answered Darla, in sophomoric fashion.

"He's already there," a suddenly resurrected Gavin corrected me.

"The Pope," Darla said.

"Hey, that makes sense," I said excitedly. "It's a big chance to proselytize masses of European youth."

But who knew if the story was really accurate? It was probably inevitable that this exact story would gain currency. After all, Pope John Paul II had appeared in Santiago on a couple occasions for the July 25th Holy Day. Other Popes actually hiked El Camino back in the Middle Ages. But would Benedict have the flair for the dramatic of John Paul II?

***

The strangest things happen in European bathrooms. No, not lewd things. No worries there. More like disconcerting things.

When you flip the light switch on in the bathroom, the lights do come on. But then comes the hard part. When you least expect it—and often at crucial times in the middle of certain essential tasks—they cut off automatically. You can be in the middle of performing a constitutional and you find yourself jumping up and groping around looking for the light switch. Presumably, Europeans learn to just bide their time and carry things out in the dark; it took me the better part of the Camino to figure this out. But what a wonderful flourish of pride once I did master this critical lesson.

Where you really had better be feeling your oats is in a European shower. Again, I'm not being lewd. It's just that approximately 9 ½ seconds after turning the water on, it will automatically cut off. At first, an American is likely to think that something is wrong. So when you get the water running again you breathe a sigh of relief that you can begin enjoying your long, hot shower. Only problem is the water is usually not steaming hot, and the moderate amount of bliss will only last 9 ½ more seconds. It quickly became clear there are no shortcuts. You're going to have to be intermittently mashing down on a knob while showering. Worse yet, you become paranoid that the water is going to cut off and you'll be in the cold, so you start hitting the button every five seconds. All I can say is I sure hope our medieval predecessors didn't have to endure anything quite so hellish.

Let me say just a bit more on this topic of supreme importance. This kind of rationing of water and lights is one of the things that make a person European, as opposed to the wonderful world of infinite hot water and lights, which constitutes the United States of America. So which is better? That is probably the wrong question. But I'm going to say that objectively—except when a person is stranded on a toilet in the dark or pumping away feverishly on a shower knob—the European way may now make the most sense in a world of depleting finite resources.

In any event, Gavin and I were suddenly having trouble finding any kind of shower to take. The albergues had begun to crack down, given the mad rush of pilgrims on each town. In Palas de Rei, we got busted sneaking into two different albergues, despite fellow pilgrims conspiring on our behalf. Finally, we were able to sneak into a third albergue. After scurrying around, we realized we were in the women's room. We fled half-robed up a flight of stairs to the men's room and were finally able to crank out enough light and water to use the toilet and bathe.

On the way out we joined a crowd of pilgrims hovered around a television set. The national news was dominated by the masses descending on Santiago. They showed one elderly man being pushed forward in a wheelchair (We had already passed a few pilgrims being pushed in wheelchairs), and another riding towards Santiago on a donkey.

"What are they saying?" Gavin asked me.

"They're talking about rumors that the Pope is going to be there."

"Uh oh," he said, "Lutherans may be planning bombings if he shows up."

"Hey, but think about the Muslim pilgrimage to Mecca," I said. "They almost always have lots of deaths (In 1994, 1,426 Muslim pilgrims were stampeded to death in Mecca. Another 345 were stampeded in 2006)."

"That's *why* they go to Mecca," Gavin explained to me.

"Honestly though," I reasoned, "in that one sense, you've got to respect them. If we knew some of us were going to die in Santiago, most of us would probably just turn around and walk the other way."

***

We joined Kip's 6:00 class under the covered pavilion in the town center. It was a good thing because, for the first time since crossing the Pyrenees in France, it began to rain. The swarm of pilgrims, the most since the Middle Ages, had overwhelmed Palas de Rei. Surplus pilgrims were being required to sleep under the pavilion on the cement. Despite the light rain coming down, Gavin and I unhesitatingly decided to blow town at twilight.

"I'm glad to see the backside of that place," Gavin said on the way out of town. Yes, but he didn't have a tent and we were walking in the rain. And given the towel-snapping banter between us, the idea of sleeping intimately in a tent was quite unappealing. Yet as the uncle I felt it necessary to remind him, "If it's raining when we stop tonight, you're gonna' have to get in there with me."

As the reader is now aware, finding a perfect spot right at dark is a roll of the dice. But that's what happened a few hours later. We were able to pull just a few yards over to the side of the Camino onto a perfectly flat, grassy spot. It had just about stopped raining, as I went about setting up my tent.

Soon a group of four pilgrims with headlights came walking by.

"*Hola,*" I said curiously.

"Hola, buenas noches," all four replied. They were Asians.

"A donde van ustedes (Where are you going)?" I asked.

"Santiago," a tiny little Japanese girl answered softly. Gavin and I immediately identified with these kindred souls. They were fellow albergue boycotters and night hikers. However, if the truth be known, our egos may have been scraped a little bit. This foursome was proving to be more unconventional than us.

"Donde ustedes van a acampar esta noche (Where are you going to camp tonight)?" I asked.

"Santiago," the little girl repeated.

"Santiago esta 55 kilometers de aqui," I said confused.

"Sabemos (We know)."

"Did you hear that?" I said to Gavin. "They're going to Santiago tonight."

"Yeah, right," he said, "Ask if they're going to hike naked."

To his surprise, I immediately asked them, *"Gavin quiere saber si ustedes vayan a caminar desnudos* (Gavin wants to know if you're going to hike naked)?"

They laughed heartily, and the girl said, *"Necesitamos decider pronto* (soon)."

A healthy-looking thirtyish male from China said, "If we want to hike with Niki (the Japanese girl), we have to walk all night."

"Stalkers," Gavin joked.

The two guys recognized the word, and laughingly agreed, "Yes, we are stalkers."

They wanted photos, which for once I was in the mood for. Before they departed, the little Japanese girl proceeded to make a series of running jumps to do high-fives with me. I kept raising my hands a little higher, which drew yelps from everyone, including Niki. And then they were off in a light drizzle for a very long night indeed. My heart went out to them.

They ended up walking all night and made it approximately half the way to Santiago. There they rested for a day-and-a-half, and actually arrived in Santiago after Gavin and me. By the tone of their voices when we saw them again, they weren't the least bit self-conscious at not having actually met their quixotic goal. The main thing was they had struggled and done it their way. They had lived. Surely they will remember this all-day and all night trek in on-and-off rain as the highlight of their journey.

For most of human history, the locus of economic power in the world has actually lain in *the East*. For the last thousand years though, it has resided mostly in the West. However, with the resurgence of China, India, and the Asian tigers, the pendulum seems to be shifting back to the East. Whether it is New York, London, Paris, or Las Vegas, increased numbers of Asian travelers are now a fact of life. Asian pilgrims have even begun appearing in significant numbers on The Camino for the first time.

When I was growing up, I used the tired old stereotypes. We said they all looked and acted alike. The Japanese were supposedly so robotic that they sang company songs at work each day. However, friends who live in Asia tell me in no uncertain terms they are great individualists.

I remember lying on my bunk in the albergue in Burgos watching a young Korean pilgrim attempting to drain the blisters in his feet. Every time he stuck the needle in the blister, he let out a grimace and jumped like a grasshopper. In TriaCastela, a Chinese pilgrim arrived in town, only to realize he had left his camera back at the previous albergue. He immediately rushed away back up the steep mountain he had just descended, stabbing wildly at the air in anger with his hiking stick.

To be sure, it was more difficult getting to know the Asian pilgrims, mainly due to the language barrier. But almost universally, they appeared upbeat, energetic, and even unusually well-hygiened. Further, they were almost always the people striving to speak in our language, rather than vice-versa. This is rather charitable of them if you consider how much money we borrow from them every year. Historically, the debtor has to learn the creditor's language.

***

"Hey Kip," I called from my tent, in what had become a morning ritual, as he raced by our camping spot.

"Is that Gavin?" Kip pointed to an inert body next to my tent.

"Yeah."

"He slept in the rain?"

"I don't think it rained here," I said, looking around.

"You're living a charmed life," he chortled. "It poured back in Palas de Rei."

Trailing behind Kip was what may have been, without exaggeration, the largest mass movement of humans in Western Europe since the Second World War. The Camino had begun to have the outward appearance of a refugee crisis. Fortunately though, instead of frightened families stuffing their remaining possessions onto rickety wagons or clinging to pack animals, you had generally well-fed, upper middle-class Europeans walking purposefully towards this apostolic mecca. And the irony was delightful. It was all happening on a continent that had supposedly given up on religion.

***

"Todos los albergues estan completos (All the albergues are full)," I yelled. *"Todo complete."* Swarms of pilgrims were rushing by a trinket stand located on the side of the Camino, without even taking notice of it. Only one person seemed to think I was funny—the owner of the stand.

This poor fella' had assembled a full inventory of all imaginable Galician souvenirs and pilgrim paraphernalia. His stand was in a perfect location right off the Camino. However, his strategy ended up backfiring. Ninety per cent of the passers-by had their ears pinned back and after-burners on as they raced for a bunk in Arzua. In fact, the only thing that slowed anybody down was *my* puerile joke that all the albergues were full. That made them anxious and the owner laugh. Gavin approved as well.

"Some trip wires would be appropriate here," he noted.

Later in the day, this bed-obsessed brotherhood of pilgrims also missed out on another worthwhile El Camino attraction. Given its long-Atlantic coastline, *pulpo* is an exotic Galician specialty. The Camino runs straight through the streets of Melida, especially renowned for its *pulperias*. Gavin and I arrived there mid-day and immediately entered a pulperia that looked like a German beer hall. The waitress brought us two orders of spiced octopus, soaked in wine, served on beer platters. We devoured the rich, nutritious Galician specialty.

"Man, if I could eat that every day, I think I could live to 110," I said.

"Yeah, that was special," Gavin agreed. It was a good thing we received this morale boost. We had another long afternoon and evening of Galician trekking ahead of us.

***

In Arzua, pilgrims were wandering around distraught. My flippant remarks had proven prophetic; all the albergues really were completely full. For all of Gavin's and my wise remarks, these peoples' concerns were actually quite understandable. The guide books had universally said a tent was unnecessary. But now, without a tent and with the albergues full, pilgrims were running out of options.

We ran into Jean Francoise and Emily for the first time in a week. Up until now, he had scheduled things for the two of them with German-like efficiency. But today he had finally been outflanked by hundreds, if not thousands of early-rising pilgrims. "They're going to let pilgrims stay in the poli-deportivo (sports gymnasium)," he said. He and Emily were marching determinedly in the opposite direction of us.

"We heard the poli-deportivo is this way," I said.

"We've already been to that one," he said tensely. "It's full. But they're opening up another one." This was gut-check time for Jean Francoise. But for Emily, it was just the opposite. She saw the possibility of liberation. "If it's full," she said, "we're going to sleep out with you."

It wasn't full. But it might as well have been. Mats with backpacks claiming a stake on them lay all over the gymnasium. The room temperature already reflected the overcrowding, and more pilgrims were on the way.

"This is why so many medieval pilgrims died," Gavin commented.

"Yeah, let's give this a miss," I agreed.

Surprisingly, Jean Francoise lightened up, and said, "Let's go with them." An Italian named Antonio in his mid-thirties, who had obviously developed a terrible fixation on Emily, made it a fivesome. Once again we headed out into the Galician countryside in the early evening. Emily was immediately in the thrall of the surroundings. "This is wonderful." Her speed quickly accelerated from its normally modest daytime pace. "Yes, we should have done this before," Jean Francoise said. Indeed, he had a newfound look of wonder on his face. Being forced to hike late and camp out was helping bring home the true mystery of pilgrimage.

Emily probably didn't get to enjoy it as much as she might have, however. Antony practically bent her ear off with chatter. "Gosh, he's throwing the Italian blitzkrieg at her," I said to Gavin. Of course, I was just trying to goad him to step out of his cool zone.

Just once. But of course he responded with typical indirection: "There are two types of wildlife on El Camino—lizards and Italians."

Jean Francoise, meanwhile, occupied himself with practicalities. Periodically, he would drop his backpack, say "Hold on," and begin running reconnaissance for camping spots. Soon we all got into the routine. At one point, the five of us were spread out in five different locations with our backpacks as the meeting point.

"My place looked pretty flat, but the grass is long," Jean Francoise reported.

"How about if we sleep right here on the Camino," I suggested. "It's flatter than anywhere else."

"Yeah, and get trampled by hundreds of pilgrims in the morning before the sun comes up," Gavin reminded me.

Others gave various assessments of the bona-fides of their stakeouts. But nobody's enthusiasm matched that of Antonio. "I've found a really good place," he reported." Please look at this." We followed him up a hill. When we finally got to the clearing, everybody went silent.

"Leaning Tower of Pisa," Gavin whispered quietly. Indeed, Antony had found a spot that looked like a beginner's ski slope. Slowly, and a little embarrassingly, we all shuffled away. The silence was pregnant.

But ultimately it was the same old phenomenon that dictated giving all five places a pass. We wanted to keep moving. It simply felt good. So we continued despite the fact it was now starting to get dark. Finally, we turned a corner and saw a gigantic open field. Emily suddenly dropped her backpack and bolted into the field at full speed, throwing her arms up in rhapsody. We all stood there laughing and admiring it.

"Wow, she's fast," I noted.

"Yes, she runs on the track team in Quebec," Jean Francoise pointed out.

Antonio practically needed a restraining order put on him after seeing another one of this French Canadian girl's talents. We all gathered in a tight circle to protect us from the stiff breeze sweeping across the Galician hills, while Antonio talked to Emily non-stop in a low, confiding tone. With plenty of company around, Emily could afford to humor poor Antonio while he flamed out.

Chapter 42

"The Church"

If you're like me, you've been hearing a steady din your entire adult life about the evils of *The Church*. Of course, this doesn't refer to the bricks and mortar of any one specific building, but rather that amorphous entity—the universal Catholic Church that so dominated Europe in the Middle Ages.

According to the narrative, human history was held back for roughly a thousand years due to this regressive institution. Scientific inventions and progressive ideas were obsessively stifled. Grotesque stupidities such as Galileo being put under house arrest for suggesting the earth wasn't the center of the universe, as well as other quaint superstitions, are routinely cited. The Dark Ages didn't finally lift until the new ideas of the Enlightenment and Renaissance liberated humanity from the iron-clad chokehold of The Church's domination.

Well, I'm now happy to report that in my extensive research for this book, I have found the above narrative—which is virtually gospel in secular, intellectual, and academic circles—to be more misleading than accurate. In fact, it was The Church that built Europe and western civilization as we know it.

***

The years from 500 to 1000 CE are inaffectionately known as the *Dark Ages*. The Roman Empire had fallen. Europe was a crude and backward land. Rule was exercised by strong men, mostly of Germanic ancestry. Cities had mostly disappeared. Life was hard, hungry, and dangerous; vagabonds wandered the countryside. In this Hobbesian world, goodness was actually mocked, beauty was scorned, cripples sneered at and beaten, scars worn with pride, and injuries boasted of. Most babies took a brief look at the world and died. Old age came soon. Death was often welcome.

Muslim nations were far more advanced. A medieval visitor would have found Baghdad or Damascus more economically developed than any of the European nations. It wasn't at all surprising that when the Muslims decided to invade Spain, they were quickly able to gain control of most of the Iberian peninsula with their superior military forces. However, a few hundred years later Europe had bypassed the Muslims and become the world's most advanced continent. How did they do it? Again, the answer is The Church.

***

The Xerox Corporation ran a very popular commercial when I was growing up in the 1970's. It featured a Xerox machine spitting out copies of a manuscript. Looking on were a group of dumbfounded monks. A holy chant then begins rising, at which point the leading monk solemnly pronounces, "It's a miracle."

This advertisement cleverly played on the stereotype that monks spend their entire lives in the mindless task of rote-copying manuscripts. Their lives were depicted as not just stupefyingly boring, but incorrigibly weird as well.

Nonetheless, when Gavin and I arrived at a turnoff that offered a diversionary route to the oldest and largest monastery in Spain, we took it, despite it adding five extra kilometers. The monastery was nestled deep in the hilly Galician woodlands, in the hamlet of Samos. The foundation for the Samos monastery was laid in the sixth century. Fifteen hundred years later, it still looks pretty sturdy.

We took a tour, along with Kip's group, through the labrynth of winding hallways, staircases, art rooms, murals, and chapels. Gregorian chants in a monadico melody slowly overcame the tour guide's voice. Eventually, we were led out to the immaculate interior courtyard.

"Man, this must have been the life."

"Don't get any ideas, Bill," Gavin checked me.

"How did they pay for all this?" I asked the guide.

"You see that statue," she pointed to a gilded statue of a noble-looking, middle-aged man. "He wrote popular books; the monastery used the money to pay for the most expensive murals of the day."

"What did most monks do with their lives?"

"They were actually quite busy," she said with conviction. "They took care of the grounds, searched for the food, cooked, studied the Bible, and chanted."

"They also converted the pagan masses," Kip, who was at our side, pointed out. "The monasteries actually kept Christianity alive in the Dark Ages."

That was no exaggeration. These marvelous towers of ivory were Europe's only centers of scholarship. History has the monks themselves to thank for the preservation of the classics. Better yet, while the Greeks had long before invented democracy as a means for choosing leaders, only the strictly wealthy were allowed to participate. These Benedictine monasteries were the first institutions in the world to actually enjoy universal suffrage.

$$***$$

The monasteries gave Christianity a beachhead in a sea of strong-man rule. In a historical irony, it fell to the greatest strong man of all to firmly root Christianity in the European Continent. Charlemagne's armies had proven invincible over all other pagan tribes roaming the bloody landscape. Yet here was a military leader who took his Christian religion seriously. Effectively, he had the Church replace the strong man rule reigning all over Europe.

This Church proved to be quite progressive, building and maintaining roads, bridges, hospitals and hospices. No one was denied admission. The poor were considered to have a right to support from the community's property. The Church fought off the remnants of slavery by repurchasing Christian slaves that had been sold off in wealthier Muslim lands. Soon Europe became more stable, and central governments more efficient. Business was good, and roads and seaways open. The warlike ideal faded. Towns and cities started growing again, adorned with noble churches, and filled with comfortable homes.

The Church's influence led to the establishment of the first universities in Paris and Bologna in the 12th century. Oxford and Cambridge were established in the 13th century. Great figures of the scientific revolution, including Mendel, Copernicus, Kepler, Galileo, and Newton were all devout Christians. Newton, in fact, wrote far more on theology than any other subject. The Church essentially initiated capitalism, by permitting serfs to buy themselves out of bondage, greatly increasing the quality of life. More and more land was under cultivation, and regularly yielding good harvests. Majestic Gothic cathedrals pierced the sky. In the words of Voltaire, "If all wasn't well, it was at least tolerable."

But the trajectory suddenly and dramatically changed. First, in the mid- fourteenth century there was the Black Death. The Church obviously didn't cause the Plague. But it did exacerbate the calamity by claims that Jews had poisoned the sewer systems. The next century saw the hideous Inquisition. Finally, the Middle Ages ended around the year 1500, about the time Europe descended into a series of seemingly interminable religious conflicts between Catholics and Protestants. In a religion of sinners, the Church sometimes committed the biggest sins of all.

Nonetheless, despite all these setbacks and disasters, Europe never fell back to the levels seen in the Early Middle Ages. The Church had put together the permanent building blocks of a civilized society. The unceasing efforts of modern intellectuals and academicians to portray The Medieval Catholic Church as inherently evil, is not just an indictment of a large religious institution. It is a virtual condemnation of all medieval humanity.

Chapter 43

Santiago Approach

"Oh, what a horror," she exclaimed. "I can feel the slime coming out. It makes me want to vomit."

"What set you off?" I asked.

"I'm reading this awful book by an American," she said. "I can actually feel the slime dripping off the pages. I'm embarrassed to be reading it."

"Any specific reason?"

"These happy endings are awful," she said with utter conviction. "I need a shower to wipe the slime off of me."

"What's wrong with a happy ending?" Gavin asked innocently.

"That's not life. It's Alice in Wonderland."

"So are all pilgrims going to get gunned down going into Santiago?" I asked her.

"Just American ones," she popped back.

Gavin and I had been lying in the middle of the Camino, taking a break, when we had become embroiled in this conversation with this tart-tongued German woman in her late twenties. Her name was Kerstin. She was from Berlin. Kerstin spoke perfect English, which she used to harness her sharp invective.

"I've got my first blister," reported her American hiking partner, Ferdinand.

"Happy birthday," Kerstin shot back at him, which left him speechless.

In case you missed the point, Kerstin was a cool chick. She was multi-lingual, physically agile, confident, and in the logic of 21st century Europe, well-versed in anti-Americanism. And given our respective histories, it is probably not surprising that a German would be more leery of happy endings than an American.

***

Pilgrims had been talking incessantly the last couple weeks about where to stay in Santiago. Some had even made reservations up to a year in advance. Others had been racing desperately for weeks to arrive a few days before the July 25th Holy Day, with hopes of securing one of the limited spots in an albergue. Gavin and I, however, had done no planning whatsoever. All we knew was that we were walking into one vast cauldron of humanity.

We joined a group of pilgrims at a sidewalk café 12 kilometers shy of Santiago.

"Where are you staying in Santiago?" I asked Kerstin.

"Ask Ferdinand," she popped back.

"We haven't decided yet," Ferdinand answered tensely. "The big hotel costs 250 Euros."

"Where are you staying?" Kerstin asked.

"Ask Gavin," I responded.

"Somewhere appropriate for the gravity of the occasion," he said.

"Such as?"

"The nearest park," he replied. "I just can't get over thinking Santiago is gonna' be like Woodstock." Even that brought a smile—and silence—to Kerstin's lips.

Other pilgrims soon plopped down alongside us in this shady redoubt. One was a slightly built, fortyish German lady that I had seen on various occasions. She had almost always been alone, and seemed to have an especially intense look about her. However, she seemed to be enjoying the light tone of our banter and joined in.

"Why are you doing the Camino?" she asked me from across the table.

"I'm here to meet European divorcees," I responded, polishing off the old stock line. Well, as they say in Hollywood, never use the same line twice. Of course, I had long ago broken that rule, and consistently drawn snickers. But immediately, it became obvious I had gone to the well once too often. A hard, unsympathetic look came across the woman's face.

"You are not having a good day," she said coldly.

"He's had a bad few days," Kerstin piled on.

"How did you decide to do the Camino?" I asked the lady defensively.

"Not because of that," she said distastefully.

Her rebuke cut into me like shards of broken glass. I tried to engage her in more conversation. But it was all met with an icy silence. She now looked at me as though she were examining a urine sample. I quickly lapsed into stereotypes—'She's just a cold German'. That's the problem. Blame her. But, of course, that was nothing but lazy (see chapter on evil) thinking on my part. Finally, I said, "Let's go, Gavin," and I slunk off in shame. Later that day, the lady passed us on the side of the trail, but barely acknowledged my salutation. I felt small.

"That which hurts, instructs," Ben Franklin said over 200 years ago. Indeed, this woman's humiliating putdown of my adolescent humor was to be the source of my greatest epiphany of the pilgrimage. *El Camino de Santiago is not the European Divorcee Trail*, after all. Yes, my Danish friend on the Pacific Crest Trail had gotten off a good line when describing the Camino to me last year. And sure, there are lots of divorcees mixed in with this sea of humanity. Good for them for being out here. But most pilgrims had more serious reasons for undertaking the pilgrimage than recent marital discord.

My mind went back to the night Gavin and I had arrived at dark in TriaCastela. All the albergues had been full. Finally, after exhausting all other potential options, we had entered the town's lone cathedral, and headed up to the second-floor balcony for the evening. Throughout the night and on into the next morning, lone pilgrims periodically stole into the terra-cotta silences of the church, and walked quietly up to the altar. Periodically, I would peer down through the railing at these scenes of pilgrims—males, females, young, old—bowed in solemnity. This was frequently followed by the jingle of coins being dropped into a donation box, before the pilgrims left the church.

In the Middle Ages, the prime motivation for many pilgrims was a deeply-held fealty to St. James, himself. He was the man who lore held had saved Christianity in Europe from extermination by the Muslims. Very few of us modern pilgrims were here out of reverence for James. Nonetheless, many pilgrims still have profound spiritual—even religious—reasons for the journey. I had been a slow learner to be sure. Thank God Christianity is especially welcoming to us slow learners.

***

In medieval times, the first actual glimpse of the city of Santiago de Compostela was often the single greatest moment of a pilgrim's life. Having come from Paris and even further, these penniless masses had most likely faced the terror of wild animals, bandits, severe heat and cold, as well as extreme hunger. In the only real trip of their lives, they had survived for months at the sufferance of theretofore complete strangers, often speaking strange tongues. Some had perished.

As they followed the Camino up a slope on the outskirts of the city, they suddenly stood on Monte de Gozo (Mount of Joy). Here they could see the great Gothic Cathedral at the center of the whole drama. According to legend that was virtually gospel to medieval pilgrims, the bones of St. James the Greater lay inside this enormous cathedral. At that point, no figure other than Jesus figured higher in the Christian imagination. Numerous paintings and chronicles of medieval times show overwhelmed pilgrims being brought to the ground in rapture and tears here on this hill overlooking Santiago de Compostela.

However, when Gavin and I lumbered to the top of Monte de Gozo on July 23, 2010, we witnessed with no such dramatic scene. Instead of the commanding heights of the seven hills outside Rome, the modern pilgrim is greeted with urban sprawl. The city skyline now blocks the view of the cathedral from Monte de Gozo. Like Mecca, Lourdes, and other pilgrimage destinations, Santiago de Compostela has become big business.

"Bill, this looks like Macon, Georgia," Gavin lamented.

"Don't be so sentimental."

"Where do you want to go?" he asked.

"Well, do we do the unthinkable?" I asked.

"What, the concentration camp?"

"Yeah."

"It's up to you."

What he was referring to in this case was the enormous campus-sized albergue here on the outskirts of Santiago, seven miles shy of the great Cathedral. The albergue reputedly held 800 pilgrims. Opinions ranged all over the lot amongst pilgrims as to whether it was tactically smart to stay here.

By default, we started wandering down to our left where it was said to be located. Immediately, we were greeted with an arrestingly ugly scene. To be fair, the Camino governing body had had a complex logistical problem on their hand—where in the world to put this mass of humanity that arrives once a year. Their solution had been to construct this *stalag*-like monstrosity.

Gavin and I joined a line that would last 2 ½ hours. Hopefully, the reader won't mind me giving ourselves a small pat on the backs. We practiced Spanish almost the entire time we waited. Yet another athletic German girl with her bicycle was right in front of us. Without actually speaking to us, she seemed to have a slightly amused look on her face, as she listened to the two Americans behind her grappling with a foreign language. *What is it about these Germans that always makes them appear so confident?* In any event, we would see her late the evening of the big festivities, and see she had a more social side.

Gavin and I got placed in a charmless block building full of strangers and hiking equipment. Ironically, this monstrous building was outfitted with miniature bunks. I immediately decided to chunk my mattress on the ground, which had me worried about getting trampled in the middle of the night. Beside me in a single bed was a couple who spent most of the night trying to decide whether or not to consummate the occasion (Alas, they didn't. Hope it didn't ruin the entire pilgrimage).

In the morning after a sleepless night, I moaned to Gavin, "I wouldn't have lasted a week in Auschwitz."

"Not many people did," he pointed out.

We got out of there for the walk into Santiago.

***

The irony was supreme. All along the way, as we had passed through countless pueblos, villages, and hamlets, it was always a church that had announced that a town was nearing. These churches had invariably stood tall and proud, beckoning to pilgrims from miles away. But now as we wound our way through the streets and alleys of this long-awaited city of destination, finding the famous cathedral became a game of blind-man's bluff.

We missed a turn and ended up way down a highway. Then we overshot in the opposite direction. Finally, though, we started to get warm. The city became denser, as it took on a medieval feel with covered granite arcades.

"Okay, Bill," Gavin said, "I'll take my cue from you about how to act upon arrival."

"You're Protestant, not Catholic," I lectured. "You shouldn't need an intermediary."

"What if we walk right past it?" he ventured.

"Then the last 500 miles have been a total waste."

"Is this it?"

"I think so."

Chapter 44

Santiago de Compostela

"Every moment is a window on all time."

Thomas Wolfe, *Look Homeward Angel*

Asking me to critique a church is probably like asking a monk to rate a Hollywood film. Well, maybe not that strange. Like most people, I've seen thousands of churches in my lifetime. Most of them do a little something for me. Generally, the older the church, the more of a holy presence I fathom. I'm consistently partial to brownstones.

Certainly though, this church—excuse me, cathedral—deserved special consideration. After all, before this my longest trip ever to a church was probably a twenty minute car ride. Unfortunately, the first thing a modern pilgrim sees looks like an extension of a nearby building. But then things get better.

The pilgrims ahead of us were hurrying under an enormous Romanesque arch. Gavin and I broke precedent and proceeded through without any irreverencies. At the end of a long barricade we took a left, where the expansive vista of *Plaza del Obradoira* opens up. Silently, we walked to the center of the square. There we turned to look at the enormous façade of the great Gothic Cathedral in Santiago de Compostela.

***

If in doubt, build a church. That has been the default position of Christianity since around the mid-Fourth Century. Magnificent cathedrals and basilicas in Jerusalem, Rome, and all over the world, honor the early founders of the Christian religion. So it was no surprise to see an enormous body of worship here in Santiago, where one of Jesus' very closest disciples reputedly lies.

This particular cathedral has an especially charmed history. From the time the foundation was laid in 1073, kings, queens, and royalty lavished it with gold. Peasants, who felt an especially deep loyalty to James, played a major role as well, donating their mites and wares well beyond any tradition of tithing. Layer upon layer of archaeology was sculpted, piled on, and attached. In 1096, one large wing of the cathedral was burned by invading Moors. But such was the dedication to this marquee church, that it was quickly rebuilt to ever-grander proportions. Finally, in the 17th century, 800 years after it was begun, the splendid, proud, magnifying towers of Babel were added that now soar dramatically into the Galician sky.

The cathedral at the heart of the whole drama.

Gavin and I stood with our pilgrim brethren staring straight ahead at the famed *Portico de la Gloria.* This façade of the cathedral is considered to be one of the finest examples of medieval sculpture still standing. Over the centuries, many a famished, weary pilgrim has knelt right here in tears over this architectural majesty. There are actually three arches, each embroidered with scores of carvings, many done by an obscure craftsman named Mateo. The style is Romanesque, which blends in well to the dominant Gothic majesty of the cathedral.

I personally prefer small when it comes to a body of worship. This cathedral is anything but. It was clearly built with the idea of being formidable. That ideal (size) seems to have triumphed over exquisite beauty. Nonetheless, my attitude towards this granite structure was, if not reverence, solid respect.

God knows we modern Christians are tired of hearing every place we go about all the crimes and atrocities supposedly committed in the name of The Church. But here in Santiago, that was anything but the case. The massive human movement in medieval times that had led to this huge cathedral in front of us had almost entirely positive wellsprings. The person it honored had been hounded to the ends of the earth before being beheaded. Best of all, his story had inspired so many to give it their very all to make it here.

***

Pilgrims were walking around looking practically dazed. The struggle they had endured to get here was palpably etched in some of their faces.

There was Rosemary, the French lady with whom I had carried on the faux-romance in the early stages of the Camino. Of course, it had never gotten off the ground. But all along the way, Gavin and I had passed her as she grinded along. She always seemed to have a slightly wincing look on her face, as if experiencing low-grade pain. In albergues, she had often hobbled around, as if in severe pain. But now here she was in Santiago de Compostela. And as far as I knew, she hadn't skipped anywhere. She looked like somebody who had lived a lot these past five weeks. Indeed, one could say she had a palpable holy air about her, that hadn't been there early on.

It's worth remembering the roots of the religion that had

spawned this pilgrimage. The central figure of Christianity, in the journey of *His* lifetime, had arrived in Jerusalem on a donkey wearing sandals. Most medieval pilgrims were desperately poor, while modern pilgrims are heavily weighted towards the bourgeouise classes. For that reason, you probably can't put our level of satisfaction and fulfillment up there—and I do mean up—with that of the medieval pilgrims. Nonetheless, there had been significant shucking of amenities among pilgrims even here in the year 2010 CE in order to make it all the way here to Santiago on foot. Pilgrims wore palpable looks of relief on their faces.

Perhaps one pilgrim expressed it best when she wrote, "Santiago had the look of a place where the game was up. And the Devil had lost."

***

"There is a service at 2:00. Are you going?"

Gavin and I were talking with one of the American students from FOCUS (Fellowship of Catholic University). They were all devout American Catholics; it seemed like a good idea to hang with them.

We followed their lead into the principal nave of the Cathedral. They headed purposefully down the aisle, before all doing that bent-knee thing that so flummoxes us Protestants. Soon we were hunkered down on our hands and knees in a pew. Gavin and I tried to quickly replicate the crucifix sign these FOCUS students so effortlessly made. Again I prayed for the priceless gift of faith. This time though, I included in my prayers all the friendly, loving Spanish faces we had seen all along the way to Santiago, but who weren't fortunate enough to be part of the pilgrimage.

The altar was a blaze of lights, displaying a brilliant baroque ornamentation. Aging cardinals and bishops in red and purple vests stood at call. Unsurprisingly, a huge statue of St. James occupied a commanding position. My first reaction was negative because of its sheer ostentatiousness. But again, one must remember that medieval pilgrims were just a step removed from pagan roots and warring tribes. Expecting subtlety was too much.

A Disney-like device is the principal attraction for many in the Cathedral at Santiago, in the form of the *botafumeiro*. It is said to be the largest incense burner in the world. Eight acolytes stepped forward to affix the botafumeiro to pulley ropes, at which point it lifted off above the hypnotic audience, dispensing copious quantities of incense. Cameras went clicking and the folks back home had another photograph to look at.

Ironically, the roots of this high-technology gadget go all the way back to medieval times. It seems that when medieval pilgrims arrived in Santiago, many stayed right here in the Cathedral. They were reputed to be so fragrant, and even disease-ridden, that the cathedral decided it needed to cleanse them. That led to the development of the forerunner device of the now famous botafumeiro.

***

The biggest event of all was scheduled for 9:00 in the evening. Gavin and I got some scoop about an obscure monastery on the outskirts of town that might still have bunks available. We hurried through the teeming masses now swarming through the streets of Santiago. Sure enough, a group of nuns were serving lemonade at a table when we arrived. We checked in.

"Are these doors going to be open for us to enter tonight after the fiesta?" I asked, just to be sure.

"The doors close at 10:00," one of the nuns immediately said.

"At 10:00?" I repeated in disbelief.

"We always close at 10:00," she said logically.

"But this is the big night," I protested. "The show doesn't even end until after midnight."

"But we close the doors at 10:00."

The Catholic Church, monasteries, and nuns had earned our healthy respect over the course of the pilgrimage. But let's face it—flexibility isn't their strong suit. Maybe that's a good thing. But not here. Just this once.

"There's no way I've walked this far and gonna' miss the celebration," Gavin said.

"No kidding," I agreed. "I may never have a chance to go on something like this ever again."

"Where are we gonna' put our stuff, if we don't stay here?" he asked.

"Let's just leave it here and come back and get it in the morning," I decided. But the nuns caught on to our plan

"If you're not going to sleep here," one nun said looking me straight in the eye, "we'd appreciate it if you took your belongings with you, so another pilgrim can have the bed."

Nonetheless, we decided on a morally ambiguous course. We told the nuns that I was leaving, but Gavin would be returning. That allowed us to leave Gavin's backpack there. I then crammed some of his stuff into my backpack. But now we had no idea where we were going to stay.

"Let's go," Gavin kept saying. But I wanted to take a shower, knowing I was going to be out, somewhere or another, all night.

"I'll just see you in the main plaza," I naively said.

"Have you seen all the people out there?"

"Look, I've got one redeeming virtue," I assured him. "You can't miss me in a crowd." Off he went. I wasn't to see him again for eight hours.

$$***$$

Church bells were ringing all over town like a war had just come to an end. Spanish, Galician, and European flags were all waving gallantly in the center of town. Buses were decanting tourists in dinner jackets who had come just for the evening festivities. I had never, ever in my entire life seen as many people as were thronging through the narrow streets.

When I finally was able to claw my way through the standstill crowd and up to the packed plaza, the police stopped me. They said I couldn't enter the plaza with my backpack. That meant I couldn't attend the celebration that I had walked 500 miles to get to.

As far as I'm concerned we Christians are too prone to stand on ceremony. But this was one ceremony I would have liked to have attended. I soon ran into other pilgrims who hadn't gotten in either, because of overcrowding. Many were incensed. The thing that irked them most was that non-walking pilgrims who had driven to Santiago that day (technically they are pilgrims also) had filled the plaza up early.

I entered a bar where the ceremony was on Galician National TV. The commentary was in Galician, which completely eluded me. But the atmosphere was unmistakable. The 1960's had sparked its own unique genre of liberation music. Regardless of what one might think of that turbulent era, you are bound to be turned on by the uplifting music. The same could be said of Christian music, only in a much more profound way. Bach had been a church cantor and the father of thirteen. The baroque music and chants that he alone wrote could fill a person's life.

The music I now heard streaming out of the plaza packed a gravity that I have rarely had the privilege to hear. For those in the audience who had invested so much of themselves in this pilgrimage, it effectively consecrated the journey. Then suddenly, out of the darkness near the top of the cathedral, a spectacular panoply of lights illuminated all at once. A biblical-looking face appeared. Having seen so many similar depictions on stained glass windows throughout my life, I assumed it was the visage of *Jesus*. Jesus. Baby Jesus of Bethlehem, Jesus of Nazareth, Jesus the Carpenter, Jesus the Jew, Jesus the Rabbi, Jesus the Crucified, Jesus Christ. But no. It was not.

It was *James*. James the unruly disciple, James the Truant, James the wandering apostle, James the Loyal, James the Martyr, James the Inspiration for medieval and modern pilgrims. The massive crowd broke into an extended roar for this embattled, but ultimately redeemed, figure.

Yes, this ceremony, so high on emotive content, is one I would dearly liked to have attended.

Chapter 45

Pilgrim Celebration

"Bill, where do you wanna' go?"

It was Gavin. The time was 1:30 a.m. Needless to say, he said it without breaking his stride. I had been making rounds of the main streets and the big park, unsuccessfully attempting to get in the main plaza, and doing anything else I could to make myself as visible as possible. Our plan had drastically malfunctioned. But now, all was well.

"There's a band playing in that plaza behind the cathedral.

"Let's go."

Off we headed with my backpack on my shoulders, towards the sound of music. We arrived in a jam-packed plaza where pilgrims were celebrating in wide open fashion. The music was rock n' roll. Gavin immediately got kidnapped by a brunette from Czech named Eva. She was nice looking, and an even better dancer. He was in his element and didn't stop moving for the next two hours.

Meanwhile, I did what a tall person instinctively does in a crowd. I headed for the wall, which I rocked up against with my backpack. A Nordic-looking woman, who also seemed to be seeking anonymity, walked over to where I was standing.

"Oh yeah," I said, "You were the girl in front of us in the line yesterday, right?"

"Yes," she smiled.

"Did you like our Spanish class?"

"Yes, it was pretty good." American hyperbole, followed by German understatedness.

"How long have you been bicycling on El Camino?"

"Ten days."

"Where did you begin?"

"St. Jean's Pied de Port."

"Wow, that's about 80 kilometers a day?"

"Yes," she said. "I've noticed."

This kindred soul and I were enjoying this conversation here on the margins of the festivities. But suddenly I, too, got hijacked, just as Gavin had before. Unfortunately, the results weren't anywhere near as fortuitous.

The woman looked to be in her mid-forties. She also looked to be recklessly drunk. Further, she had made the classic mistake of the pop-singer Madonna—a middle-aged woman trying to dress like she was 18 years-old. She commenced dragging me away from a good conversation, my backpack, and the wall.

"Dance, Bill," she began to shout. I would soon learn these were the only two words in English that she seemed to know. Efforts to converse in Spanish were no more successful.

If you saw me dance, a smile would likely purse your lips. You would quickly understand how I've made it 49 years without ever getting married. Nonetheless, I gave it as good of a try as I ever had, pitching about in awkward *WASPy* gyrations. Everybody was so obviously having a great time, and I halfway even enjoyed it myself. But this woman had a wild, untamed look about her. I fended off her more aggressive approaches with embarrassed looks back at my former German interlocutor.

"Is this lady German?" I yelled back to her.

"I don't know," she laughed.

I finally freed myself and returned to the wall. But this insatiable pilgrim of indeterminate origin was back on me. I had seen her before. *Was this Laura, the short-haired German girl's, mother?* Wow. All the seemingly *ES* (eat s__t) *looks* she had given me, and now she was hurling herself at me in pell-mell fashion.

I looked out and saw the Colombian pilgrim, *Shakespeare,* who was now in full-rhythm with a dancing partner. Better yet, he had a smile on his face a mile-wide. Next to him was his Brazilian companion, Felipe, also dancing away in high gear. Unlike most stereotypes, the one about great Latin American dancers needs to be amped up, rather than toned down.

In desperation, and perhaps counter to the spirit of pilgrimage, I asked Shakespeare, *"Tu podrias bailar con esta mujer? Yo no se como bailar* (Can you dance with this lady. I don't know how)." Effectively, I was asking him for a bailout. He proceeded to take over from me and carry the task out with great panache. Confidence and fun beamed all over his face.

This also led to my third and final epiphany on the Camino. Shakespeare had frequently and proudly told Gavin and me all about the intensive English language immersion program he had been taking in Ohio for the last two years. Unfortunately, these conversations had always been in Spanish—never in English, for the simple reason it didn't seem like he actually spoke any English. In adolescent fashion, Gavin and I had dubbed him 'Shakespeare' for his English, or lack thereof. But now he was proving to be a helpful friend and a great pilgrim. Look at him out there. For the second time in two days, I felt downright small.

Finally, the music ended, and Gavin and I were reunited.

"I couldn't believe how drunk Laura's mother was," I exclaimed.

"Laura's mother?" Gavin said. "What are you talking about?".

"Yes, wasn't that Laura's mother that was all over me?"

"No, Bill," Gavin shot back. "Do you know who that was?"

"A very drunk pilgrim."

"It was Eva's (the Czech girl he had been dancing with) mother," he laughed.

"Well, why didn't you and Eva control her?"

"Relax, Bill."

The German bicyclist was enjoying this exchange, as she walked out of the plaza with us.

'Where are you planning to stay tonight?" I asked her.

"I have no idea," she smiled.

"Neither do we."

We headed to a park bordering the church. It clearly wasn't a solution. Small skits and rag-tag musical groups had sprung up on the far end. "I'm checking this out," Gavin said. Off he went at 3:30 in the morning. Right then, a familiar face appeared out of the dark.

"Blondine," I immediately exclaimed. We embraced. Gavin and I hadn't seen her since Gavin's vomiting episode, about 400 kilometers back. She was traveling with the athletic Norwegian girl we had met in Roncesvalles.

"Where do you stay tonight?" she immediately asked. It was

a logical question, given I had been her original mentor on stealth camping. "I have not slept inside since I last saw you," Blondine proudly reported.

"I've heard this from other pilgrims," I said in a congratulatory tone. That was a white lie, but I felt she deserved kudos.

"Somebody told me there is a park about a kilometer in that direction," I said. It was only a vague directive. But we soon rounded up Gavin. Then Blondine, the Norwegian girl, the German bicyclist, another German guy, Gavin and I all began trooping to the north side of town at 4:00 in the morning, with me in the lead. Once we got out of the immediate center of town, we passed through what appeared to be a housing project.

"This would probably be pretty good," I said, when we came to a flat plot of grass.

"What about those guys over there," Gavin pointed out. Indeed, a group of hysterical-sounding males were gathered about a hundred yards away. Worse yet, they seemed to be taking notice of us. "Let's keep moving," Gavin said. Déjà vu—always keep moving. We continued on through a residential area.

"Hey, that looks like the park," I said when an expansive green area appeared. Everybody murmured a mild assent. It was closer to the road than desirable.

"You shouldn't put up your tent," Gavin suggested.

We commenced divvying up the flattest spots over by the far wall. But I couldn't resist. I erected my tent. Everybody went about their business, except the German bicyclist, who sat up against the wall, with her knees up against her chest.

"Do you have a sleeping pad?" I asked confused.

"No, it's okay," she answered.

"You can sleep in my tent," I offered. "I'll put my sleeping bag out here."

"That's okay," she said evenly. "I'm not planning to sleep."

"But you're riding your bicycle to the sea tomorrow."

"That's fine," she said matter-of-factly. "I will wait for the sunshine."

So everybody got some sleep for two or three hours, except her. At first light she was gone, headed off for Finistierre on the Atlantic coast.

It's so easy to depict modern Europe as effete, lacking in dynamism, and hopelessly attached to old ways. But nights like this show the Old Continent still had it. In some ways, it still is the

Great Continent.

As for us pilgrims, the best was yet to come.

Chapter 46

The King vs. the Galicians

"It's funny, but I don't recall seeing a lot of these people on the Camino," a lady from Texas drawled.

Gavin and I were standing in a line that stretched all the way up two cobblestoned streets. Everybody was applying for a Compostela, certifying completion of the Camino. We had walked up to the building with Darla, who had taken one look at the line and said, "Five hours,", then turned and walked away.

"Hey, join us," a pilgrim we knew at the front of the line had offered us.

"Thanks," I had responded, holding my palms out. "But we'll wait." Gavin and I had then made the long walk back to the end of the line. Perhaps this rejection of temptation offered small redemption for my subtle deception of the nuns yesterday afternoon (Or maybe things don't quite work that way).

This lady from Texas may have been technically correct. I didn't recognize a lot of the people queued up either. But my gut told me there weren't many, if any, cheaters in this crowd.

TV camera crews were on hand filming the occasion. That was no surprise. Heck, even New York City might be jarred by the sudden influx of so many people, especially considering *the way* most of us had made it here.

"That's Galician National TV," someone said. They certainly had plenty to choose from in this pageantry. But, lo and behold, they began training their klieg lights on none other than the tallest pilgrim in the line. I had been chatting in Spanish with lots of people we were seeing. They must have heard that because a man soon came up with a microphone and the camera crew moved in to focus. I was now on national television for the first time in my life. For several minutes, the interviewer peppered me with questions that I did my best to answer.

I have met a grand total of three people in my entire adult life that were taller than me (the tallest, in fact, was a 7'6 ½" guy I met at the London Tall Person Club). As best I could tell, the average Galician was a bit shorter than the average European. So very few Galicians would have ever encountered a single person in their lifetimes as tall as me. This was reflected in the wonderment of the interviewer's voice.

"*Hay mucha gente como usted en los Estados Unidos* (Are there many Americans like you)?" he asked. I went out of my way to alleviate any fears he might have that America was a land acrawl with *faux giants.* I further pointed out how I often got passed by much shorter pilgrims. Finally, I told him something that I considered very important—namely, that Americans have just begun to discover El Camino. Everybody has had such a great experience, that they are sure to go home and tell all their friends about it. I'm glad I got to do the Camino while it was still 95% European.

The interview went on for several minutes. "I was a little nervous," I said to Gavin when they finally stepped away. "Only sleeping a few hours in the last two nights, and then doing an interview in Spanish. I hurried my answers."

"Yeah," he said softly. "I could tell."

***

"I'm telling you, Pope John Paul would never have passed up such a perfect opportunity as this," I said to Gavin.

"You wouldn't have made a good Catholic anyway," he replied.

"Think about it though," I protested. "In a continent that is losing Catholics by the day, you've got all these impressionable young people that have walked 500 miles to get to this Catholic shrine. That's a belt-high fastball for any Pope." But what do I really know about Popes? I guess I was partial to John Paul for a special reason. He had stood up Madonna in 1996 when she went to Rome seeking a papal audience, after the filming of *Evita* (Madonna has bad-mouthed the Catholic Church ever since).

He wouldn't come downstairs for a meeting with the world's most famous pop star. But he had been plenty happy to venture all the way to Santiago de Compostela to greet salt-of-the-earth pilgrims. By my lights, that's what you call a well-balanced individual. "My vision extends over the immense network of routes that unite Europe," he had told the roused faithful. "I see that since the Middle Ages, the Caminos have all led and all lead to Santiago de Compostela."

We didn't have the Pope. But we did have the next 'best' thing on hand. King Juan Carlos. He and his wife, Sophie, had jetted in for the occasion. (Pity the two of them for cheating themselves out of the glory of walking here!). They were staying at the luxury hotel off Plaza Obradoira. That same hotel used to be a hospital that treated indigent medieval pilgrims who had trekked from the other side of Europe. Now they put up royalty—a decided step downward. Like most Americans, suspicion of royalty is practically embedded in my DNA.

But I later learned that I was perhaps being too judgmental about this Juan Carlos. Apparently, he wasn't just any ol' stodgy ceremonial figurehead. To be sure, he and his family been forced to make an accommodation with Franco to maintain their positions (and necks). However, upon Franco's death Juan Carlos stepped in and demanded democratic elections. He was tired of Spain being viewed as a backwater—a country in, but not of, Europe. In fact, the King is known around the country for his populist touch, often mingling with people on the street. Better yet, he recently told the voluble Venezuelan President Hugo Chavez to shut up *("Por que no te callas"),* after Chavez had called the Spanish Prime Minister a fascist. For once in his life, Chavez was rendered speechless.

Seemingly the entire town had been cordoned off to cut a swath for the King and Queen's route to the Church.

"I'm gonna' give this a miss," I said to Gavin.

"Ditto."

Perhaps we were just being ogres. But I don't think I'll be regretting on my death bed that I wasn't one of the faces in the massive crowd to see the two of them walk into the church. They were just doing what any two pilgrims would.

Instead, Gavin and I were drawn to a rally on behalf of Galician autonomy in a plaza behind the church. Speaker after speaker took to the stage to produce rousing, oratorical flourishes in Galician. The crowd swelled, and the mood verged on ecstatic. You couldn't blame the central government in Madrid for bringing in the heavy artillery for a bit of pomp and circumstance. But honestly, the stronger undercurrent seemed to be here in this plaza behind the church.

"Wow, I had known about the Basque independence movement," I said to Gavin. "But this seems like it almost might be even stronger."

"I would like to learn Galician, and live in Galicia someday," Gavin declared. It had taken him 500 miles, but at last he had gotten over his juvenile fixation on *ETA!*

***

"Bill, I'm gonna' go down and dance," Gavin said. It was our last night in Santiago, and we were again piling into a packed plaza where a band was going to play Galician folk music.

"Hey, there's Laura," I said. *That* slowed Gavin down. Laura sat there on the steps chatting with her always serious-looking mother. There was something especially pilgrim-like about their modest eastern German style. What a great learning experience this Camino was, no matter where you come from.

We swapped e-mail address with her, as I did with other pilgrims. I began receiving regular e-mails from Laura, who was chafing at her provincial lifestyle back home in eastern Germany, and angling for a way to liberate herself. Per my suggestion, she and other pilgrims started making plans to hike the much more difficult Appalachian Trail, which runs 2,175 miles through fourteen American states. This exemplifies a powerful dynamic of travel by foot—once you've done it this way, you are never quite the same again. Adventure calls.

Gavin walked down the stone steps to the floor of the plaza and quickly took up with Kip's group and the FOCUS students. I stood at the top of the amphitheater with our two backpacks, taking it all in. The tunes, the dancing, the atmosphere were almost surreal. Folksy-looking middle-aged Galician men hopped along on one foot, and the women moved gaily in their dresses. The music streamed out like the deeply held product of its Celtic and mountainous origins. Its sheer authenticity was overwhelming.

Periodically, during the evening people strangers approached me to say they had seen the interview I had done on the national news. "When? What did it sound like?" I kept asking. "Will they show it again?" It was probably the only interview I will ever do on a national television station. But I never got to see it.

The dance ended after midnight. Gavin and I then trooped across town to bivouack in the same park as the evening before.

"Man, that was the best music I've ever experienced," I said before getting in my tent.

"I shall make Galicia my home someday," Gavin again solemnly declared.

Part Two

The End of the World

*"We had longer ways to go.
But no matter, the road is life."*

Jack Kerouac, *On the Road*

Chapter 47

March to the Sea

"You really should do the extra 60 miles to *Finistierre*," everybody had advised me before leaving for Spain. "It's beautiful."

"Is Finistierre where Columbus set sail from?" I had asked time and again.

Surprisingly, nobody really seemed to know the answer. Most people thought he probably had. It wasn't illogical given it was the shortest distance to the New World. In fact, though, he had embarked from the Canary Islands. But most of the other Spanish explorers—Magellan, Balboa, Cortez, and Pizarro, had taken off from Finistierre, whose name is derived from the conventional wisdom of that time that it was the end of the world.

Gavin and I hoped to make the 61 miles to Finistierre in three days, which would be an acceleration of our pace up to this point. Further, the terrain was reputed to be more mountainous on the way to the sea.

Kerstin and Ferdinand came out of the luxury hotel, as we were preparing to leave town. Kerstin had her arm wrapped in Ferdinand's arm in a playful manner.

"Wow, looks like it was a happy ending for you," I said mischievously.

"It's not over yet," she popped back.

"Is it true that this hotel serves free meals to pilgrims?" I asked.

"I don't know," she said. "The guests get all the food we want at the hotel." Kerstin had apparently found just the right balance of amicability and worldliness to keep her naïve American suitor off balance.

In reality, this hotel had long ago made an agreement to serve free meals to pilgrims. The concierge sent us to the garage where pilgrims queued up to eat for free. He also told us that only the first ten pilgrims get this privilege. Not terribly surprisingly, when we arrived in the garage, exactly ten pilgrims stood in front of us. The five at the very front were Asians. I wanted to ask them if the ten places were already taken. But their eyes were glued to the pavement. They seemed embarrassed.

"They've probably been here since 6:00," I commented knowingly.

"6:00 last night," Gavin corrected me.

Two guys at the end of the line came up to say, "We just heard you need your Compostela for a free meal. You can have our two spots."

"Thanks a lot." We were tired and hungry after all the confusion, revelry, and adrenaline of the last three days. A five-star breakfast sounded therapeutic. However, a young German girl steeled herself to politely come up and give us the news. "We are saving spots for our mothers," she said, looking me straight in the eye. "The line is full."

We sighed and headed off on the march to the sea, with growling stomachs.

***

"Man, it feels great to be moving again, after being surrounded by all those people for days," I said.

"Yeah, I'm looking forward to the sea," Gavin responded.

"Do I smell some saltiness in the air, or am I imagining it?"

"You have extra-perceptive powers, Bill."

"Honestly, how far from the sea do you think we'll be when we first spot the ocean?"

"How do I know?"

"I say 30 kilometers," I ventured hopefully.

The climbs became steeper. The weather was sultry hot. Gavin got ahead of me, which kept me in a state of low-grade worry about losing him. Technically, this was no longer the Camino, and the trail wasn't as well marked. We were used to seeing many of the same pilgrims day after day. But now there were all kinds of new faces.

After a particularly long, winding climb, I finally found Gavin waiting on me. A lone Peruvian girl stood there panting. I had briefly lived in Peru, and even hiked a short distance on the *Inca Trail*. We had an entertaining chat with her, and might even have chosen to hang back with her. Gosh, these people from poor countries sure are pleasant to be around. But a new logic had set in. Kilometers. Everybody was walking at their maximum pace through this isolated region to hurry up and get to the sea.

No longer were we passing through towns every six or seven kilometers. Finally, after 18 kilometers, we came up on a country store, where we were able to conjure up some cold cuts, chocolates, and milk. We lay sprawled out on the ground ingesting these calories. The German girl who had bumped us from the breakfast line came by. Perfect timing.

"Would you like some?" I tweeked her.

"No thank you," she said gravely.

"Why not?" Gavin asked.

"We've already eaten."

"We remember," I said. "I hope you enjoyed it half as much as this."

"We are really sorry," she said. This wasn't just a pro-forma response. She really did seem embarrassed that they had out-consumed a couple of Americans, especially when it came to food. It is an article of great faith amongst Europeans that we Americans can't control our appetites in any way. Unfortunately, there is some credence to this view. A recent survey showed that the average American emits 25 tons of carbon dioxide each year; the average European emits only 11 tons (Africans less than one ton).

"Where are you going to stay tonight?" I asked the German girl.

"We've heard there is an old schoolhouse off the road, where pilgrims can stay," she reported. "But we don't know if we'll make it that far tonight." They didn't.

Gavin and I were destined to rejuvenate our twilight hiking schedule that had served us so well in the approach to Santiago.

But this time we were forced to hike throughout the day, instead of taking a several hour break in some pilgrim town. Darkness slowly descended. Trekking through the darkening green forests was again exhilarating. I am so easily depressed at the anarchy that indiscriminate technology seems to be wreaking on humanity. But nights like this, when everybody is trooping along at their maximum speed on foot and that *quicksilver feeling* sets in, leave me hopeful.

Gavin and I had already backtracked twice from missed turns earlier in the day. We ended up on an abandoned country road as the last light vanished. Finally, we came up on a modest-sized building that we dearly hoped was our destination.

"That's the smallest schoolhouse I've ever seen," I said.

"That's the largest outhouse I've ever seen," Gavin retorted.

"We'd better be careful," I said. "It may be somebody's house."

But it was the schoolhouse. Better yet, when we entered there were mattress pads spread out over the floor, instead of tiny bunks. There was no hospitaleiro. A lone Frenchman lay on a pad, trying to sleep. Soon other pilgrims arrived in the dark. Their faces had *that look*. After struggling all day and finally making their destination, endorphins were surging. Everybody wanted to talk.

"Wow, I didn't know where we were going to sleep," a young pilgrim from Ireland said.

"Yeah," I agreed. "We weren't even sure we were on the right trail."

The Frenchman rose up. "Could everyone please be quiet?" he asked. "I've been here for five hours." I almost went into a state of shock. A Frenchman had told me to be quiet, instead of shut up. And he had done it in English. More amazingly yet, he had been polite. After 800 kilometers, the spirit of El Camino was sinking in to everyone.

However, maybe his gentlemanly approach was all wrong. We kept jabbering as the adrenaline was flowing from our all day hike.

***

Our last night before reaching the sea was even better. The day had been insufferably hot. In the mid-afternoon, we had reached a small village where all kinds of pilgrims were holed up.

We had even given serious thought to staying right there with everyone else, perhaps a sign our fortitude was in retreat. But that would have meant not arriving in Finistierre for two more days. So we had again set off on an open-ended hike at twilight.

There was no need to hold anything back. We galloped through the increasingly steep Galician hills at full speed. Several potential spots had appeared. "How 'bout this?" I would say. Gavin no longer felt any need to pay lip service to these mild suggestions. He would just come to a standstill, slowly grab his water bottle, gulp down a large swig, and begin sauntering onward. Continuing had become the path of least resistance.

"Man, it's gonna' be a long time before I feel this free again, (a statement which unfortunately proved prophetic)," I said.

"Yeah, I hear ya'," Gavin said softly. Even a teenager recognized this Galician ambiance was special.

Right before dark we came to a small chapel with a relatively flat lawn out front. "Hey, this must be that chapel we heard about," I said. We knew each other's routine well enough now that we automatically walked over to set up camp. This would prove serendipitous. For not one single flat spot would present itself between here and the sea, over 20 kilometers away.

"They said there was water down below this church somewhere," I said hopefully. But when walked down to a boggy area, only a trickle of sketchy water was actually seeping out.

"Did they mention whether the water was actually wet?" Gavin asked.

"Man I don't know," I muttered.

We walked back up the hill. If absolutely necessary, we had enough water to make it to the next town. But it wasn't a pleasant prospect. Unexpectedly, we saw the headlights of a car coming down the dirt road that ran right by the church. "I'm gonna' stop this guy and ask about water," I said.

"Let's hope he speaks something other than Galician," Gavin reminded me. I held up my hand, and the driver dutifully stopped at my summons.

"Disculpame, usted sabe donde esta agua?"

"Por debajo (down below)," he said.

"Hay casi nada (almost nothing)," I reported helplessly.

He jumped out of his car and ran down the hill to inspect the water source. Once he was convinced of the lack thereof, he immediately said, "Ya me voy por mi casa por el agua (I'm going to my house for water)."

Off he whooshed in his car, kicking up a cloud of dust in his wake. Twenty minutes later the man returned in the pitch black dark with three liter bottles of clear water, and a beaming smile. The milk of human kindness runs strong yet.

"Viva Galicia," we joked with him, and parted ways with everybody happy.

Chapter 48

Finistierre

"Life, if you know how to live it, is long enough."

Seneca

Gavin was unusually quiet this morning, as we followed the path along an open, windswept plain. Soon the trail began losing elevation in an uncharacteristically sharp manner. Looking out into the distance, a bleak, hazy, *nothingness* prevailed. At first, I regarded it absent-mindedly. But then I perked up.

"Hey is that the sea?"

"No," Gavin said. But after a few more steps, he hedged himself. "Well, maybe." As we kept walking, the blue outline of the Atlantic slowly revealed itself. We were 21 kilometers from Finistierre.

"This would have been really cool to do last night," Gavin commented sincerely.

"No kidding, with the sun setting in the West." Objectively, though, any campers would have to be prepared to be totally exposed to the elements. This morning it was the sun and wind.

"You know, it's ironic," I analyzed. "The first and last day on the Camino are the hardest."

"What's the message in that?"

"Well, I'll just say that it's all been a little harder than I had thought it might be." Indeed, if you added in our first day going backwards to France, the alternative route we had taken to the Samos monastery, and now the trip to the sea, we were looking at about 600 miles in under six weeks. That's roughly equivalent to an Appalachian Trail pace.

***

It should have been magical cruising into Finistierre. Instead, it was little shy of hellish. The heat was cloying, sticky, and heavy. We spoke little. Today it wasn't the journey that mattered. It was all about the destination.

We skirted a tortuous path along the edge of the pewter-colored sea. Sand, white waves, and sea spray down below stood out in stark relief. Most coastlines this gorgeous would have long ago been inundated with popular resorts. But not here in Galicia. This is the single most isolated part of Western Europe outside of northern Scandinavia. We entered the fishing village of Finistierre—witness to so many historic events—around 6:00 in the afternoon.

"This place reminds me of Key West," I said.

"Why?"

"They're both out on the tip of something," I said. "Endings and beginnings." We were to see in the next couple days that there was a lot more than meets the eye to this village. Like Key West, it attracts a disproportionate share of renegades. Pilgrims had arrived here and stayed, either because they had fallen heavily for the exotic ambience or run out of money.

French pilgrims celebrating their arrival in Finistierre, French style.

By the time we got to the far side of town, it was 7:00. The albergue was full. That would also end up being serendipitous. For starters, we weren't *there* yet. The trek to the End of the World didn't end here, but at the lighthouse—four kilometers away up a winding mountainous road.

We ran into Jean Francoise and his cousin, Emily, along with Antonio. They were planning to climb to the top tonight.

"Hey, let's go up with them," Gavin suggested.

"We can do it tomorrow," I demurred. "I'm exhausted."

"But you said we should spend our last night in front of the sea."

"Alright," I relented. "Are we gonna' leave our backpacks here or carry them?"

"Where do we leave them down here?" Sometimes an 18 year-old makes sense. Slowly I hoisted my backpack for the last big effort. We were soon marching up a paved road featuring a sharp fall-off to the sea on our left. Hordes of pilgrims marched doggedly in pursuit of this final shrine. The heavy din of footsteps brought back memories of leaving St. Jean's Pied de Port to ascend the Pyrenees on the very first day.

"Where are we possibly gonna' camp tonight?" I wondered out loud.

"It's a heckuva' time to bring that up."

The traffic was all in one direction. Everybody wanted to see the End of the World at dark.

"Hey, see the lighthouse," I said.

"Where's the diving board?"

"Hey man," I warned. "Do you know how many pilgrims have died right here?"

"That's why they call it the end of the world."

***

Gavin and I came to a precipice. Black sea extended in three directions, roaring its warning back up at us. The only thing that lay between here and there was a steep, rocky drop-off—the same netherworld that has at turns exhilarated and horrified mortals through the ages.

We tiptoed around some large boulders towards the lighthouse. A crowd of pilgrims had gathered. Everyone was uncharacteristically quiet. The cold, bullying winds and crash of the sea were the predominant tunes. These dark waters, known by medieval pilgrims as *La Costa da Morte* (the Mansion of the Dead) have been the site of countless shipwrecks and human catastrophes. Rare would be the mortal who could confront such a powerful scene and not consider the greatest mystery of all—death.

In one sense, it is indisputably and ominously true that we humans are in fact a doomed race. But since time immemorial, humans have bravely confronted this specter of oblivion, annihilation, nothingness.

"Where oh death is your victory," the Apostle Paul wrote defiantly. "Where is your sting?"

"Death be not proud," Donne wrote in his third elegy fifteen centuries later. "Some have called thee mighty and dreadful, for thou are not so."

***

A group of pilgrims wandered over to the far end of the parking lot and started down towards the water. Gavin and I tentatively followed.

"For God's sake, please don't go down too close to the water," I pleaded with him. He stuck close by. Somebody managed to get a fire started. Pilgrims then began pulling various items out of their backpack and engaging in the purification ritual of burning them. After all, it's the end of the world.

"What's it going to be, Bill?" Gavin asked. I found a pair of hiker socks with gaping holes in them. "It's the thought that counts," I muttered self-servingly and tossed them into the fire. As unimpressive as my sacrifice was, it was in fitting with my philosophy. Religion should be unconcerned with the material. Granted, we had the ultimate physical panorama right in front of us. But it was like a pilgrimage—simply a means to an end.

As pilgrims, we were striving to reach the deepest recesses of our souls, the very ground of our beings. Indeed, it is through the very ordinary acts of walking, resting, walking, heeding nature's call, walking, finding a place to eat, eating, praying, sleeping, and walking some more, that pilgrimages have always given us ordinary humans the opportunity to do something extraordinary.

Pilgrims' voices sounded hushed, even grave—as if this was more consequential, perhaps a final act of some sort. I chatted briefly with a Mexican girl and a Polish man. But we avoided the usual banter of home countries, etc. Nationhood seemed inconsequential at this moment.

Gavin and I soon began the dark trek back down the mountain. About halfway down, two Spanish girls we had met the very first evening on the Camino recognized us. They excitedly summoned us over to an inlet just off the road. "Can you camp here?" I asked them. "Yes, why not?" Their voices betrayed elation at the pilgrimage's completion. But it quickly became clear that their two male counterparts didn't share these girls' enthusiasm at our presence. So we continued down.

Near the bottom, we came to a small park overlooking the sea. We had been sternly warned by the hospitaleiro there were stiff fines for stealth camping in Finistierre. But there was nowhere else to go. Besides, this was too good to pass up. The black as pitch night was broken up by millions of stars twinkling straight above and the deep undertow of the dark ocean below. It is easy to forgive humans for long thinking this really was the End of the World.

Jean Francoise, Emily, and Antonio were lying on the far side of the park. "I'm gonna' go over there," Gavin said. We traipsed over to where they lay on a thin sliver of grass next to a wall. It immediately became clear that poor Antonio was still in the throes of a super-heated passion for young Emily. He was leaving tomorrow and bearing down at full speed. I found a spot well away to camp, while Gavin threw his sleeping pad down next to them.

From inside my tent I could hear their chatter going on for hours. This was intermingled with the faint voices to my rear of pilgrims dutifully marching back down the mountain upon completion of their pilgrimages. But it was all gradually drowned out by the mighty rhythm of the sea.

Part III

The Camino in the
non-Holy Year of 2011

"I travel for travel's sake. The great affair is to move."

Robert Louis Stevenson

Chapter 1

In Search of Different

"A bewildering variety of motives drives our great traveler."

Milton Rugoff, *The Great Travelers*

When a person travels overseas, the main thing he or she is looking for is something *different*—maybe even strange. For that reason, I decided to return and do El Camino de Santiago for a second straight year. More than any other foreign trip I have ever taken, the Camino had represented a kind of United Nations of adventurous souls.

Gavin had contracted hiking fever himself and was racing up the Appalachian Trail as fast as he could after his freshman year at Virginia Tech. So immediately I was looking for interesting trekking partners. And this being the Camino, I was to find them. It just kinda' happened by chance. Well mostly, anyway.

***

"Chinches, chinches, chinches, hay chinches."
It was 3:00 in the morning in Najera, Spain. A middle-aged Italian lady was frantically beating on the door of the hospitaleiro.

271

When he finally opened the door, the woman again screamed in horror, *"Chinches, chinches."* I vividly remembered that word from last year— *chinches*, bedbugs.

"Donde?" the hospitaleiro asked defensively.

"Hay cien chinches en mi cama (100 bedbugs in my bed)," she shouted in an accusatory tone. The drama quickly unfolded. Pilgrims *en masse* went running out into the common area with their sleeping bags, shaking them hysterically. The hospitaleiro, a kindly middle-aged man, was doing his best to project calm.

"Did you find them on one bed," I asked him, "or all over the place?"

"They were largely contained in one area," he assured me, "not more than six or eight."

"That is not true," a Swedish girl named Petra immediately interjected. "I saw close to a hundred of them over where I was." Petra proceeded to throw her sleeping bag into the trash can for fear of the bedbugs spreading into all the rest of her equipment. Another pilgrim became so distraught that she threw her entire backpack away. Meanwhile, the albergue rapidly changed policy. They suddenly decided to shove us out the front door at 4:00 into the nighttime rain.

"You said last night we weren't even allowed to leave until 6:00?" I asked him in confusion.

"We need to kill all these bugs before today's pilgrims arrive," he explained.

Off we all dubiously went into the dark.

***

The Spanish are more provincial and less well-traveled than the other western European peoples. For that reason they tend to hang more with their fellow compatriots on the Camino. However, when they do get with a foreigner who shows interest in them, they often get quite excited. I spent the first two weeks with mostly Spanish pilgrims. All manners of questions, jokes, and stories were directed at me. Several Italians – who seemed to pick up Spanish at the speed of light – also joined in with us. These people were truly great fun. Maybe it's because I'm a southerner myself, but these denizens of southern Europe felt like kindred souls to me.

But by the time we all got to Burgos, I was mentally exhausted from trying to comprehend all this colloquial Spanish. Perhaps fortunately, the two groups of Spaniards and Italians I had been bouncing between were getting off here.

A festive air again dominated Burgos. I wandered around the town's annual food festival with a large group of Basques. At each booth, one of them would launch into an enthusiastic explanation of all the foods and wines. At my height, I sometimes have difficulties communicating while standing in noisy places, even in English. I was relieved when we finally sat down.

Between enthusiastic ministrations of sangria, these Basques were in an especially uproarious mood. *"No podemos esperar decir todos los cuentos a nuestra gente (*We can't wait to tell everybody back home all the stories)," they kept repeating between deep pulls on Sangria. And wow. Being a southerner, I've seen some great raconteurs in my time. But nobody could recount events with greater flourish than these Basques. The bedbug story back in Najera received especially prominent billing.

My comprehension leaked and leaked all night. But I was powerless to steer the focus away from me. They kept reaching crescendo points, while I crashed helplessly. Finally, it had become so embarrassing that all I could do was stand up, say *'Adios',* give out hugs, and walk back to the albergue.

***

When I had spontaneously decided to do the Camino for a second time in 2011, I had expected a vastly reduced population of pilgrims from the Holy Year of 2010. I'm glad to be able to report that I was 90% wrong. To the naked eye, there were not any fewer pilgrims in 2011.

In Tosantos, I wandered the cobblestoned streets, futilely looking for somewhere to stay. Finally, I ran into the mayor who good-naturedly opened up the gymnasium for us surplus pilgrims.

At dinner that night, I noticed a pair of very noticeable ladies laughing, chatting, eating, and drinking. It wasn't just their looks. They also looked fun. *Where* are they from, I wondered. *How* do I meet them? *What* would I say? And given the complex mosaic of the Camino, what language would I speak?

Chapter 2

The French Connection

"When all is said and done, Great Britain is an island, France is the cape of a continent, and America is a whole different world."

Charles de Gaulle

"**W**hat time is it?" one of the two girls asked me the next morning, before leaving Tosantos.

Her question concerned the most banal subject. Worse yet, it had come in the language of commerce—English. When I later got to know these two girls very well, I derided them for not being able to come up with a more imaginative *pickup line* than that. However, my answer—"No idea"—wasn't any more inspired. The two of them set off up the Camino with no further ado.

I trailed a couple kilometers behind them and caught up with (but did not stalk!) them in Villafranca. They were taking their morning cappuccino with gusto and patience. We exchanged salutations. However, by the time I ordered a bocadillo inside, they had blown town. These girls were French—those ancient European people of such great sophistication and self-esteem. That had to be the answer. They were doing the Camino their own way, and at their own pace.

***

"Ah, the Swedish bikini team," I said when I came upon a group of girls that I had gotten to know. No, it wasn't the actual Swedish bikini team to whom I lobbed this irreverent remark. And it certainly wasn't the two elusive French girls. Rather, it was a group of American college students that had been wowing both pilgrims and townspeople with their height and physical attributes. The girls were all in the 6-foot range. They were volleyball and soccer players at universities in Kentucky and Arkansas, and preferred trekking in their sports outfits.

"You're not gonna' believe what happened last night," Brittany exclaimed.

"Bedbugs?" I guessed.

"No, we caught this creepy old man spying on us at 3:00 last night," she said in disbelief. "He's been following us around the last few days."

"I hope it gave him an epiphany," I responded nonchalantly.

"We're gonna' walk with you tomorrow," Roxanne said.

"Sure, sure," I said. I hung out with them for a couple days, and they were plenty fun. But soon I reverted back to just seeing them here and there. We simply weren't strange enough or different enough for each other, which is what a good overseas trip demands.

***

Finally though, I did meet a group that easily met the strangeness test. In Borcianos, a Latino-looking guy in his mid-thirties arrived with *two* attractive women. One was a short, thin, athletic-looking lady in her early thirties. The other was a softer, feminine-shaped blonde in her late twenties.

First, I thought this guy was with the shorter girl. But then it began to look like he favored the blonde. My confused first impression can be forgiven, if I may say so myself. In fact, I would soon see that the two ladies were also quite confused. So was he.

I was a bit reluctant to approach a group with such a complex *omerta code*. But the man wasn't at all stingy about the company he was keeping. One day as I was passing through a small pueblo, I came across them on one of their signature coffee breaks.

"Come join us for a drink," he said invitingly.

"Sure."

"I'm Fernando," he held out his hand.

"Where are you from, Fernando?"

"Mexico and Spain, but I have an American passport."

"Ah, perfect combination."

The thin, wiry girl with pretty blue eyes was shy on the surface. But she would prove to be quite the woman. Her name was Angelica. She was a full-time architect in Milan, as well as a ski instructor in the Italian Alps. Angelica spoke six languages. Every time she addressed somebody at the table, it was in a different language. She had met Fernando on her second day on the Camino; they had been together ever since.

Fernando, himself, wasn't the most impressive of physical specimens. Somehow though, this seemed to add to his aura. He had the appearance of an aging hippie, or perhaps a ruffled intellectual. His forte was putting people at ease. This was a good antidote to his shy, but intense, hiking partner. I assumed Fernando and Angelica were—or at least had been—an item. But they hid their secrets better than most Camino romances. So I really didn't know.

The other girl, Eva, was a classic Bavarian fraulein. She

had hooked up with Fernando and Angelica a couple weeks into the Camino, presumably also at the behest of Fernando's welcoming personality. Besides being quite pleasing to the eye, a few other things stuck out about Eva. She was very nice

Fernando, Eva, and Angelica in Plaza Obradoira.
Three cool customers.

in a plain, nature-loving way. She, too, seemed shy. And perhaps not coincidentally, she, too, was utterly in the thrall of Fernando.

The thing I found so impressive (well okay, there were a few things about this that were impressive) is that the two ladies steeled themselves to get along well with each other. And it was in more than just a grudging way. Angelica had gone to graduate school in Austria. She regularly conversed with Eva in fluent-sounding German.

Is this complex triangle a new 22d century type relationship, or is it a throwback to the 14th century? Maybe I'm just another naïve American who doesn't understand our more worldly European cousins.

But I reckon a lot of people would have had trouble figuring out this sublime mystery. If Angelica seemed to be most in favor with Fernando one day, you could bet your bottom dollar that the next day it would be Eva. And, of course, vice-versa. Often things would shift subtly several times a day. The girl that was temporarily out in the cold was relegated to walking with—you guessed it—*me*.

Even some of its members seemed caught off balance at times by the changes in momentum. One day as we stood in line at an albergue in Leon, I heard Fernando explaining to Angelica in a softly apologetic voice, *"Solo por el corto plazo* (only for the short-term)."* Presumably, that meant he was making a tactical adjustment in favor of Eva. Angelica's eyes had shown a wide-eyed bewilderment at his explanation. But she didn't complain—nothing to rock the boat or jeopardize her position in the triangle.

However, once when Fernando was having an especially saturated 'Eva day', Angelica had decided to break ranks. At 9:30 in the evening, she had bolted out of the mountainous village of Foncebadon alone, with the purpose of sleeping at 5,300 feet beside the Cruz de Ferro. She had no tent and had lain there shivering all night in a cold mist.

"I could hear wolves howling," she said in her soft voice the next day.

But it had proven to be a brilliant ploy. Fernando greeted her heroically upon reuniting the following day. She regained her most-favored pilgrim status for the entire day. Likewise, Eva got hurt one day, and had to stay back. The next day she was forced to take a taxi to catch up with Fernando and Angelica. But her absence quickly put her back in primary favor with Fernando.

Obviously, this was trying at times for the two girls (not so much, Fernando). Yet, the God's honest truth is that the two girls really seemed to enjoy each other's company. There were three different cultures at work here, and they had assimilated fabulously. So in that sense this was all very much in the spirit of the Camino.

***

"Fernando." I said one day at our coffee break. "You're a classic *Epicurean.*"

"What's an Epicurean?" he asked in a seemingly innocent display of ignorance. The ever-resourceful Angelica pulled out her dictionary and looked it up.

"An Epicurean," she reported, "is someone who avidly pursues pleasure and avoids pain." She laughed uncontrollably before finally responding, "Yes Fernando, you're an Epicurean." But I must say this for Fernando. He was comfortable in his own skin, and a pleasure to be around. And he honestly didn't seem to be one bit possessive about either of his two fine-feathered hiking partners.

As you might expect, other pilgrims were wondering about the internal dynamics of this hermetically sealed group. And since I had walked with a lot of other pilgrims prior to hooking up with this threesome, people were asking me for intelligence, gossip, or whatever I would offer up ("Hey Bill, let me ask you just one thing real quick. That group you've been walking with. I, uh,uh, who's with who?") Few seemed to completely believe my true answer that I honestly didn't know the *ultimate* truths about this triangle. And a triangle is what it remained, rather than a quadrangle.

I would see them off and on again until the end (Yes, it lasted all the way to Santiago). But ultimately, I found the role of being a supernumerary in the group, rather than a principal, to be unsatisfying. So I began looking for new hiking partners.

***

I had continued seeing the two French girls at various points and had kept wondering about them. Incidentally, they later told me that they, too, had wondered what in the world was going on with the exotic threesome that I had been with.

Finally, one afternoon, I was walking through Hornillos del Camino during siesta hour. True to my nomadic style, I wasn't sure whether I was going to stay here, or continue on. To my surprise, the two French girls were sprawled on park benches in the blazing heat.

"*En Espana, se usan las camas* (beds) *por las siestas,*" I remarked in jest.

"No," one of the girls addressed me in English, "it's not possible. The worst snorer on the Camino is in the room next to me."

"Is he that big French guy?" I asked. Like everyone else, I had my 'favorite' snorer.

"No, it is this Asian man," the other girl responded feistily. "He sounds like a dying animal." Actually, that's a pretty good description of what a truly horrible snorer sounds like. It's awful, bordering on morbid.

"You know what they say in Spanish to somebody they want to be quiet?" I asked them.

"No, please tell us," they eagerly requested.

"*Callate gusano*'. It means shut up worm." That drew their laughs. They proved to be good students as well, repeating this line several times per day in jest. "Come inside and have a cold drink with me," I offered. We went into the bar where I introduced them to the wonderful world of Aquarius, Spain's favorite soft drink.

"Where are you from?" I asked.

"We both live in Paris."

"I've heard of it," I said, polishing off Gavin's old line.

"Actually, it's a foreign country to us, too" one of them said laughingly.

Their names were Veronique and Audrey. They were 35 and 26 years old, respectively. We left the bar and walked around town looking for a supermarket. Then I joined another group for a delightful dinner in the center plaza with the enchanting magnificence of the town's Gothic Cathedral towering over us. While eating I got to witness Veronique and Audrey playing with dogs and singing along with a group of Spanish kids in the red and orange glow of a Spanish dusk. It was an early glimpse of what I would later see was their trademark characteristic—happiness.

The revelry got cut short when the albergue called us in at 10:30, while it was still light outside. Fortunately, the hospitaliero had seen that I didn't fit in any of the bunks, and had put me in an empty guest room. Ten minutes after getting in bed, I heard a frantic knock on the door. I opened the door and saw the silhouettes of my new friends, Veronique and Audrey.

"That man is still snoring," Audrey said in disgust. "Can we stay in here?"

"Sure, there are all kinds of extra beds," I answered. "The only thing I'm worried about is bedbugs."

"Are there bedbugs?" Audrey asked in panic.

"I don't know," I said sincerely. "But it has that kind of musky smell in here."

"What does musky mean?"

"Damp, slightly wet."

A fast conversation ensued between them in French.

"We decided snorers are worse than bedbugs," Veronique reported to me. They entered, jumped in two bunks, and were out within minutes.

Bedbugs create their own brand of paranoia. The slightest tinkle in a bodily hair can engender fear of a bedbug bite. That is why you often heard *slapping sounds* in albergues during the evening. However, this almost never worked. They are amazingly covert. I never once heard of anybody killing one that way.

As for the Asian man, I began a daily gig to blunt his sleep-destructive potential. I would gingerly approach him whenever we saw him on the Camino and chat about how far away the next pueblo was. *"Planeas quedar alla* (Do you plan to stay there)?" I would ask nonchalantly. This intelligence-gathering proved highly effective. Because of the frequent pueblos along the way, we could quickly call an audible and divert to another pueblo for the evening. Better yet, Veronica and Audrey were almost always doubled-over in laughter as I went about schmoozing this snoring monster.

***

Veronique, Audrey, and I started into the most isolated stretch

With Veronique and Audrey in the meseta.

of the Camino together. It was 18 kilometers of completely flat terrain without any water. However, Old Lady Luck was to be on our side. Last year the heat had been outright diabolical through this dreadful section. But now we were treated to a cool breeze and perfect overcast weather. Perfect, I might add for shooting the breeze ourselves.

When I found out Audrey's mother was from Germany, I began taunting her by goose-stepping to the German national hymn: *Deutscheland, Deutscheland, uber alles.*

Then, I asked them about, *Frere Jacques.* Of course, this 18th century French nursery melody about a sleepy young French boy named Jacques is famous world-over to grade-school children. I had only taken one year of French in the fourth grade, and it had seemed like we spent half the year on just this one song.

Needless to say, French adults don't go around crooning this song regularly. But my prompting gave them a chance to sing something they probably hadn't sung since they were little girls. They gamely rose to the occasion. With voices soaked with hilarity, they enthusiastically sang out:

Frere Jacques, Frere Jacques,
Dormez Vous, dormez vous,
Sonnez les matines! Sonnez les matines!
Din, dan, don. Din, dan, don.

For the next hour, we traipsed through the Spanish meseta blasting out various combinations about the sleepy little French boy. Obviously the renditions I participated in stuck out like a sore thumb. But after several kilometers, I could finally sing it better than I ever had been able to in the 4th grade.

It was never obvious where to take a break in the meseta, given the lack of tree cover or natural features. Finally, we just sprawled out on the ground, *pilgrim style*, with our backpacks as headrests. This is often when the best conversations occur.

"So what finally ended up happening to Frere Jacques?" I asked languidly.

"He died," Audrey shot back right away.

"Why did he die?"

"He slept too much," she responded, with just a split second of hesitation.

"FrereJacques is dead?" I repeated in disbelief.

"Yes," Audrey said sternly.

"Frere Jacques is dead," I yelled out.

"I can't live without him," Veronique screamed. Fortunately, we were in the vast nothingness of the meseta.

My lifetime's worth of experience has yielded this conclusion: Nothing builds camaraderie like self-deprecation. In this case, it was doubly effective. These two French girls had just made fun of a song that is virtually iconic in France. And they had done it to an American. One of the knocks against the French is that they take themselves too seriously. Henry Kissinger spoke repeatedly in his memoirs of, "the congenital French tendency to overrate their importance." But these girls, Audrey and Veronique, hadn't allowed their high self-esteem to prevent them from joining in any Camino ribaldry. I quickly became an unabashed admirer.

Chapter 3

Repartee with the French

"What are most Swedes? I had recently asked a young Swedish pilgrim. "Lutherans?"

"Atheists," she had answered plainly, and if you don't mind me saying, a bit uppitily. "About 3% of Swedes go to church." And her tone of voice left little doubt as to what she thought of those three percent. But then she thought a second and said, "Actually, Islam is the most popular religion in Sweden. They're about 5% of the population. They're all religious."

Actually, I found her answer quite forgivable. Like most college students, she wanted to be part of the 'in thing', which religion certainly is not in Sweden. Perhaps it's trendier to partake of the Swedish national sport—suicide.

Veronique and Audrey, however, couldn't have been more different. Both faded the Euro-trend and were, in fact, quite religious. "I go to mass every day at lunch back in Paris," Audrey said. Periodically when passing through pueblos, they would spontaneously enter churches and hit their knees. I'm normally quite voluble commenting on things. But at times like this it seemed best to just sit back and witness, and hopefully learn from them.

Audrey preferred to speak in English because she had spent two years on a humanitarian project in India. Say what you want about them—and I'm a bit of both a Francophile and Francophobe—but the French do often walk the walk. It is quite a bit more common for them to head off on far-flung humanitarian pursuits in parts yonder. It is much less common, on the other hand, to live their lives in naked pursuit of money than us Americans. One could even say they have a healthy boredom with the subject of money.

Actually, I've noticed that when the subject of the economy comes up amongst these Latino peoples (French, Spanish, etc.), a grim look tends to come across their faces—almost as if they're discussing the enemy.

But I don't want to get too mushy. I once heard a critique of the great European novelists. "Yeah, the romance, heartbreak, and drama are all great. But nobody ever worked a day in any of them." While working in London, it often seemed like the English cringed at even being seen to try. My point is that American ambition shouldn't be frowned on per se.

My best friend while living in South America had been a Frenchman, named Bruno Montanaro. He was twenty years older than me and well-versed in anti-Americanism. *"La política exterior de los Estados Unidos esta bastante fea* (American foreign policy is more than ugly)," he often said with great conviction. But I never got bent out of shape listening to his critiques. They were so obviously sincere.

One day right before I departed from Argentina, Bruno and I were sitting outside a café in Buenos Aires. He was carrying on about various American actions in his usual colorful fashion. Suddenly, however, he seemed to be struck by a revelation. *"La gente tiene parece muy determinada* (The people seem very determined)." Indeed, it's not that well known that France actually tried to build the Panama Canal before the United States, but gave up in the middle of the project due to malaria. At that point, that ultra-American cowboy, Theodore Roosevelt, stepped in and finished the project, despite stern warnings about the dangers from an array of experts.

Bruno followed his revelation up with another authentic moment. *"No queremos estar como los Estados Unidos* (We don't want to be like the United States)." *"Pero nuestra gente necesita mas iniciativa* (But our people need more initiative)." That's it. Initiative and entrepreneurship are what keep Americans in the game versus our European cousins. On things like educational testing, health care indicators, and crime rates, Europeans consistently rank better than us. But most of the great breakthroughs come from the New World. So which system is better?

In Asuncion, Paraguay, another young group of French later became friends with Bruno and me. Let me say, these French people are good talkers. They would analyze every film, food, wine, political event, you name it—exhaustingly. Right before we all left Asuncion, we finally came to a meeting of the minds.

"I hate to admit," I said, "but the system that combines the best aspects of the French social safety net and American incentives is Great Britain (although I'd never have admitted this to the British while living there) of all places."

"Creo que estas corecto," these French had reluctantly agreed. Months of debate had yielded this entente. That's the point of intensive traveling. We really can learn from each other.

***

"What about the Resurrection or the Virgin Birth?" I stuck my neck out and asked Veronique and Audrey. "Do you believe in the literal interpretation of the Bible?"

"Why do you ask?"

"Well," I started into my relatively inarticulate religious views, "my father died seven years ago. Do I expect to ever actually see him again? No," I answered my own question. "But I bet just today I've consciously done a dozen things that he taught me, and subconsciously countless more. So doesn't that give him some form of life after death that is ultimately more important than his actual body resurrecting?"

I might be booed out of town by an American audience for the total heresy of these impure religious views. But the French have a great tradition of intellectual debate. Veronique responded calmly, "That is fine. But I choose to believe the Bible."

"God, it's refreshing to hear this out of Europeans," I said.

"Bill, all you have to do is open your heart up to God," Veronique said in a lovely voice. *That* kind of innocent, trusting faith is so beautiful. Yet I've always found it so elusive.

"But what about Nietzschke?" I asked. "He wrote that God is dead (in the famous 'parable of the madman'). But you European intellectuals love him."

"No, it's wrong," Audrey quickly corrected me. "Frere Jacques is the one who is dead. But God is alive!"

We all picked up on this refrain, screaming the joyous news that despite what had happened to poor Frere Jacques, God was indeed alive. And not only was God alive, He (She) was alive on the European Continent of all places. The three of us sounded more like Bible-thumping Baptist preachers, than French Catholics and a reserved Episcopalian.

I was lamb happy walking with these girls the next few days. We couldn't get over this revelation, as well as our cleverness at figuring it out. I know. It's terrible when people laugh too much at their own jokes. Our fellow pilgrims looked at us like we were having spasm attacks. But many of them also got caught laughing uncontrollably at our revelation about Frere Jacques, who is famous in all European countries. Better yet, they treated respectfully our good news about God Almighty.

More balanced people, including my two French hiking partners, never had doubted God's existence for a second. But hey, I'm a sinner par excellence, which is another reason the Camino was a good match for me. The ascetic aspect of a pilgrimage brings a pilgrim closer to that which is ultimate. And in my best moments—which are somewhere between 49% and 51% of the time—the most important thing of all is indeed, God Almighty.

***

Audrey had to return to Paris for a wedding.

"Be careful Audrey," I warned, "a lot of men will be stalking you at the wedding, with your girlish figure from the Camino."

"Yes, but everybody I talk to, I'm going to be looking at their nose."

"Their nose?"

"Anybody who looks suspicious, I'm going to say, 'Get away from me, you fucking snorer'," she shocked me. Too often religion and humor are an either/or thing. But the last week these two French girls had proven they could complement each other quite nicely. In Sahagun in the central town square, I gave Audrey a big 360 degree whirling farewell hug with several rotations. Cafeteria dwellers all over the plaza looked on in amazement.

Then I looked at her one last time before finally saying, "You're cool."

She blushed a second and said, "You're cool, too." I don't know if she meant it. But I sure as heck did.

Chapter 4

Epicurean or Calvinist

Fortunately, Veronique had two more friends coming from Paris. Their names were Berenice and Maria. Hiking now with three fun-loving Parisian madamoiselles quickly made me the most envied man on the Camino (I didn't discourage rumors!).

One impressive thing was that each one of these girls could have mischievously had sycophants, supplicants, and the like around them. It would have put them in temporarily advantageous positions. Many a female pilgrim has opted for just such a stratagem. But these girls didn't feel the need to draw undue attention, or otherwise resort to pouting, hauteur, or guile. Rather, they were self-possessed and very comfortable with whom they were.

Again, I was to be surprised at the authentic religious devotion each of them spontaneously showed. Often when we entered a pueblo, a quick conversation would ensue between the three girls. Soon we would be entering the hush of one of the modest Romanesque churches that run in perpetuity throughout the tiny villages of Spain. The sound of four sets of hiking shoes would be the only thing to break the total silence. Usually, I would choose to sit in the row behind them, mainly because of language differences. But also for religious differences. They were Catholic, and I was Protestant.

They often recited Hail Marys and the Lord's Prayer. Usually they did it in Spanish. Sometimes they did it in French, and other times in English. They seemed more surefooted in these liturgical activities than me, even in the English prayers. Finally, they would sing some solitary baroque tunes in French, and then we would solemnly walk out of the church.

Quickly, they would get back on *their game.* When passing through pueblos, one or the other would suggest "una copa (cup of coffee)" or "una cana" (mug of beer). Maria carried a water color set in her backpack; she would pull it out on breaks and, to my amazement, draw admirable sketches in ten or fifteen minutes. None of it—the religion, the coffee, the beer, the painting, the walking—seemed obsessive nor addictive. Rather, it just looked fun.

French girls jousting.

As they went about stick fighting, making animal sounds (*onomatopoeia*), and other incommunicable pleasures that probably eluded me altogether, they would be laughing like little girls. Veronique continued shouting, "Quiero una cama, quiero una cama (I want a bed)," like she was racing them and everybody else to get a bed in the albergue that night. At times, they would all be gasping in laughter so much they could hardly pronounce the others' names. Once when Veronique realized she had left her hiking stick at a watering spot, she went dashing at full speed through the Galician wilderness, as the three of us fell to the ground in hysterical laughter. To say that these girls enjoyed life is to flirt recklessly with understatement. This was especially impressive given they were all reaching an age when unmarried American women are often entering intensive psychotherapy.

***

"Bill, why is it that we only see you talking with women?" Berenice and Veronique had begun needling me.

"I talk with lots of male pilgrims," I had predictably protested. But then I felt compelled to add, "Males my age are suspicious of each other. It's just too weird trying to meet each other."

Nonetheless, they had put me on the defensive. I didn't want to become known as another grasping American male who had arrived on the Old Continent with his ears pinned back. The honest fact, though, was that my height just naturally drew attention, which allowed me to meet an inordinate number of people. But from now on, whenever a girl would yell out, "Bill," I would become sensitive about it. "I met up with her at the beginning of the Camino before I met ya'll," I would quickly explain to them. They certainly weren't jealous (Gosh, that sure would have been a heckuva' ego boost if they had been).

One afternoon the four of us were all traipsing along through Galicia on a cool, overcast, Irish-looking day. We were universally seized by Galicia's majestic beauty, but repelled by the daily rat race for a bed. We had no idea where we were going to stay tonight. Palas de Rei, the biggest city up ahead, was already rumored to be full. I kinda' enjoyed the uncertainty. We turned a corner through another tiny Galician village. The not entirely unpleasant aroma of cow manure pervaded the olfactory senses. Sitting on a stone wall by herself was Miriam.

Miriam. If a gorgeous blonde who was a professional classical music flutist is your cup of tea, then you would probably find Miriam quite alluring. She had been playing professionally in Hamburg for the last eleven years, but had grown up in Bavaria. That was all impressive. But there was more. Maybe I was imagining it—or maybe I was just confusing it with the rest of Miriam—but she spoke beautifully lilting English. I theorized that her music career demanded such soft pronunciation.

Certainly I would have liked to get to know Miriam better. Who wouldn't? But I was very content with the group I was already with, and didn't want to get separated from them. Besides, Miriam was quite elusive in her own way. She had set out in early June from St. Jean Pied de Port with no trekking experience, and little shy of terrified. But she was independent enough to steadfastly avoid getting pinned down with any one hiking group. "Every time I try walking with people, I injure myself," she said. But there was probably more to it.

Call Miriam entrepreneurial, even cagey. By my lights, she was a pretty good example of how lone female pilgrims should conduct themselves. She hiked with lots of different people from different countries. I would see her chatting with people as diverse as buffed-up Italian bicyclists, an urbane lawyer from Oslo, and a group of rugged-looking trekkers from Germany. Oops, I didn't mention any women. But Miriam has the same excuse as me. Beyond a certain age, it's just easier to get to know people from the opposite gender.

As Veronique, Berenice, Maria, and I approached Miriam

Miriam in the classic pilgrim resting position.

sitting on the wall, I was holding my breath a bit. I could just hear more Gallic sarcasm directed my way.

"Hello Bill," Miriam said gamely.

"Yes," I said trying to strike the right balance. Meanwhile, Veronique, Berenice, and Maria approached this blonde-headed German woman warily. Very, very warily. Like dogs warily circling around a cat. Again, not because they were trying to preserve their resident male—no such dynamic at all.

My immediate worry was that my three French friends would think, "Oh, there he goes again with another floozy." But Miriam, despite being little shy of voluptuous, didn't fit the profile of a bimbo in the least.

My second concern, though, was a bit more ominous—bitter

old history buff that I am. The Latino Gallic peoples and the Saxon German peoples haven't just bled themselves white fighting wars. They have so often proven themselves to be diametrical opposites in the most basic cultural ways.

"Where are you staying tonight, Miriam?" I asked.

"This building right here is a parochial albergue," she said, pointing at the modest stone edifice in front of us. "They are going to let twelve pilgrims in at 5:00. I had a look around inside and it's nice."

Silence from my French companions.

"Do you want to stay here?" I quietly asked them.

"It is not important to me," Veronique answered very softly. Meanwhile, Maria had begun walking on to the next pueblo.

"They're serving dinner as well," Miriam volunteered cheerfully. "And at 6:00 they're showing a movie about Jesus' life."

"That sounds pretty good," I said, not wanting to sound too enthusiastic. "I'll run and retrieve Maria."

But Veronique and Berenice began running down the dirt road and called Maria back. Through indirection, we had all agreed to stay.

***

The sit-down dinners in parochial albergues were always special.

On this occasion a German man arrived at the albergue right before dinner. He politely asked the hospitaleiro if he could stay for free. The man, who was in his thirties, explained that he had started in Berlin and planned to eventually walk all the way to Jerusalem. His cause was world peace. The albergue readily took him in. At the dinner table he pulled out his pilgrim's passport, which stretched all the way around the table, and showed the stamps he had accumulated in his long journey all over the Continent, including a visit to Auschwitz. He was making the entire pilgrimage based on donations received along the way.

"How long will it take you?" someone asked.

"Four years," he answered plainly. He then began soliciting people to walk with him through Italy next year to all the holiest sites. "Forty-seven people have already told me they want to walk with me." I began considering making it 48.

At the dinner table, I was seated next to a petite Mexican lady in her sixties, who was doing her admirable damndest to complete the Camino. Juxtaposed next to her was a group of Danes, who once again shined with their own compelling brand of healthy appearance and genuine camaraderie. Further down the table, Veronique appeared over-the-moon happy while chatting with an Italian speedster who was a good ten or twenty times more dashing than the lanky American she had been with for weeks now. Miriam and the French girls slowly warmed to each other in European style. Because there had not been immediate American-style demonstrations of warmth and kinship, I had assumed there was destined to be poor chemistry between them. Fortunately, I had misread all of them. If you're looking for an analogy, the Europeans (except, of course, the Italians!) are more oriented towards the tortoise, while we Americans favor the hare.

You never know what surprises lie ahead. I sure was surprised that the tiny Mexican lady blew the roof off the small bunk room we were in with grotesque snoring.

* * *

"Can I give you my vision of the perfect day as a pilgrim?" I asked the four girls at the table.

"I want to hear this," Veronique said with an amused look.

"It would be struggling all day in bad weather and going thirty kilometers," I waxed. "Then you arrive at a nice restaurant like this. The minute you sit down the voice of Jimmy Hendrix comes piping out of the loudspeakers."

"Yes, that would be fabulous," Miriam, the musician, agreed.

We were at a pulperia in pulpo-famous, Melida. Everybody was taking "canas" of beer before the rich pulpo arrived at the table. It was one of those rare occasions of perfect equilibrium.

We had arrived in Melida a couple hours before only to hear, once again, that all the albergues were full.

"Are they going to open the *polideportivo*?" I had immediately inquired at one of the albergues.

"*Ya esta completo* (Already full)," a surly receptionist had told me without looking up. But when I had gone outside, somebody had told me they hadn't even opened up the polideportivo yet. So I had gone back in and fired right back at her, "*Porque mentiste* (Why did you lie?)". In Spain, people in positions of authority aren't used to having their authority challenged. The lady had looked staggered. I had walked out thinking that just maybe I had done future pilgrims in this town a favor.

We had then headed across town and finally located the mostly empty polideportivo. After getting situated, the five of us had headed out to the pulperia. On one side of the table were the three French girls. On the other side were Miriam and myself. It was a fitting juxtaposition.

Morale was high after walking all day, and then finally getting the confusing logistics straightened out. At least for Miriam and me, it was higher than normal. But for Veronique, Berenice, and Maria, apparently morale was just running at normal levels. Veronique immediately took issue with my analysis of the perfect day.

"Why do you have to suffer first to have the *alegria* (joy)?"

"You're Catholic and you ask that question?" I countered, only half in jest.

"Yes, but we're also French."

"But you told me St. Francis was your favorite saint," I countered. "He was all about suffering."

"I love him," Veronique responded. "But I don't want to live like him." Now *that* was a sentiment I could understand.

The French, being a Latin people are more likely to pursue a diversion without regard to what preceded it, or what lies in the aftermath. They live for the moment. This in no way implies they are lazy. Veronique, Berenice, and Maria had shown they had prodigious energy and a dazzling variety of life's juices. It just shows they are less Calvinist, less focused on accumulation and final outcomes, than Americans and Germans, who come from Anglo-Saxon cultures.

I vividly remember the month of March, 2003. That was the month the U.S. attacked Iraq. I was living in a boardinghouse in Lima, Peru. My roommate was an American who may have been the only person on the entire South American continent who thought the invasion was a good idea. At nighttime he would quiz me obsessively about the postwar reconstruction contracts in Iraq. "Do you think the French are gonna' get any contracts? There's no way they deserve any contracts. Honestly, we don't have to give them any of the contracts, do we?" This went on every night, sometimes into the wee hours of the morning. *You mean it was about contracts?* It was hard to imagine a group of

French having a similar type of conversation.

I'm still on the learning curve on this particular issue. But spending so much time around these Latino peoples (Spanish, French, Italians, Portuguese) on the Camino was not only proving to be a profound pleasure. It was also helping me search for that ever-elusive balance between a Calvinist and Epicurean orientation.

"Are you going to come visit us in Paris?" Veronique asked.

"I've always been intimidated by the city," I responded.

"But now you have friends to visit," Miriam reasoned with me.

"You haven't heard?" I asked Miriam. "All these French you meet out here on the Camino who seem so nice and charming—wait until you visit them back in Paris. All of a sudden they're arrogant and impossible."

"That's not true," Miriam said. "I love Paris." But she didn't know these girls as well as me, and didn't feel comfortable joking with them. In any event, these types of conversations are the reasons you go overseas in the first place.

***

More cultural differences emerged the following day as the masses had begun rounding in on Santiago. Periodically, we would pass through apple groves where the French girls would snag an apple, lay their teeth in it, and toss it into the bushes after a few bites. This was plenty acceptable etiquette, as the apple cobs would quickly be devoured by various scavengers.

We came to a berry patch, where they dropped their backpacks. Soon they were delighting in plucking berries from the bushes.

"Are the red berries okay?" I asked.

"No," Maria immediately said. "Only the blue ones."

All along the way these girls had proven to have the golden touch as to when and where to take breaks. But this one, where we lay eating berries in a windswept field looking out into the Galician hills as droves of *bed-obsessed* pilgrims stormed past us, was one of the most memorable.

A group of four college-age American girls arrived and saw the berry feast underway. They immediately dove in and started plucking berries. That was all cool. But the next step is to then enjoy the berries. Don't worry. They didn't try to sell them or anything quite that crass. Rather, they continued picking berries. And picking and picking and picking. After a while, each one of them had filled up large plastic bags full of berries to feed themselves all the way to Finistierre, with enough left over to bake a few pies. I didn't think much of it. However, it drew Gallic wrath from my trekking partners.

"Look how many they took," Veronique noted with consternation.

"They're hungry," I said amused, especially since one of them was a 4'9" girl that everybody had been angling to photograph with me (to her horror and my boredom) in various pueblos along the way.

"But look what they've done," Veronique snorted. "There aren't any more berries for the other pilgrims." Indeed, I looked over and noted with some amusement that the grove of bushes had been mostly denuded. It never would have occurred to me, without Veronique pointing it out. Berenice and Maria joined Veronique in a cacophony of criticism.

Perhaps the American girls' actions could be described as *Darwinian*—survival of the fittest. This contrasted with a *Rousseau*-like ("Rights of Humankind") attitude on the parts of the French girls. These two contrasting philosophies have helped shape the history of the last couple centuries, and I won't attempt to expound on them here. But it does seem like the latter philosophy may be more appropriate for a spiritual pilgrimage.

Chapter 5

Christianity and the Future?

On June 2, 1939, a 32 year old internationally renowned theologian arrived by ship in New York Harbor to a hero's welcome. Morale was high all around. The United States finally seemed to be emerging from the Great Depression. Yes, war clouds were gathering in Europe. But this man was one of the key leaders in the German resistance against Hitler. His name was Dietrich Bonhoeffer.

Bonhoeffer, a Lutheran minister, had just been banned from public speaking and removed from his teaching position at the University of Berlin. The near-constant surveillance of the Gestapo had rattled him. Reluctantly, he had accepted an offer to come to the United States.

His treatment in New York couldn't have been more different than back in Germany. Bonhoeffer spoke good English and seemed comfortable chatting and joking in all circumstances. An extensive lecture tour of the United States was scheduled. Indeed, his every utterance was greeted with great adulation. Alas, it was not to be.

"I have made a mistake in coming to America," Bonhoeffer wrote to fellow theologian, Reinhold Niebuhr. "Christianity in Germany will face the terrible alternative of either willing the defeat of their nation or destroying our Christian civilization. I know which alternative I must choose." Bonhoeffer valiantly decided to return to Germany after just 26 days in America.

There he embarked on what could only be described as a morally ambiguous course. He began spying *for* the Third Reich. However, soon he was using his position with the German spy agency to smuggle Jews out of the country under Code Name Operation 7. He was also allowed to travel outside of Germany with the ostensible purpose of collecting information on his church contacts in England and Switzerland. But what he ended up doing was briefing them on his plot to kill Adolf Hitler.

Bonhoeffer admitted to his colleagues his doubts as to how well he might hold up under torture. And to be sure, his time was to come. The Gestapo arrested him in 1943, his cover was completely blown in 1944, and he became one of the last people executed by direct order of Hitler himself on April, 9, 1945.

This is a classic tale of old-fashioned sacrifice and suffering on behalf of a religious cause. Indeed, the biblical passage Bonhoeffer was reading before being led to the gallows was Isaiah 53:5—"By his wounds we are healed."

Is suffering what religion is all about? The question seems relevant here in the twenty-first century for a reason that may surprise many people.

***

Christians are now the most persecuted people in the world. Many secular intellectuals will greet this news with great hostility. *Their* deeply-held faith is that Christianity is a staid white person's religion that systematically persecutes minorities. But by the millions, Christians are being silenced, discriminated against, jailed, and executed in parts of China, India, Egypt, Pakistan, Myanmar, Indonesia, and Iran. Churches are routinely burned down. Having said that, there is some very good news as well. A quick look at Christian history demonstrates that the persecutors are destined to miserably fail.

In the first three centuries of Christianity, the Romans tried all manner of beheadings, crucifixions, burnings, and humiliation to stamp out Christianity. But it all failed dramatically. In the midst of the general urban squalor, plagues, and pagan decadence of imperial Rome, the Roman people noticed Christian families lived profoundly different and more hopeful lives.

Likewise, the Soviet Union was the world's first and largest officially atheist society. Christians were systematically hounded to gulags and their death from one end of this vast empire to the other. The result is that Russia may now be the most Christian country in the world.

When China was taken over by Mao in 1949, there were approximately 4 million Christians. Mao immediately began a savage campaign of reprisals against these Christians. Now, after more than sixty years of constant state-directed persecution of Christians, including burning of tens of thousands of churches, it is estimated there may be over 100 million Christians in China. It now appears likely that *China will one day be the largest Christian country in the world*.

Here in America, I'd look for Mormonism to become less of a curiosity, and more of a mainline faith. The Mormon Church has traditionally been the most persecuted religion in the United States, having suffered unspeakable atrocities. Yet as we've seen, persecution traditionally strengthens a faith. Mormons already outnumber mainline denominations such as Episcopalians, Methodists, and Presbyterians. Conceivably, they could become the major religion in the United States.

Two hundred years ago, Voltaire predicted that within a hundred years nobody would practice Christianity or even read the Bible. But from its earliest days, Christianity has always demonstrated an astounding ability to renew itself. It survived the beheading of the top echelon of its leadership for the first three centuries. There was the monastic movement that helped move Europe out of the Dark Ages. The Protestant Reformation gave the Church new life after the Catholic Church's corrupting monopoly. The Great Awakenings in 18th century England and America evangelized the English-speaking peoples in unprecedented numbers. Now in the 21st century, the greatest irony of all appears to be unfolding.

Christianity is staging its most dynamic revival in the Global South. Its future may now lie most critically with white-robed priests dancing and chanting their way through the streets in places like Nigeria, Pakistan, Egypt, and Brazil.

At the end of the day, there is something about this religion of the masses and human beings that is a good match.

Chapter 6

Camino Glory

I had found a certain novelty in being part of the masses that had held Santiago in a virtual state of siege in the Holy Year of 2010. However, it still nagged at me that I hadn't gotten into the great culminating festivity in front of the Cathedral in Santiago. I had wondered if 2011 was destined to be another virtual 'refugee' situation. To my relief, it wasn't.

The albergues were thronging and the plazas were bustling, to be sure. Regardless of the year, July 25th is always the biggest holiday of the year in Galicia. But at least you could take two free steps without having to apologize for colliding with somebody's camera. I found an albergue to stay in within a chip shot of the grand cathedral. Best of all, I got in the big festival.

On the night of July 24th, I stood in Plaza Obradoira, waiting for the much ballyhooed fireworks show. I was surrounded by Germans. Several hospitaleiros had told me that they are inundated by Germans in the spring and fall, when the weather is cooler. But the late stages of the Camino this year had seen legions of Germans as well. Anybody who tells you Germans can't be fun either has had their country invaded by them in the too recent past, or doesn't know what they are talking about. My unequivocal attitude is, the more Germans the better.

In the midst of this sea of Germans were two American college professors, a father and son. The son, Benjamin, had convinced his father, George, to do the Camino to help recover from the death of his wife. Benjamin's strategy had proven to be fabulously successful. George was in his seventies. Walking the Camino was the challenge of a lifetime. But like many older pilgrims, his secret was discipline. He had religiously gotten out at first light and kept up a steady pace. They had unabashedly hurried to their daily

George and Benjamin with their Scandinavian dancing partners in Finistierre. Everybody looks pretty happy.

destinations to get a bed. At night, though, George had taken his game face off and enthusiastically joined in whatever revelry lay at hand.

"Where are Caroline and Petra?" I asked George. I was speaking of the pretty young Norwegian and Swedish girls we had been with in the early going.

"I danced with Caroline until 3:30 last night in Finistierre," he beamed.

"The whole thing has been just what he needed," Benjamin later told me. "He was really a wreck after Mom died."

Benjamin, himself, was a 39 year-old bald-headed, bearded college professor; he had had what is known in Camino parlance as a 'hookup'. He had romanced with a cool, hippie-looking German pilgrim. The father, son, and I sat there in the square surrounded by all these northern-Europeans. There sure as hell weren't any regrets.

"Man, I've taken all kinds of trips to Europe over the years," George said. "But this Camino is far and away the best way to see this continent."

"Amen," I said.

***

The show finally got going. It was indubitably the single most powerful 30 minutes of religious exultation I have ever had the privilege to witness. The music was choral, thunderous, and dramatic. The light displays were equally scintillating, including a flaming red devil chasing St. James around the building.

Such a powerful performance is bound to bring all kinds of human emotions to the fore. In my case, one in particular stood out. More than perhaps any other time in my life, I felt my own selfish *ego* being submerged. In its place, was the common glory of the masses. It's easy to say, "We're all in this together." But for that 30 minute period, where everybody stood entranced by this brilliant production, it honestly felt like it. Never had I felt closer to this religion of masses that I have practiced so unevenly since I was a little child. And never had I seen such a moving tribute to either Christ or any of his martyred apostles, as what unfolded here in Santiago de Compostela.

Yes, there are many strategies and approaches to walking this great Christian pilgrimage. But twice now I had done it the conventional way, beginning in St. Jean Pied de Port and arriving in Santiago five weeks later with the crush of pilgrims for the great celebration of the July 25th Holy Day. And I can say without any hesitation that, whatever inconvenience it entails in crowds and heat, I would not change a thing.

***

The band party afterwards was telling. Everybody looked like a pilgrim who had covered significant distances on foot to get here. So many had struggled so hard. And you never really knew just what anxieties and fears people had endured along the way.

I ran into Midan of South Korea for the first time in a few hundred kilometers. She had arrived in Spain with her best friend from Korea. In the early days on the Camino the two of them had struggled mightily to make the paces, getting out at first light and hiking until late in the day. Better yet, Midan had developed a reputation as a crack cook in the albergues. I had benefited disproportionately from some of the *curries* she had meticulously prepared. Theirs was an inspired effort, to be sure. But I had been dubious as to whether they could make it all the way to Santiago in time for the Holy Day.

Things had then become more complicated. Midan's svelte

friend, Eun Jin, had the fortune (or misfortune) of meeting an especially confident American pilgrim named Roland. He had taken an immediate shine to Eun Jin and had thrown on the full-court press. Soon Midan had begun to feel like a supernumerary. Saving face is everything in Asian cultures. Midan had begun walking all out every day to escape from her friend, Eun Jin, and this new suitor.

"Where's Eun Jin?" I would ask Midan. She wouldn't answer. "Where's Eun Jin?" I kept asking. But she always acted like she didn't even know who I was talking about. She must have been deeply upset.

Meanwhile, in a Shakespearean twist, Eun Jin had been suddenly tossed aside by Roland, who had found new prey to track. So now Eun Jin had been jilted by both her best friend and her paramour. Life can be pretty complicated on the Camino.

Soon, I had begun to see Eun Jin on her knees at churches in various pueblos, always in deep prayer and solitude. Sometimes she would spend hours all alone in a church. She had even started taking an organizing role in some of the pilgrim masses held in pueblos. Eun Jin wasn't actually Christian. However, she appeared in the midst of a profound, perhaps even life-changing, epiphany, of which the Camino has historically been a great incubator.

Finally, here in Santiago there had been redemption and reconciliation. The two girls' valiant struggles had paid off. They had both arrived in Santiago in time, although separately. There was still the issue of Roland. He had fallen short in his extra-prospecting and in the process earned widespread criticism in the pilgrim community with his overly forward ways. He was now trying to re-integrate with Eun Jin. But now *he* had become the supernumerary, as he stood to the side shuffling his feet around the two reconciled Korean girls. Yes, this Camino was indeed a learning experience.

When I ran into Midan her eyes lit up. I spontaneously picked her up and twisted this tiny Korean in 360 degree rotations until she was begging me to let her down. "Please, please," she shouted. "I can't stop, I can't," I screamed. Finally, I let her down as we both saw stars. Her English was only basic, and there was loud noise all around. This was the best way I could think of to say goodbye forever to this doughty Korean girl.

***

Now came the most important goodbye—to my French friends. My experience has been that any planning of a goodbye is bound to backfire. I can probably think of no more than a few memorable farewells my entire life. And those just sort of happened spontaneously.

I distinctly remember leaving London after 4 ¼ years on the trading floor. British traders with whom I had been in close daily contact for years would approach me and softly say, "So long, mate." That was it. There was no exchanging of e-mail addresses, promises to write, call, etc. To be sure, it was a little bit spare for my taste. On the other end of the spectrum is the overwrought American goodbye, replete with hyperbole, emotion—either feigned or real, and extravagant promises to write and stay in close contact.

As the reader might surmise, I'm a bit partial to British goodbyes. They seemed to capture the crux of the situation best. It really is over. Get on with it. Now I would like to be able to report to you that another part of the vaunted French culture is the perfectly equilibrated good bye or *au revoir*, combining the best aspect of the American and British models. Alas, I didn't find out.

The albergue in which I was staying strictly locked the doors at 2:00.

"What time is it?" I suddenly asked.

"Almost 2:00," Veronique reported.

"Oh my God, I've got to go."

I quickly hugged Veronique and Berenice.

"Where's Maria?" I asked hurriedly.

"Talking with Miriam."

"Give her my regards," I said hurriedly, and ran off.

***

"The Appalachian Trail is the best way to see America," I had repeatedly promised these French girls all along the way, "just like the Camino is the best way to see Europe." *That,* incidentally, is not hyperbole. We have been in periodic contact since returning to our respective countries. Hopefully they will give it that once-in-a-lifetime shot on America's trail of the masses.

For myself, I'm immensely grateful to have had the privilege the last two years on the Camino to personally witness the glories of both Old *and* New Europe. The key to the success of both of this route, and the Appalachian Trail lies in the wisdom espoused a millennium-and-a-half ago by that great chronicler of Christianity, St. Augustine. *"Solvitur ambulando,"* he wrote. Walking solves all.

Regrettably, I haven't religiously followed many Christian precepts and practices very well over the course of my life. But on this score—solvitur ambulando—I have been quite faithful indeed. My strongest feelings are that walking, along with the attendant ascetic lifestyle, brings us mortals helplessly toward that which is *Ultimate*. It is humbling to think of the literally tens of millions of pilgrims over the centuries that have discovered that exact truth right here on this old pilgrim's road.

About the Author

Bill Walker was born and raised in Macon, Georgia. He received a Bachelors and Master Degree in Accounting from the University of Georgia. From 1985-1999 he was a commodity futures broker at the Chicago Board of Trade and London International Financial Futures Exchange. Later he taught English as a Second Language in five Latin American countries.

His first book, *Skywalker—Close Encounters on the Appalachian Trail* (2008), was a narrative of his 2005 thru-hike of the Appalachian Trail. His second book, *Skywalker—Highs and Lows on the Pacific Crest Trail,* was a narrative of his 2009 hike of the 2,663 mile Pacific Crest Trail. Mr. Walker, who is 6'11", is currently working on a book on the subject of height. He lives in Asheville, North Carolina.

Acknowledgments

Several people helped turn out this work in purposeful fashion. Andy Livingston, a close friend in Honolulu, Hawaii put his sharp eye to the manuscript and made several keen observations. Among them, he thought the chapters on miracles and relics were integral to the work and that I should keep them in the final product. So if you happened to not like those two chapters, Andy deserves a healthy share of the blame!

Because I am not a prodigious photo snapper (Gavin and I didn't even carry a camera in 2010), I had to call on some of my fellow pilgrims for assistance. Veronique Landwerlin of Paris, France, Sarah Sissuka of Madrid, Spain, Meawes Groschopp of Berlin, Germany, Eva Ritter of Stuttgart, Germany, and Dr. George Steger of St. Louis, Missouri were able to help me fill the breach.

Thank you.

Message from the Author

I would like to express my sincere gratitude for you choosing this narrative. The fondest hope of any author is to inspire readers to undertake some theretofore unknown pursuit. Indeed, the Camino de Santiago represents the most fulfilling way I have ever found to travel. Those of you who are interested have a bright new chapter ahead in your lives.

Finally, if you see fit, a written review on Amazon would be greatly appreciated (three or four lines is plenty). These reviews are tremendously helpful to us independent authors.

Thank you, and *buen camino,*

Bill Walker
January 15, 2013

Suggested Readings

Alcorn, Susan: Camino Chronicle, Shepherd Canyon Books, 2006

Christmas, Jane: What the Psychic Told the Pilgrim, Greystone Books, 2008

Coelho, Paulo: The Pilgrimage, Harper One, 1995

Cousineau, Phil: The Art of Pilgrimage, Council Press, 2000

Davidson, Linda Kay and Gilitz, David: The Pilgrimage Road to Santiago, St. Martin's Griffin, 2000

Freeman, Charles: Holy Bones, Holy Dust, Yale University Press, 2011

Frey, Nancy: Pilgrim Stories, University of California Press, 1998

Hitt, Jack: Off the Road, Simon and Schuster, 1994

Kerkeling, Hape: I'm Off Then, Free Press, 2009

Melczer, William: The Pilgrim's Guide to Santiago de Compostela, Italica Press, 2008

5289071R00177

Made in the USA
San Bernardino, CA
01 November 2013